Understanding
the Literature of
World War II

The Greenwood Press "Literature in Context" Series
Student Casebooks to Issues, Sources, and Historical Documents

UNDERSTANDING
the Literature of
World War II

A STUDENT CASEBOOK TO
ISSUES, SOURCES, AND
HISTORICAL DOCUMENTS

James H. Meredith

The Greenwood Press
"Literature in Context" Series
Claudia Durst Johnson, Series Editor

GREENWOOD PRESS
Westport, Connecticut • London

Library of Congress Cataloging-in-Publication Data

Meredith, James.
    Understanding the literature of World War II : a student casebook
to issues, sources, and historical documents / James H. Meredith.
      p. cm.—(Greenwood Press "Literature in context" series,
ISSN 1074–598X)
    Includes bibliographical references and index.
    ISBN 0–313–30417–3 (alk. paper)
    1. American literature—20th century—History and criticism—
Sources.   2. War stories, American—History and criticism—Sources.
3. World War, 1939–1945—Literature and the war—Sources.   4. War
poetry, American—History and criticism—Sources.   5. Authors,
American—20th century—Interviews.   6. World War, 1939–1945—
Sources.   I. Title.   II. Series.
PS228.W37M47   1999
810.9'358—dc21   98–44591

British Library Cataloguing in Publication Data is available.

Copyright © 1999 by James H. Meredith

Library of Congress Catalog Card Number: 98–44591
ISBN: 0–313–30417–3
ISSN: 1074–598X

First published in 1999

Greenwood Press, 88 Post Road West, Westport, CT 06881
An imprint of Greenwood Publishing Group, Inc.
www.greenwood.com

Printed in the United States of America

The paper used in this book complies with the
Permanent Paper Standard issued by the National
Information Standards Organization (Z39.48–1984).

10 9 8 7 6 5 4 3 2 1

Copyright Acknowledgments

The author and publisher gratefully acknowledge permission for the use of the following material:

"An Interview with Richard Wilbur," by Joseph Cox. *War, Literature & the Arts* 10, no. 1 (Spring/Summer 1998). Reprinted with permission from *War, Literature & the Arts*, Joseph Cox, and Richard Wilbur.

"An Interview with Paul West," by Thomas McGuire. *War, Literature & the Arts* 10, no. 1 (Spring/Summer 1998). Reprinted with permission from *War, Literature & the Arts*, Thomas McGuire, and Paul West.

"Conversations with Joseph Heller," by Kathi Vosevich and James Hughes Meredith. *War, Literature & the Arts* 11, no. 2 (Fall/Winter 1999). Reprinted with permission from *War, Literature & the Arts*, Kathi Vosevich, and Joseph Heller.

"A Conversation with Joseph Heller at the United States Air Force Academy." From "Yossarian at the United States Air Force Academy," a conference presented by the Department of English, USAFA. Reprinted with permission from Joseph Heller.

"Hang the Enola Gay," by Alfred Kern. *War, Literature & the Arts* 7, no. 1 (Spring/ Summer 1995). Reprinted with permission from *War, Literature & the Arts* and Alfred Kern.

"A G.I.'s Perspective: An Interview with Robert B. Ellis, Author of *See Naples and Die*," by James Hughes Meredith. Reprinted with permission from Robert B. Ellis.

"Interview with Paul Frank: A Second-Generation Lithuanian," by James Hughes Meredith. Reprinted with permission from Paul Frank.

Every reasonable effort has been made to trace the owners of copyright materials in this book, but in some instances this has proven impossible. The author and publisher will be glad to receive information leading to more complete acknowledgments in subsequent printings of the book and in the meantime extend their apologies for any omissions.

This book is dedicated to Kathi and the du Fallu sisters because I could not have finished this project without their support.

Contents

Introduction

On the morning of 1 September 1939, the German Wehrmacht (Army) invaded Poland and opened the hostilities of what would become the second major war within a twenty-year period. The seeds of World War II had been planted after the end of World War I in the Treaty of Versailles. In this document the victorious Principal Allies (the United States, the British Empire, France, Italy, and Japan) and the Associated Powers (Belgium, Portugal, and Romania) levied strenuous conditions against the defeated German empire.[1] In addition to the onerous financial burden Germany had to carry, the most distasteful aspect of its reparations was the subjugation of millions of outlying German-speaking people to Poland and Czechoslovakia. After having forced Austria into political union in March 1938, Adolf Hitler, during the summers of 1938 and 1939, began bringing the world closer to war over the fate of these Germans in what was known as the Polish Corridor and the Sudetenland. Germany's two other allies, Japan and Italy, had been engaged in militaristic conquest throughout the decade, starting with Japan's invasion of Manchuria in 1931 and Italy's attack on Ethiopia in 1935.

Although World War II ended a full decade before I was born, I have always felt a strong connection to it. I distinctly remember in the 1960s sitting on the spacious front porch of my grandmother's

Greenville, Mississippi, boarding house drinking cold, southern-sweet iced tea out of ample glasses. On that porch I listened to my uncles talk about their experiences during World War II. These two men were reluctant storytellers about their combat experiences. My father had to fill in the details later.

I mention my family in this way not only out of sentiment but also to explain why understanding this war—especially the literature and the context in which it was written—is vitally important today. What I heard on that porch was surely repeated not only throughout America but probably throughout the entire world as well. I am confident of this assertion because I have had the occasion to talk to people of many nationalities about this war. As much as my family suffered (one of my uncles had two ships sunk underneath him, and one of my grandmother's brothers died in a B-26 airplane crash), many other families suffered much, much more. In fact, because of World War II whole families in other parts of the world no longer exist.

The World War II generation is dwindling, and the generation that fathered and mothered those men who left their homes to fight the war has been gone for quite a while now. Soon only those will remain whose connection to the war, like mine, will be what they have either heard or read. It is important to get the story right. The lessons of World War II are so great and so weighty that we cannot afford to repeat them.

My approach to such a vast topic (World War II is the most written-about topic in the twentieth century, if not in the history of humankind) is one I have tested in the classroom. I choose to personalize the war as much as possible because it affected more people than any other event in human history. In this volume I have tried to cover as many important topics as possible; however, my guiding principle has been to describe how the conflict affected individual people and to scrutinize aspects of the war close to places where I have lived and traveled. For example, when I lived in the Netherlands my house was right off the Hell's Highway made famous in the Market-Garden operation (see Chapter 1).

For the purposes of classroom deliberations, I have found some aspects of the literature useful in evaluating the vast amount of writing concerning this war: although the literature of World War II recognizes the global scale of the conflict, it focuses largely on the plight of the individual. Although the forms such literature takes do reflect traditional literary types, sometimes these types are transformed to express a new reality in the post-Hiroshima world. (Very little literature about World War II would be considered experimental, yet the literary world radically changed after 1945, affecting much of the literature about World War II as well.)

Chapter 1 of this volume concerns the experience of combatants during the war. I use the term *combatant* to describe any individual who served primarily at the front. Although a naval combatant is not represented here, I do not mean to slight the seaman. Because this book is meant to be representative and not comprehensive, I had to leave out a lot of worthy material. The writers whose work is presented in Chapter 1 used their experience of combat as the basis of their stories and art, and they all eventually became famous literary professionals. Chapter 1 also provides a brief historical overview of World War II as well as interviews with three combatants who subsequently published books about their experience.

Chapter 2 is a study of the home front during World War II. Like no other war before it, this war brought radical change not only to the battlefield but to the home front as well. Chapter 3 addresses the issues of occupation, resistance, and espionage. During World War II the level of brutality reached unprecedented levels— the world had never before seen such inhumanity on such a large scale. This chapter includes an interview with a novelist who has not only written about the ravages of this war but lived through the German bombing of Britain, the Blitz, as well. Chapter 4 focuses on the Holocaust, the persecution and attempted annihilation of the Jews by the Nazis. Finally, Chapter 5 considers the devastation of Hiroshima and Nagasaki by atomic weapons, events that have changed humanity forever by initiating a post-war arms race that would threaten the world with nuclear annihilation.

Documents presented in this work include the instruments of surrender by both Germany and Japan, transcripts of certain speeches by President Franklin D. Roosevelt, a snapshot collection of historical perspectives, a historical case study, and interviews.

Topics for written and oral exploration, and suggestions for further reading, are found at the end of each chapter.

Page numbers set within parentheses refer to the particular text referenced in the related endnote.

NOTE

1. Martin Gilbert, *The First World War: A Complete History* (New York: Henry Holt, 1994), 518.

World War II Chronology

October 1929

Benito Mussolini and the Italian Fascist Party as-sume power and eventually bring an end to democratic government in Italy. Under Musso-lini's leadership Italy joins Germany and Japan as one of the Axis Powers in a fascist alliance.

September 1931

The Japanese Imperial Army occupies the Man-churian area of China. During their brutal oc-cupation the Japanese exploit the area's natural resources and people in support of the Japanese war machine.

February 1933

After becoming chancellor of Germany in Janu-ary, Adolf Hitler gains dictatorial control over the German government. Hitler uses the burn-ing of the Reichstag (the German parliament building) to increase his control over the coun-try. One month later Dachau, the first concen-tration camp, is built near Munich.

October 1935

Mussolini's Italian Army invades Ethiopia. Brit-ain and France attempt to impose sanctions against Italy, causing Mussolini to move politi-cally closer to Germany. Although the Italian Army possesses modern weapons of war, the

Ethiopians prove difficult to defeat. This conflict continues until May 1936.

July 1936   The Spanish Civil War pits the Soviet-backed Republican forces against General Franco's fascist army sponsored by Germany and Italy. Germany uses this conflict to try out its new war machines, such as the dive-bomber, and to strengthen its alliance with Mussolini's fascist military. After years of bitter fighting, Franco's forces prevail in 1939.

29 September 1938   After annexing Austria in March 1938, Hitler turns his attention to the German-speaking people living in Czechoslovakia. Attempting to avoid an armed conflict, Britain's prime minister, Neville Chamberlain, negotiates an appeasement to Hitler in Munich, which allowed Germany to occupy the German-speaking areas of Czechoslovakia (eventually, however, all of this country would be forcefully occupied). Chamberlain fails to understand the true madness of the man with whom he is negotiating.

1 September 1939   The German Wehrmacht invades Poland, and Britain and France respond by declaring war against the aggressor nation. World War II begins.

9 April 1940   The Wehrmacht invades Norway. On 10 May 1940, Germany launches an offensive against the Allies on the Western Front, and by the end of the month it forces the Allies to begin the evacuation of the continent at Dunkirk. France falls to the German onslaught on 22 June 1940. The Battle of Britain begins on 10 July 1940 when German planes attack British port targets.

6 April 1941   German forces conquer both Yugoslavia and Greece, and by the end of May Crete is taken as well. On 22 June 1941, Germany launches Operation Barbarossa by invading the Soviet Union. Japan bombs the U.S. Navy at Pearl Harbor on 7 December 1941. The United States and Great Britain declare war against Japan the next day.

4 June 1942	The U.S. Navy decisively defeats the Japanese Navy at Midway Island; in August the U.S. Marines land on Guadalcanal with an amphibious assault. On 8 November the Allies invade North Africa in Operation Torch.
2 February 1943	In arguably the most decisive event of the war, the German 6th Army surrenders to the Soviets. The remaining Jews in the Warsaw ghetto revolt against German forces during April. On 9 July the Allies begin Operation Husky, the invasion of Sicily, and by September the Allies begin the Italian campaigns.
6 June 1944	The Allies begin the reclamation of the European continent with the D-Day invasion of Normandy. In September the Allies launch a major airborne offensive in Holland called Operation Market-Garden. In the Pacific Theater the Americans invade occupied Philippines during October. On 16 December the Germans initiate a desperate offensive against the Allies on the Western Front known as the Battle of the Bulge.
19 February 1945	U.S. Marines land at Iwo Jima in Operation Detachment, and then U.S. forces land at Okinawa on 1 April. The deaths of President Roosevelt, Mussolini, and Hitler occur during April. On 8 May the German forces finally surrender, but Japan continues to hold out until the United States drops atomic bombs on Hiroshima and Nagasaki in August. The Japanese finally surrender on 15 August 1945.

1

The Combatants

An Analysis of Martha Gellhorn's *A Stricken Field*, Joseph Heller's *Catch-22*, Kurt Vonnegut's *Slaughterhouse-Five*, Norman Mailer's *The Naked and the Dead*, James Jones' *From Here to Eternity*, Irwin Shaw's *The Young Lions*, and the Poems of Richard Wilbur, James Dickey, and Randall Jarrell

LITERARY ANALYSIS

Somewhere in the overlapping of fact and fiction presented in this chapter lies art in a most sublime form: in the survivor's bittersweet expression of both relief and awe at having escaped death, the ultimate tragedy of war. Although the works of literature discussed in this chapter represent different perspectives, narrative styles, and genres, the one similarity among them is that they are the voices of individuals who directly participated in the great global conflict called World War II. Some other war veterans have told me that there is no more horrible or degrading experience in life than combat; if these works of literature are any indication, it would be hard to argue with their assertion. None of these works glorify war in any way.

The following literary analysis provides only a brief synopsis of the works studied in this chapter. The analysis is not meant to be an exhaustive discussion of each work of World War II combat, but a representation of how some writers and poets approached their experiences and their craft. The one common characteristic of all these works is a de-romanticized view of war: war indeed is hell.

A STRICKEN FIELD

Adolf Hitler, appeased by British prime minister Neville Chamberlain at Munich in September 1938, was allowed to conquer Czechoslovakia without firing a shot. This appeasement allowed Hitler to occupy all areas of Czechoslovakia that contained German-speaking people. Martha Gellhorn, a correspondent who personally covered the Nazi takeover of that country, describes in *A Stricken Field* (1940) how Czechoslovakia changed almost overnight from a peaceful land into a hellish nightmare under fascist rule. Although *A Stricken Field* is a novel, Gellhorn approaches the takeover of Czechoslovakia from a more journalistic standpoint than a purely imaginative one. The reader soon discovers that in this world turned upside down by Nazi domination, facts have truly become stranger than fiction.

The novel's protagonist, American journalist Mary Douglas (a fictional representation of Gellhorn herself), reports the horrific fate of this stricken country. The story begins with Douglas flying into the Czech capital from Paris. The Germans she sees at the airport stand out with their strange swastikas and boisterous swagger: these men already possess the arrogance of world conquerors. As the novel develops, Douglas realizes that these Nazis are bullies who mean serious business. Shocked by what she sees in Czechoslovakia, Douglas soon takes the side of the innocent Czech citizens. In fact, by the novel's end Douglas is smuggling out a narrative describing the Nazi atrocities in that victimized country.

Reading this narrative, Douglas discovers that it

> was a simply worded statement, made by a postman, whose name and town address were inked out, telling of the Nazi invasion as he had seen it. It read flatly, being written with no emotion. He described first the local terror, practiced by the triumphant and unleashed Henleinists [Czech fascists] in his village, before the actual entry of the German army. He then told, in less detail, of one night and day after the Reichwehr [the Nazi forces] took over, during which Sudeten citizens had been summarily arrested and transported by truck to concentration camps.[1]

The "middle-aged, drawn, weary and uncared-for woman" who brought this narrative to Mary explains how people risked their

lives to get the story out (284). Douglas, who then drops her journalistic objectivity and her previous fear of smuggling even cigarettes, decides to join the movement and risk her own life to get
the story out. The more she reads of the narrative, the more con-
vinced she is that she has made the right decision:

> She read of night executions and how the shots sounded to people
> locked in their dark homes, praying there would be no sudden foot-
> steps coming up their paths, no muffled, commanding knock at
> their doors. She read of the sick being hurried from the hospitals,
> since even hospitals offer no protection; of concentration camps
> springing up, and reported in whispers through a countryside
> where jails had always been small and cozy-looking and uncrowded,
> and law courts were proud public monuments; of the immediate
> Jew-baiting, described by a shamed and heartbroken Czech woman
> who had seen children called Jew in the street, painted with the
> word, placarded, mocked and hounded, but the children only wept
> and were afraid and did not understand what this meant; of sin-
> gular, painless but revolting humiliations, invented to hurt a whole
> people's pride. (287)

The novel ends with Mary safely on the plane to Paris with her
"contraband" securely hidden, the narrative waiting to be shared
with an unsuspecting world.

Gellhorn, who had also previously covered the Spanish Civil War
for *Collier's* magazine, was no stranger to the destructive force of
Nazi hatred. During the Spanish Civil War the Germans had used
the occasion to try out their new war machines that terrorized the
Spanish countryside from 1936 until the war's end on 1 April 1939.
However, the atrocities in *A Stricken Field* eventually pale in comparison to the ravages the continent experienced by Hitler's forces.

Spare in emotion, *A Stricken Field* is written in an elegant style
that exemplifies the new approach to literary discourse about
atrocities after the Nazi reign of terror. In writing of the nightmare
brought on by Hitler, writers used understated language to balance
the extraordinary images they saw and were compelled to describe.
The cruel barbarity against innocents and utter astonishment at the
scope of the inhumanity forced Gellhorn (like most contemporary
writers) to hold in her emotions and language because the experience was almost too difficult to describe. This was a world both
figuratively and literally turned upside down.

CATCH-22

Joseph Heller's novel is arguably one of the most important American novels published in the last forty years. *Catch-22* (1961), a dark comedy about life in the U.S. Army Air Force (USAAF) during the last stages of World War II, is set on the fictitious island of Pianosa off the coast of Italy. Although essentially a war narrative, this novel is also about life under any form of bureaucratic repression whereby the individual has been dehumanized by power, greed, hubris, and other aspects of moral confusion.

Because of the immense popularity of this novel, the phrase "catch-22" has become common in the English language. We hear it almost every day when someone is put in a no-win situation, mainly because of bureaucratic double-talk and twisted logic: when you are "damned if you do" and "damned if you don't."

As the novel begins, the protagonist, Yossarian, has "pain in his liver" and lies in the hospital, a place of refuge where he can avoid going on yet another bombing mission.[2] Yossarian clearly expresses his anxieties about this phase of the war:

> Men went mad and were rewarded with medals. All over the world, boys on every side of the bomb line were laying down their lives for what they had been told was their country, and no one seemed to mind, least of all the boys who were laying down their young lives. There was no end in sight. The only end in sight was Yossarian's own, and he might have remained in the hospital until doomsday had it not been for that patriotic Texan with his infundibuliform jowls and his lumpy, rumpleheaded, indestructible smile cracked forever across the front of his face like the brim of a black ten-gallon hat. The Texan wanted everybody in the ward to be happy but Yossarian and Dunbar. He was really very sick.
>
> But Yossarian couldn't be happy, even though the Texan didn't want him to be, because outside the hospital there was still nothing funny going on. The only thing going was a war, and no one seemed to notice but Yossarian and Dunbar. (25)

In countless interviews (including one in this book), Heller has unequivocally stated that he was not opposed to the American war effort during World War II. In this passage, however, Yossarian (and Heller agrees with what Yossarian says) is instead articulating his opposition to senseless slaughter. Yossarian does not want to die for a leader who would manipulate his personnel by telling them that it is good to die for their country when they are in fact at war for other, unstated reasons. *Catch-22* is not so much anti-war as anti-misuse and -abuse of power.

Heller, himself a veteran of sixty combat missions as a bombardier in the USAAF, draws on his own experiences during World War II, giving the story a manic sense of authenticity. In *Tilting at Mortality: Narrative Strategies in Joseph Heller's Fiction*, David M. Craig writes that Heller's

> experiences as a bombardier over Avignon during World War II were catalytic to his career as a writer. In them *Catch-22* begins. Their spark was not to his desire to be an author, for that had burned unabated since childhood. Nor did the reaction that they occasioned occur quickly, regularly, or consciously. Rather, Avignon provided in highly compressed form his essential subject, human mortality, and engaged his imagination in a way in which this subject could eventually be given expression. No *Catch-22* reader is likely to forget the result, the Snowden death scene over Avignon or the secret of entrails: "[m]an was matter. . . . Drop him out of a window and he'll fall. Set fire to him and he'll burn. Bury him and he'll rot, like other kinds of garbage."[3]

Yossarian, who has been deeply affected by Snowden's death, fights to save his own life. For him, war is personal, an act of self-survival. He now realizes that people are actually trying to kill him and that there is nothing more personal than dying.

Anxiously aware of his own mortality, Yossarian is "deathly" afraid of participating in more bombing missions. This fear is made more acute because Colonel Cathcart, eager for publicity, keeps raising the number of missions an airman must complete before being sent home. In this no-win situation, this catch-22, the Germans are no longer the enemy—Yossarian's own commander is! Unable to negotiate in the insane world that Colonel Cathcart has created, and with the war's outcome already clearly decided in the Allies' favor, Yossarian asserts his independence from the system. He decides to desert and so declares, " 'I've got to get to Sweden' " (462). Sweden becomes his goal, a more secure and permanent haven than the hospital had proven to be.

In part because its intensity never lets up, *Catch-22* is an extremely effective work of fiction. Heller breaks apart the narrative flow, often repeating important thematic and emotional scenes throughout the novel, to create a work of art in which form truly equals meaning. The story is about a crazy world, full of crazy characters, and told in a "crazy" way. But what is most important in the novel is not the telling of a traditional story but rather the conveying of the theme about the importance of the individual surviving in an especially hostile, absurd world. *Catch-22* is a wholly satisfying novel about a wholly unsatisfying situation.

SLAUGHTERHOUSE-FIVE OR *THE CHILDREN'S CRUSADE: A DUTY-DANCE WITH DEATH*

Kurt Vonnegut's dark satire, *Slaughterhouse-Five* (1968), is about the survival of Billy Pilgrim, a disoriented officer captured by the Germans during the closing phases of the war and sent to Dresden just in time to experience that city's horrific fire-bombing by the Allies. Like the novel's protagonist, Vonnegut, a soldier in the U.S. Army, was also held captive by the Germans and witnessed the destruction of Dresden during World War II. The main title comes from the disused slaughterhouse number five where Billy and other American prisoners-of-war (POWs) were being held when the bombing occurred on 13 February 1945.

Billy, who seems overwhelmed by life's devastations, epitomizes the ultimate survivalist: he literally becomes "unstuck in time."[4] Because Billy can travel easily to several different dimensions of time and space, he knows before it will happen that Dresden will soon be incinerated—with thousands of buildings destroyed and countless people killed—and there is nothing he can do about it. "So it goes" is all that he can say, as he surrenders to the inevitability of it all. Despite his other experiences (such as surviving a plane crash or captivity on Tralfamadore, a planet 446,120,000,000,000,000 miles from Earth), nothing compares with the senseless destruction of Dresden. With Billy providing a perspective like no other person on Earth, the bombing of Dresden becomes not just another routine of war, one more bombing raid to hasten the war effort, but a senseless atrocity—a calamity, literally of universal proportions.

As Vonnegut transports this "Pilgrim" through both time and

space, he unhinges traditional narrative form to correspond with Billy's unworldly experience:

> Billy has gone to sleep a senile widower and awakened on his wedding day. He has walked through a door in 1955 and come out another one in 1941. He has gone back through that door many times, he says, and pays random visits to all the events in between. (23)

By using this particular narrative form, borrowed from the science fiction genre, Vonnegut stresses Billy's role as an individual who transcends the boundaries of normal existence and perspective.

The preposterous paranormal adventures of Billy Pilgrim's progress, especially his trips to outer space, underscore the hitherto unimaginable nature of the World War II Dresden experience. Until World War II, who would have thought that the militaries of the United States and United Kingdom, two democratic countries, would be capable of the utter destruction of a city like Dresden long after its strategic value had disappeared? No one, as Vonnegut's novel makes abundantly clear—not even someone from outer space.

THE NAKED AND THE DEAD

This novel by Norman Mailer is the closest book twentieth-century America has to Tolstoy's *War and Peace*: it is truly a modern classic. Among the various duties he performed in the U.S. Army during World War II, Mailer served as a rifleman in a reconnaissance platoon stationed in the Pacific Theater. The setting for *The Naked and the Dead* (1948) is Anopopei, a fictitious island in the Pacific. The novel begins with an army division about to make an amphibious landing; its objective is to defeat and destroy the Japanese forces defending the island.

The novel focuses primarily on a handful of people: the invading force's commander, Major General Cummings; his aide, Lieutenant Hearns; and a reconnaissance platoon led by Sergeant Croft, a war-hardened veteran. The book, in realistic and illuminating detail, is ripe with examples of the jealousies, humiliations, tensions, and fears the modern combat experience has generated among all the ranks. The reader never sees the enemy, despite their eminent threat, because the true danger to the individual soldier actually lies among his own comrades.

As this novel develops, the invading army's offensive is stalled: Cummings, the consummate strategist, begins making elaborate plans to outflank his opponent. Hearns describes Cummings thus: "He had known men who were casually like him, the same trace of effeminacy, the same probable capacity for extreme ruthlessness, but there was more here, more complexity, less of a congealed and overt personality to perceive comfortably."[5] Because Cummings needs more information about the enemy's status, he sends the reconnaissance platoon on a dangerous scouting mission behind the lines. He is the ultimate manipulator and uses these men to hatch his scheme for glory. Lieutenant Hearns, finally having enough of Cummings' mindgames, asks to be placed in charge of the platoon, a request that puts him at odds with Sergeant Croft, the absolute leader of the unit.

Croft is resentful of Hearns' insertion into his unit, and he will not let anything get in the way of maintaining his position. Because Croft is an intuitively skilled soldier, the platoon is drawn to follow his lead:

> Croft had an instinctive knowledge of land, sensed the stresses and torsions that had first erupted it, the abrasions of wind and water. The platoon had long ceased to question any direction he took; they knew he would be right as infallibly as sun after darkness or fatigue after a long march. They never even thought about it any more. (550)

In the end, Hearns is killed on the mission largely because of Croft's subversive insubordination and, quite frankly, his own inexperience. Hearns proves to have had more skills in military politics than in the vagaries of combat. The unit's survivors return from their dangerous mission only to find that the battle is over— the division gained the victory without their help.

Coincidentally, while Cummings is away from the island, the offensive seems to take a life of its own. Despite the absence of its leader, the division makes remarkable progress under the unremarkable Operations Officer, Major Dalleson, against an unexpectedly weakened enemy. Eager to take the initiative (and the credit) upon his return, Cummings makes the most of mopping up the enemy; but because he had so little to do with the actual victory, he is disappointed in how things went overall:

> He had never quite freed himself of the shock Major Dalleson's victory had given him. To leave his battle front on a quiet morning and return the next day to find the campaign virtually over was a little like the disbelief with which a man would come home to find his house burned down. . . . What irritated him most of all was that he must congratulate Dalleson, perhaps even promote him. To snub Dalleson now would be too patent. (622)

The petty concerns of this self-absorbed officer seem chillingly inappropriate and in complete disregard for the men who fought and died in the battle. All Cummings seems to care about is self-promotion and his own career.

The "time machine" chapters are the feature through which the novel tells the full story of these men. In these various interluding chapters, the reader discovers the pre-war lives of the characters—their backgrounds, fears, joys, and disappointments. Bitterly honest and highly developed, *The Naked and the Dead* tells the naked truth about the harsh reality of World War II and the flawed men who fought it.

FROM HERE TO ETERNITY

Set in Hawaii right before the Japanese surprise attack on Pearl Harbor, this novel (published in 1952) by James Jones is a prime example of American literary realism. It concerns the condition of the U.S. Army on the verge of its most challenging war. Jones based this novel on his experiences as a serviceman in the U.S. Army from 1939 to 1945. The picture of this between-the-wars army is at once fascinating and revealing: without an "external" enemy to fight, the soldiers spend most of their time and energy fighting each other. The chief characters are Robert E. Lee Prewitt (a private who has not only stopped boxing for his unit but also ceased playing the bugle for the Army as an act of contrition for the man he killed in the ring) and Sergeant Milton Anthony Warden (a manipulative, cynical Army lifer who finds unexpected redemption in the love of Karen, his company commander's wife).

All the characters in this novel face a host of problems. The company commander, so obsessed with his own career that he neglects his wife, is also ironically a poor military leader. Karen, who has grown tired of being neglected by her ambitious husband, has drifted from one meaningless affair to another until she finds Warden. And for the time being he becomes the one lover who seems to make a difference in her life. Prewitt becomes bitter about the brutal murder of a fellow soldier, so he murders the perpetrator, Staff Sergeant Fatso Judson, and then goes AWOL, hiding out in his prostitute girlfriend's house. After weeks of hiding, Prewitt eventually decides to go back to his unit after the Japanese surprise attack; but before he can reach his barracks he is shot dead by nervous Military Police (MPs) who mistake him for an enemy infiltrator.

Warden's and Karen's fates are far less tragic. After turning down an officer's commission, which would have made him a gentleman forever in the eyes of the Army, Warden and Karen drift apart. At the book's end, after saying goodbye to both Warden and her husband, Karen is on board a ship carrying her back to the mainland. But before the ship leaves the harbor, she has already attracted the affections of another man.

Besides concentrating on the love interests and personal problems of the main characters, this novel depicts interesting scenes of the Japanese surprise attack. For example, after recovering from the initial explosion of the Japanese bombs, Warden and a few of his troops muster to shoot down the attacking aircraft:

> Another plane, on which they could clearly see the red discs [the rising sun emblem of the Japanese military], came skidding over the trees firing. . . . The plane flashed past, the helmeted head with the square goggles over the slant eyes and the long scarf rippling out behind it and the grin on the face as he waved, all clearly visible for the space of a wink, like a traveltalk slide flashed on and then off of a screen.[6]

Although Warden and his men have now seen the face of the Japanese enemy, in this case, ironically the real "enemy" is still themselves (as in the saying, "I have seen the enemy and the enemy is us"). This pre-war portrait of disorder, with all its murders, sexual affairs, and tragedies, amazes readers by the fact that this army was eventually able to win the war. A bickering tradition-bound army, these men seemingly had to overcome themselves first before they could think about defeating the Japanese.

THE YOUNG LIONS

This neglected novel (published in 1948) by Irwin Shaw is about the lives of three combatants who find their fates determined by a war that turned the whole world upside down: Noah, a sensitive American Jew; Michael, a Hollywood star; and Christian, a handsome yet insensitive Austrian. These men, born on opposite sides of the geographic and social scale, cross paths with one another and dramatically change each other's lives. Shaw's own experiences in the U.S. Army in Europe during World War II had a profound influence on his writing of *The Young Lions*.

The title of the novel comes from a minor book in the Old Testament about the prophet Nahum, who celebrates the coming destruction of Nineveh, the capital of Assyria.[7] The novel's opening epigram voices the apocalyptic vision of Nahum: "Behold, I am against thee, saith the Lord of hosts, and I will burn her chariots in the smoke, and the sword shall devour thy young lions: and I will cut off thy prey from the earth, and the voice of the messengers shall no more be heard."[8] Like this Old Testament story, *The Young Lions* is also about atrocity, death, and revenge.

The novel has biblical proportions as well: it is about men who are forced to disrupt their lives, lives not without troubles, to die or be radically changed forever. The opening setting is pre-war Austria, where Christian is attempting to rape an American girl. His sexual assault, as unconscionable as it is, is a situation he has apparently been in before. It is also a prelude to the barbaric violence about to occur throughout Europe: a foreshadowing of a loss of civility ravaging the world.

As self-absorbed and hard-hearted as Christian is, over the course of the story, even he becomes disillusioned—not by the atrocities of war but by the petty corruption of his comrades in the German Army. It is easy to see that despite his sterling qualities as a soldier Christian severely fails as a human being.

Noah, who possesses few obvious characteristics of an exemplary soldier (except for a strong heart), is ultimately a success as both a soldier and a human being. Because he is Jewish, Noah experiences bigotry from fellow soldiers in the U.S. Army; he is an outcast. Despite his difficulties in military society, his love for Hope, his faithful wife, redeems him from his tribulations. The experience of war, however, proves no less difficult for Noah than what he experienced in civilian life. The recipient of a Silver Star, he is wounded in battle only to return to combat to be killed by Christian. Shaw describes his fatal shooting:

> Noah had been hit in the throat, low and to one side. He was bleeding badly, but he was still breathing, shallow, erratic gasps. He was not conscious. Michael crouched beside him, putting a bandage on, but it didn't seem to stop the blood much. Noah was lying on his back, his helmet in a small pale bed of pink flowers growing very close to the ground. His face had resumed its expensive, remote expression. His eyes were closed and the blond-tipped lashes, curled over his pale-fuzzed cheek, gave the upper part of his face the old, vulnerable expression of girlishness and youth. (598)

Noah's body does not survive the war, but his memory survives in the hearts of his wife and Michael.

Whereas life has always been a struggle for Noah, life is ironically easy for Michael. Self-assured and a part of the social elite, Michael has had everything go his way—until a bad marriage and the military draft. Michael eventually befriends Noah when they end up in the same basic training unit. Separated at the front because Michael gets a safe assignment to Civil Affairs, the two are reunited after D-Day and remain together until the end, which occurs when Michael witnesses Noah's death. Michael then kills Christian, the man who has killed his friend. Michael returns Noah's body to the unit commander. Now a chastened, new man, Michael survives and is transformed by his combat experiences.

This novel, arguably Shaw's finest work, excels at describing the lives of the combatants. Following a more traditional form than other novels discussed in this chapter, it sensitively develops the often-desperate experiences of individual soldiers on all sides. Because Shaw describes the experiences of these three combatants with such vivid detail and with such sympathy, it is easy to forget that these were fictional soldiers and not real ones.

THE POETRY OF WILBUR, DICKEY, AND JARRELL

Images of combat are rare in poetry. Indeed, poetry is primarily a philosophical, reflective form of artistic expression, and despite the subject matter, the poem has to work like a poem—with irony and imagery. As celebrated poetic craftsmen, Richard Wilbur, James Dickey, and Randall Jarrell used combat images very sparingly and wrote only a few war poems. However, those that they did write are evocative of both the horror of war and the balm of hope.

Although these poems begin within the realm of realism, describing actual features of the combatant's world—a landscape littered with mines, the death of just men, or the last handstand of a doomed man—each one eventually moves beyond mere realism and ends almost transcendently hopeful. It is poetry that seems to come from two minds.

Richard Wilbur's war poems are based on his military service with the 36th Infantry Division during World War II, and his best one is "Mined Country" (1947), which is about the betrayal of nature—a beautiful landscape mined with explosives.[9] Instead of being the poet's traditional refuge from the discomforts of life, this pastoral setting has ironically become a place of great danger. In fact, because there is little mention of the people who actually laid the mines there, the inanimate woods have replaced the flesh-and-blood enemy—at least in the poet's mind. In a world turned upside down, turned "wild" as Wilbur says, even old poetical traditions and places of refuge have become threatening.

Like the irony Wilbur employs in "Mined Country" to help explain the seemingly inexplicable, Dickey's best war poem, "The Performance" (1957), uses irony for the same reason. During World War II, Dickey served as an USAAF airman in the Pacific Theater. "The Performance" is about the brutal execution of an American by the Japanese, and it conveys this scene of violence with ironic disregard. The poem is devoid of the anger seemingly appropriate to the occasion. Although the poet should be outraged at the senseless death of his comrade, his friend's comic handstand before the execution will not allow it.

Thus, the poem is not about the act of dying but about the process of living life to the fullest. When the poet's comrade, Donald Armstrong, meets his fate, it will not ultimately matter because he has lived life to the fullest. In other words, Armstrong (whose name contains an obvious pun) has done all things in life but stand on his hands in the moments just before being executed—that is, until now.[10]

Randall Jarrell, who joined the USAAF in 1942 and flew combat missions in Europe throughout the war, writes more about the war in his poetry than either of the other two poets. In the poem he thought best expressed his views of the war, "Eighth Air Force" (1948), Jarrell, like the other two poets, relies on irony to convey the unease of his own contribution to the war's killing. He describes the bivouac of aviators as a place where men play with puppy dogs.[11] The sentimental image of the puppy exists here incongruously with that of the "murderers," the "guilty" airmen who have dropped tons of bombs on "innocent" civilians. J. A. Bryant Jr., in *Understanding Randall Jarrell*, writes:

> the principal function of the men, actually boys, viewed here in the evening before a mission is simply that of effective instruments and the nature of their moment of rest, a countdown to further deployment. The speaker, himself a survivor of bombing missions, contemplates the men. . . . He reflects that, for all their appearance of innocence, these men are murderers.[12]

In the end, Jarrell resolves this incongruity by drawing on an allusion to Pontius Pilate, the man who "washed his hands" of the death of Jesus: although he could find no fault in that just man, circumstances forced Pilate to sacrifice the Nazarene. Without this sacrificial death, however, Jesus could not have become the Messiah, the transcendent figure in one of the world's most pervasive religions. Like Pilate, the poet can find no fault in the representative "just man," the airman who is one mission away from going home, because circumstance often compels people to commit evil in order to combat an even greater evil. Readers are also forced to ask the same question Pilate faced: How could we condemn a man such as this one? Jarrell thus suggests that one should not find fault with this airman who has been bombing "innocent" civilians.

Like the novels, these poems convey the difficulty of combat: its hardships, degradations, fears, and bitter ironies—life with very little joy. Despite the fact that the intensity of combat compresses a lot of life into a small amount of time (the essence of poetry and fiction itself), all these fiction writers and poets quickly went on to other literary subjects besides war. Apparently they did not want to dwell on war too long. But before they did get on with their lives, these artists (and many others) gave the reading world valuable reflections on their experiences at the front.

NOTES

1. Martha Gellhorn, *A Stricken Field* (New York: Penguin, [1940] 1968), 280. All subsequent quotations of this text come from this source.

2. Joseph Heller, *Catch-22* (New York: Scribners, [1961] 1996), 15. All subsequent quotations of this text come from this source.

3. David M. Craig. *Tilting at Mortality: Narrative Strategies in Joseph Heller's Fiction* (Detroit: Wayne State University Press, 1997), 40.

4. Kurt Vonnegut, *Slaughterhouse-Five* (New York: Dell, 1968), 23. All subsequent quotations of this text come from this source.

5. Norman Mailer, *The Naked and the Dead* (New York: Holt, Rinehart and Winston, 1948), 70. All subsequent quotations of this text come from this source.

6. James Jones, *From Here to Eternity* (New York: Scribners, 1952), 744. All subsequent quotations of this text come from this source.

7. "Nahum," *The New American Bible for Catholics* (Washington, DC: World Catholic Press, 1986), 970.

8. Irwin Shaw, *The Young Lions* (New York: Signet, 1948). All subsequent quotations of this text come from this source.

9. Richard Wilbur, "Mined Country," in *New and Collected Poems* (New York: Harcourt Brace Jovanovich, 1989), 343.

10. James Dickey, "The Performance," in *The Norton Anthology of Modern Poetry*, eds. Richard Ellmann and Robert O'Clair (New York: Norton, 1973).

11. Randall Jarrell, "Eighth Air Force," in *The Norton Anthology of Modern Poetry*, eds. Richard Ellmann and Robert O'Clair (New York: Norton, 1973), 880.

12. J. A. Bryant, *Understanding Randall Jarrell* (Columbia: University of South Carolina Press, 1986), 51.

HISTORICAL CONTEXT

CZECHOSLOVAKIAN ANNEXATION

After the peaceful incorporation of Austria into the German Third Reich (the title Hitler gave his Nazi regime) in March 1938, Hitler focused on annexing the area that had been given to Czechoslovakia under the 1919 Treaty of Versailles. This area had a majority of Sudeten Germans. In 1938, 14 million people were living in the Czechoslovakian Democratic Republic: 10 million of them were Czechs and Slovaks; 3 million were Sudetens; and the rest represented various eastern European ethnic groups.[1] Konrad Henlein, the leader of the Sudeten German Party and Hitler's Nazi ally, was politicizing the German cause in Czechoslovakia.

On 26 September, Hitler claimed that the Sudetens were being mistreated by Czechoslovakia and gave the European powers until 28 September to restore the Sudetenland to the German Reich, or else he would mobilize the Wehrmacht, thereby implementing an invasion (code-named Fall Grun).[2] Italy's fascist leader, Benito Mussolini, hurriedly organized a meeting among the leaders of Britain, France, Italy, and Germany in Munich. (Interestingly, no one was there to represent the Czechoslovakian people.) The result of this meeting was the complete appeasement of Hitler's demands to control the German-speaking territory of Czechoslovakia. For his part Hitler promised that he would diplomatically consult with the other European powers instead of making shrill demands, but of course he never intended to keep any of his promises. Britain's prime minister, Neville Chamberlain, failing to comprehend Hitler's intentions, returned from the meeting and claimed he had brokered peace, when in fact he had unwittingly brokered eventual war. The war would begin a year later. Chamberlain never figured out one could not reason with a madman.

By the middle of March 1939, Hitler had gained complete control of what was the former Czechoslovakian Republic, replacing it with the Protectorate of Bohemia and Moravia—and Baron von Neurath as a puppet *Reischprotector*. Although the German occupation of the Czechoslovakian people may have been somewhat less harsh than it later was in other countries, 350,000 people eventually perished there under Nazi domination.[3]

THE INVASION OF POLAND

The immediate opening of hostilities during World War II involved the invasion of Poland on 1 September 1939.[4] Without any declaration of war, the Wehrmacht rushed fifty-three divisions, including six armored divisions and all their mechanized infantry, into Poland along a broad front.[5] Although the ill-equipped Polish Army troops doggedly attempted to hold on, the result was their inevitable and swift capitulation. By 14 September—only two weeks after the invasion began—the German Army had Warsaw surrounded. Then, Hitler insisted that the city be bombed into complete submission.[6]

On 27 September, embattled Warsaw surrendered to the Wehrmacht. The German Army was concerned that this rubble of a city would now be hazardous to their soldiers' health, so they waited several days before going in. Because the city was completely without food, water, and adequate medical capabilities, this delay resulted in the deaths of many Polish soldiers and citizens. Soon the Polish leaders, professionals, and intellectuals who had managed to survive were rounded up and murdered.

The reason that the German Army had such an easy time in this military operation was that the Polish Army was an ideal opponent—weak and mistake-prone. Moreover, the Polish troops were fitted with obsolete equipment and led by an inferior general staff.[7] The Polish geography also provided a flat terrain with few natural barriers, and the Polish military possessed very few fortifications to stop the Germans.

Hitler's aims in invading Poland were not only to restore German territory lost through the Treaty of Versailles but also to initiate the complete conquest of Europe. The prelude to the Polish invasion had followed Hitler's typical pattern—he made demands and threats, and the other European powers attempted to appease him. However, Poland, unlike Czechoslovakia, resisted his demands for repatriation of ethnic Germans in its territory. Poland felt empowered because it had signed a Mutual Assistance Pact with Britain on 25 August 1939, and it also had a long-standing alliance with France.[8] However, the Germans had signed the Nazi-

Soviet Nonaggression Pact on 23 August 1939 in Moscow, opening the way for Germany to invade Poland and eventually all its eastern neighbors. While the main purpose of this pact was to prohibit both the Soviets and the Germans from attacking each other, it also allowed either country to act aggressively against other nations in Europe.

As a pretense for the actual invasion, the Germans faked a Polish attack on a bordering radio station. Martin Gilbert notes that the first victim of the war was "most probably a common criminal," killed on 31 August 1939 by the Schutzstaffen (SS, protection squads) as a part of the deception.[9] Heinrich Himmler, the Nazi head of the SS from 1929 to 1945 and leader of the Gestapo (the Nazis' secret police) from 1943 to 1945,[10] led this special operation. Because of long-standing strained relations with both Germany and the Soviet Union, Polish forces before the invasion had been split between both the Western and Eastern Fronts. Polish forces were stretched to the breaking point. When the German Army penetrated the Western defensive line and had the Polish Army encircled, those forces were essentially doomed because there were no reserves. The war, for all practical purposes, was decided in just four days. Before the war, Poland's overall strategy for defense had been to mobilize quickly and maintain a continuous defense, and more important, for France to intervene if Germany attacked. None of these actions ever took place because the German Army moved much more rapidly than anyone had imagined possible.

The Wehrmacht soldiers outperformed their opponents at a remarkable level. For example, the marching achievements of the German infantry were phenomenal, traveling close to twenty miles a day—not far behind the twenty-two miles their mechanized comrades averaged. The German onslaught was not completely flawless, however: the armored XIX Corps ran out of gas only on the second day of combat.

Hitler wanted to impose absolute German "will" over this country, so he turned the infamous SS Death's Head regiments loose behind the Wehrmacht's advances. Hitler wanted to destroy all forms of Polish culture—particularly in the Wartheland, the area of western Poland that had historically been under Prussian control. Within a week of the Polish invasion, 24,000 officers and men of the Death's Head regiments had begun the extermination of

Jews and anyone else who might pose a "threat" to Nazism.[11] To hasten Poland's destruction Himmler began many special "actions," such as mass deportations of unwanteds, outlawing the Polish language, and implementing the *Lebensborn* program, a procedure by which to Germanize Polish children by removing them from their natural parents to adoptive Germans in the fatherland.[12] Poland ultimately suffered the worst of all Nazi atrocities, as all Polish cultural institutions were destroyed.[13] According to John Ellis in *World War II: A Statistical Survey*, Poland's prewar population was 34,800,000; of those, fully 4,800,000 citizens were lost in concentration camps and about 500,000 from other causes.[14]

THE CONQUEST OF THE CONTINENT

Compounding the weakness in the Polish defense was the fact that Germany was employing revolutionary blitzkrieg tactics. In fact, these tactics were so revolutionary that the entire German Army was not completely won over to them. The main architect of blitzkrieg, General Heinz Guderian (the commander whose tanks ran out of gas on the second day of fighting), was considered an unpopular maverick among the German military establishment, but his new tactics were highly favored by Hitler.

After the defeat of the Imperial German Army in World War I, Guderian (like other younger German officers) was determined to avoid costly trench warfare. The primary principle of blitzkrieg was the elevation of the mobile tank as the most important weapon in a concentrated attack.[15] Moreover, the principle of attacking became the primary strategy. In supporting the tank on the attack, other modern weapons, such as mechanized infantry and airpower, formed a combined arms force. These combined arms were controlled by a sophisticated communications system and aided by a thorough campaign of misinformation. A key to modern warfare's success was to break the opposition's spirit.

After conquering most of Norway in April 1940, Hitler quickly moved against the Continent's remaining free countries in the west. Operation Yellow (Fall Gelb), the western offensive, began on 10 May 1940 when 136 German divisions, roughly half the size of the Allied forces, stormed into the Low Countries.[16] Although Holland and Belgium were neutral, Hitler needed to control them so that his forces could bypass the Maginot Line to attack France. The Maginot Line was an elaborate system of fortified French defenses that ran from Switzerland to Luxembourg. Contrary to the Germans' new offensive strategy of blitzkrieg, France's Maginot Line represented a defensive mentality. France was obsessed with winning the last war instead of the next one. By invading the Low Countries west of France's "impregnable" defenses, Hitler's forces could render them utterly useless because they were prepared only to defend against a German frontal assault from the east.[17]

The peaceful Dutch, who had traditionally relied on flooding as a defense against raiding forces, were not at all prepared for the German onslaught. The German 18th Army quickly overran the three fortified positions that the Dutch had previously organized: the Ijssel, the Grebbe, and the Peel-Raam lines. Although the German 22nd and 7th Airborne Divisions met stiffer resistance than they had expected, these two Wehrmacht units eventually prevailed. By 12 May, the larger German Army had linked up with airborne units that had been dropped on key positions ahead of the main force—the Germans now controlled most, although not all, of Holland. On 14 May, Hitler was impatient that the Dutch were hanging on (although barely), so he ordered the Rhine River bridges at Rotterdam to be bombed immediately. The 1.1 square miles of the city's central district were heavily destroyed, resulting in the deaths of 814 civilians (although the casualty figures were rumored to be much higher).[18] The senseless bombing of this city—the Dutch government had already initiated peace negotiations before the attack began—became an important example of Nazi ruthlessness for Allied propaganda and ended the British reluctance to bomb civilian targets. Consequently, on 15 May, the Royal Air Force (RAF) bombed the Ruhr industrial area, thus beginning a massive strategic air campaign against Germany.[19]

In Belgium on 11 May, the defenders of the important Eben-Emael fortress, a fortification that controlled the strategically essential Albert Canal and Meuse River waterway to the port in Antwerp, surrendered after a crack unit of fifty-five German paratroopers attacked it on 10 May. By 11 May the offensive was going so well for the Germans that their generals were competing with each other to see who could advance the furthest along the entire Western Front that then stretched from Sedan, France, in the south to the Waal River in the north. British air support was attempting to slow the German advance in Belgium and to keep them from completely encircling all the Allied forces in that area. Within a month, however, not only would the Germans have the British Expeditionary Forces cut off from other forces in France, but Paris would also be left vulnerable as well. French forces were doing no better either, as German Panzers (tank forces) continued rumbling through the Ardennes. A French counterattack on 15 May at Sedan failed miserably. On 17 May, the German 6th Army entered Brussels, the fifth European capital to surrender to the Wehrmacht.

Despite the dire situation that the Allies faced in early May, one event took place that was of tremendous strategic importance in the eventual outcome of the war: the naming of Winston Churchill as prime minister of England on 10 May. The power of his oratory and the force of his will made him one of the most important leaders of World War II.[20]

After the fall of Brussels, British general Bernard Law Montgomery's 3rd Division withdrew to a new defensive position at the Dendre River due west of the Belgian capital city. On 18 May in France, Guderian's Panzers occupied St. Quentin and General Erwin Rommel's forces reached Cambrai; the month-long encirclement of the Allies in northwest Europe, therefore, was about two-thirds accomplished.[21] By the night of 20 May, Panzer units had reached Amiens and were headed for Abbeville, completely severing the main Allied forces on the Continent. Hundreds of thousands of Allied troops were now surrounded in northwestern France and Belgium. However, a spirited British counterattack at Amas stunned Rommel's 7th Panzer Division; for the first time since their offensive began, the German soldiers had been checked.

But the Allies were still crumbling. Inexplicably, instead of pressing their offensive, the Wehrmacht stopped and regrouped. With the German forces pausing in their offensive, the British took advantage and planned a massive evacuation of their troops from Dunkirk. Although the reasons for Hitler's decision to stop his indomitable offensive at this time are not completely understood, one possibility was that Goering persuaded him that the Luftwaffe (German Air Force) could finish off the enemy all by themselves—a bold claim that proved to be entirely baseless.

With the remaining Belgian forces collapsing around them, on 27 May the British and other Allied troops began the Dunkirk rescue. This rescue mission lasted until 2 June and involved between

850 and 950 ships and small vessels. Although only 8,000 soldiers were evacuated on the first day,[22] eventually 338,226 personnel were rescued by the end of the operation.[23] The Dunkirk evacuation was one of the most miraculous events of the war and a rallying point for the British people. The British success in this rescue arguably lost the war for Hitler, as it allowed enough Allied forces to remain in the war to fight again.

Despite the success of the Dunkirk operation for the British, the Germans soon continued their blitzkrieg with the bombing of Paris on 3 June. The full-fledged battle for France began on 5 June. By 10 June, the Allied troop evacuation began from Le Havre, Cherbourg, and other ports on the Brittany coast.[24] On 11 June, Paris was declared an open city (which meant that while Hitler would not exploit it for military purposes, the Allies would not bomb it either) and what remained of the French forces retreated in chaos to the south.[25] Paris fell to the Germans on 14 June, and on the same day parts of the Maginot Line were breached from the front as Guderian's forces swept to the east and trapped the French forces garrisoned there. On 16 June, the democratic government of France collapsed and Marshall Philippe Pétain, an 84-year-old hero of World War I, negotiated an armistice with both Germany and Italy (which had only begun hostilities with France on 10 June). Pétain then formed a new, collaborationist French government in the city of Vichy.[26] France was thus divided between the German-occupied zone in the north and Vichy in the south. With the capitulation of the French Republic, England was the only democratic country left in Europe to combat the fascist governments of Germany and Italy.

THE BATTLE OF BRITAIN AND THE BLITZ

Although the Luftwaffe did not launch its main offensive, code-named *Adlertag* (Eagle Day), until 13 August 1940, the air war for the British Islands actually began in the early summer of 1940. The Luftwaffe orchestrated its air offensive in preparation for Operation Sealion, the planned invasion of the United Kingdom that never occurred.

Despite their enormous victories so far in the war, the Germans were beginning to demonstrate a weakness in strategic thinking. Whether they ever realized it or not, the Germans had to have air support to invade Britain successfully. Thus, before the Luftwaffe troops began concentrating on Royal Air Force targets, they misguidedly bombed British channel shipping and ports along the southern coast. Then, beginning, with an intense aerial bombardment on 7 September, the Luftwaffe started a bombing campaign against the city of London, once again ignoring military targets. But by 15 September, also known as the Battle of Britain Day, the RAF had successfully adjusted to the Luftwaffe's city-destruction strategy and effectively destroyed the Luftwaffe's air offensive. The RAF's convincing victory in the air destroyed the Germans' belief that they were on the verge of victory, and it was no coincidence that Operation Sealion was postponed two days later. Besides the RAF's superior leadership and organization, technological advances (such as high-speed aircraft—the Spitfire and Hurricane fighters—and radar) proved to be important factors in the eventual defeat of the German Air Force by the end of September 1940. Ultimately, the Battle of Britain extinguished an estimated 1,294 German and 788 British aircraft.[27]

With the indefinite postponement of the invasion of Britain, Germany began night bombings, or the Blitz, on London and other cities in the United Kingdom. The complete focus was now on civilian targets; the German bombing strategy had fully developed to terrorizing citizens. The Blitz lasted from August 1940 to mid-May 1941 and brought considerable destruction to Britain: 43,000 civilians lost their lives and another 139,000 were injured, along with the demolition of a vast amount of infrastructure.[28] In all, Germany dropped 30,541 tons of bombs during 30,881 sorties from September 1940 to February 1941.[29] This air offensive, however, did not curtail British aircraft production (the RAF had more aircraft available at the end of the battle than it did in the beginning) or make a dent in morale. In fact, the wanton bombing of civilians proved to be an important propaganda factor in arousing American public support for the Allied war effort.[30] The Germans renewed the Blitz in 1944, this time using the V-weapons instead of conventional bombers. The V-1 (a pilotless aircraft powered by a jet engine) and V-2 (an unmanned, long-range rocket propelled by a liquid-fueled rocket motor) were the *Vergeltunsgwaffen*, or retaliation weapons. The Germans decided to send these so-called special weapons over the English Channel in retribution for the destruction of German cities by Allied bombings.[31] Approximately

A B-25 Mitchell bomber static display at Maxwell Air Force Base, Alabama. Yossarian served on this type of airplane in *Catch-22*.

10,000 V-1 flying bombs (3,957 of which were shot down) and 1,054 rockets (517 of which actually landed) fell on England; these weapons killed 8,884 British citizens.

STRATEGIC BOMBING

Although the modern foundation for the idea of taking the war to civilian areas goes back to the American Civil War with Sherman's March to the Sea and to the long-range bombing in World War I, World War II was the first major engagement in which civilian populations were systematically bombed. As Stephen E. Ambrose notes in *D-Day: The Climactic Battle of World War II*, strategic bombing was such a major feature of the Allied strategy that General Dwight D. Eisenhower threatened to resign as the Supreme Allied Commander to force the Air Force high command to divert strategic assets for tactical ones in support of D-Day. In fact, Eisenhower faced a severe shortage in landing craft and a delay in mounting the invasion because of the large amount of raw materials that went into producing bombers instead of making the boats that would take the infantry ashore at Normandy.[32] Having finally made his point to Allied planners, Eisenhower subsequently directed bombings against tactical targets important for the D-Day landing and the invasion of occupied France.

Owing to the perceived vulnerability of heavy bombers to faster, more maneuverable fighter aircraft, much strategic bombing originally began at night because darkness provided the bomber suitable protection. This meant that targets had to be large urban areas—nothing else would be visible. In May 1940, with Germany enjoying incredible success on the ground, bombing was the only means by which Britain could fight effectively. It also did not take long for the British air leadership to move targeting considerations beyond operational and tactical reasons, since they wanted to retaliate against the Blitz. British fire bombing of German cities originally began against Lübeck and Rostock in the spring of 1942. In May 1942, the British launched 1,000 airplanes in a coordinated attack against Cologne and began the systematic destruction of the industrial Ruhr valley and Berlin.

The United States preferred daylight bombing, not only because it considered night bombing a less precise method but also because its primary bomber at the time, the B-17, was ill suited for night aviation. Initially, daylight bombing not only limited the range of American bombing—the single-engine fighter could not carry enough fuel to escort bombers deep into enemy territory and back—it also maximized the risks as well.

A prime example of the risks taken by American bomber forces came against the Schweinfurt ball-bearing factories. A major element of the Allied strategy was to prioritize important industries whose destruction would bottleneck the whole German military industry. Because these particular ball bearings were an essential component of the German fighter, a restricted supply of them would thoroughly complicate German aircraft production. American forces bombed Schweinfurt on both 17 August and 14 October 1943, with a 40 percent aircraft loss rate, losing 147 bombers out of 376 during the first raid, and a loss of 60 airplanes out of 291 (a loss rate of 19 percent) on the second raid.[33] Not only were these casualty rates unsustainable, but German production quickly returned to normal after the raids.

Besides bombing strategic industrial centers in Germany, Allied bomber forces made sorties against enemy production centers in

Italy and the occupied countries. Again, priority was given to those targets considered critical to the fascist countries' military production and operations, such as oil refineries and submarine bases. Like Germany, the Italian industrial cities and suburbs became primary targets for both British and American bombers. The Allies calculated a 60 percent destruction of Italian industrial production by the time of Italy's surrender in September 1943.

In the Pacific Theater, the American Air Forces maintained primary responsibility for bombing Japan's industrial complex and cities throughout the war. The Americans first began the systematic bombing of Japan, using fifty B-29 Superfortress from the 20th U.S. Army Air Forces at Yawata Kushu, on 15 June 1944.[34] Jack Delano (et al.), in *Superfortress over Japan*, states:

> All told, B-29s were responsible for leveling about 40 percent of the 66 principal Japanese cities. Some 602 major war factories were destroyed. Fire raids destroyed 2.3 million homes and killed an estimated 330,000 Japanese civilians, injuring another 476,000. Approximately 8.5 million civilians were made homeless. Twenty-one million were displaced. Impoverishment and exhaustion were everywhere in Japan. Her economy was destroyed. Morale was declining. The newest bombing strategy of World War II—producing civilian terror, fatalism, defeatism, doubt, confusion, helplessness, hopelessness—had been successfully tested. Japanese appeared disenchanted and separated from their leadership.[35]

These conclusions about the effectiveness of strategic bombing are arguable, however, as many Japanese people seemed willing to continue the war even after the dropping of atomic bombs.

In Europe, the British Bomber Command dropped a total of 883,328 tons of bombs during 623,288 nighttime and 67,598 daylight sorties from September 1939 to May 1945.[36] The 8th and 15th U.S. Air Forces combined to drop 967,591 tons of bombs during 499,841 sorties from August 1942 to May 1945. On the Japanese mainland, the 20th U.S. Air Force dropped a total of 71,437 tons of high-explosive bombs and 107,263 tons of incendiary bombs during 30,928 sorties from June 1944 to August 1945. In comparison, the Germans dropped 74,172 tons of bombs (including the V-weapons) on the United Kingdom from 1940 to 1945. Statistics demonstrate the diminution of the Luftwaffe as the war progressed; it dropped 36,844 tons of bombs during its first year of air operations over Britain, but only 761 tons during 1945, its last year of operations.[37] When World War II initially broke out, the British had the most developed strategic bombardment doctrine and Germany had the largest air force; but by the time the war ended, the United States had far outstripped these two countries in both categories.

BARBAROSSA AND THE EASTERN FRONT

The barbarity of fighting on the Eastern Front between Germany and the Soviet Union during World War II is unparalleled in human history. The Romans originated the term *barbarian* from what they discerned as a "ba, ba" sound coming from the warriors of ancient Scotland, the men who had harassed the Romans so much that they built Hadrian's Wall. The only thing resembling a wall between Germany and the Soviet Union, however, was Poland. But by 0330 on 22 June 1941, the exact time the German invasion of the Soviet Union began, Poland had already ceased to exist—the Soviets themselves had had a hand in demolishing the one "wall" that stood between them and the Germans.

Barbarossa was the German code name for this blitzkrieg offensive into Soviet territory. Conceptual plans for the operation had begun as early as the summer of 1940—about a year before the invasion actually began. The conquest of the Soviet Union had always been a priority for Hitler, dating as far back as the writing of *Mein Kampf* (Hitler's political autobiography, which was first published in 1923).

The invasion was organized into a three-pronged attack. The northern army's objective was to capture Leningrad, the central force was to take Moscow, and the southern force was to occupy Ukraine. Because of supply and reinforcement complications, Hitler eventually concentrated resources in the two pincers forces and put the center force on the defensive—the goal was to encircle the Soviet forces and then completely destroy them. When the attack on Moscow began in late September, the Wehrmacht experienced such significant early success that the Kremlin prepared to remove Lenin's body to a safer place.[38] (If the Germans captured the remains of the Soviet's first and most revered former leader, the end would surely be near.) However, the effects of weather eventually took a toll on the German Army battling on the outskirts of Moscow—within about eighteen miles of the city. In the beginning of December, the Germans halted operations to hunker down for the onset of the harsh Russian winter.

The Soviets, fully recovered from their previous bruising defeats, soon launched an unexpected counterattack that broke through the German lines and threatened to encircle several pockets of Wehrmacht forces. Despite urgent pleas to withdraw to save the entire Eastern Front, Hitler refused and ordered his soldiers not to give up an inch of ground. By the end of December, the Wehrmacht had been pushed back about 175 miles from Moscow, suffering appalling casualties along the way. Combined with the German declaration of war against the United States after the Japanese surprise attack on 7 December, the defeat at Moscow and the general failure of the Barbarossa offensive marked the highwater mark of Hitler's dream of global conquest.

Despite the tremendous successes that the Wehrmacht had already accomplished in the war, its task in defeating the Soviet Army had been especially daunting:

> The initial German front was 995 miles long, and there was another 620 miles along the Finnish border. The main front would soon expand to 1,490 miles, and extend to a depth of over 600 miles. Into this great space of steppe, forest, and swamp marched the best of the German Army, amounting to three quarters of its field strength; by the end of the year, 3,500,000 Red army soldiers were in captivity, and 4,000,000 had died in battle. At one time the Germans occupied some 900,000 square miles of Soviet territory. It had been an historic campaign, a remarkable achievement. But at the same time "Barbarossa" was a significant failure for German arms.[39]

By the end of the Barbarossa offensive, only one of its pre-invasion objectives had been met, and that was the occupation of Ukraine. All other objectives had failed: the Soviet Army had not been decimated, Moscow remained unoccupied, and Leningrad had not been demolished. The failure to achieve these strategic goals eventually came back to haunt the German Army and was the main element in its ultimate defeat.

One of the reasons for the eventual defeat of the Germans by the Soviets was that early successes had led Hitler to over-confidence. As Hitler pushed his army more deeply into Russian territory, he ignored warning signs of trouble. Like Napoleon 129 years before him, Hitler underestimated the staying power of the Russians. Despite the huge losses they had initially absorbed, the Red Army troops maintained a will to fight and defend their territory. As the Germans were having to stretch their supply lines to the breaking point, the Soviets were contracting theirs.

In essence, the Soviets were strategically retreating to reconstitute a more powerful army that would eventually not only push the Germans back but completely destroy them as well. The speed at which the Soviets were reconstructing a new industrial base also surprised the Nazi leadership.[40] In the end, there is little question that World War II in Europe was won by the Soviet strategic victory.

Although Barbarossa ended with the German defeat at the gates of Moscow, the war on the Eastern Front continued until the Soviets captured Berlin on 1 May 1945. Along the way to Germany's final capitulation was the most horrific and atrocious warfare. The annihilation of the German 6th Army, losing about 230,000 troops at Stalingrad on 31 January 1943, was the turning point in the war on the Eastern Front. From September 1939 to December 1944, the Germans sustained a total of 5,913,750 casualties on the Eastern Front. During the same time, the Soviets lost approximately 17,000,000 soldiers.[41] The total losses in this one theater of the war alone, about one-half of the total casualties in the war, were equal to the current approximate populations of the U.S. states of Georgia and New York combined. No matter how one regards the activity that took place along this front—from SS atrocities against both soldiers and civilians, to the brutal treatment of POWs on both sides—man's inhumanity to man was disgraceful.

PEARL HARBOR

On 7 December 1941, a day President Roosevelt said "would live in infamy," the Japanese Imperial Navy attacked a surprised and unprepared U.S. Pacific Fleet anchored at Pearl Harbor in Hawaii. This operation was planned and directed by Admiral Isoroku Yamamoto (who had always maintained that a prolonged war with the United States could only lead to a Japanese defeat[42]) and led into combat by Vice Admiral Chuichi Nagumo. Shrewd signal intelligence had allowed the Japanese Navy to slip within aircraft range of Hawaii without being spotted by U.S. intelligence forces.[43]

The U.S. Opana Mobile Radar Unit made first contact with the oncoming Japanese aircraft, but because of inexperience and a lack of attention these forces were not reported to U.S. fleet leadership. Soon, the first wave of dive-bombers and torpedo boats dropped into attack formation on the unsuspecting seventy warships, including eight battleships, and began the deadly assault that finally brought the reluctant United States into the fray.[44] In total, 2,403 U.S. combatants and civilians were killed and 1,178 wounded; it could have been worse, however, had Nagumo launched a third wave of aircraft instead of ending the attack prematurely because he was afraid of a counterattack (which never occurred).[45] Despite the overwhelming success of the Pearl Harbor operation, this attack eventually proved to be the beginning of the end for Imperial Japan's war effort.

Shocked by this surprise attack, the United States firmly united after Roosevelt went before Congress on 8 December 1941 to ask for a declaration of war against Japan, which he soon received. Japan's Axis ally, Germany, then declared war against the United States on 11 December.

NORTH AFRICA AND ITALY

Operation Torch was the code name for the Allied landings to remove German and Italian forces from North Africa. Since the beginning of the war, British forces had been battling the Italians and Rommel's infamous German Africa Corps—and losing. With the arrival of General (later Field Marshall) Montgomery to the North African Front, the British began pushing the Germans back from their earlier gains throughout North Africa. The climactic British victory at El Alamein in Egypt, in early November 1942, sent Rommel's forces reeling in retreat across Libya. This important victory also helped persuade some members of the Vichy French government to assist in the Torch landings. After these landings, the Allies, led by General Dwight D. Eisenhower (later the Supreme Allied Commander in Europe), quickly established control over Vichy French territories and began operations to drive the Germans completely out of North Africa. Because of their superior logistical support and manpower, it was only a matter of time before the Allies defeated Rommel's combined forces, especially since Hitler would not let Rommel act as freely as he needed to, considering his inferior forces. Squeezed by an effective Allied naval and air blockade, the Germans were forced to surrender on 13 May 1942, after their remaining Panzer forces had disintegrated into scattered pieces.[46] In all, the Allies had sustained 76,000 total casualties, and the Africa Corps sustained 35,000 killed or missing and 266,600 POWs.[47]

With North Africa securely in Allied hands, freeing both troops and equipment, a successful invasion of Italy was now a possibility. Prodded by Churchill, who considered the Italian peninsula the soft underbelly of Axis Europe, the Allies organized the invasion of Sicily with the idea that it would lead to the overall invasion of Italy itself. The initial aim of the Italian campaign was not only to keep the German forces pinned down on a southern front but also to keep Allied troops properly occupied until the major invasion of Europe could be launched. Despite these rather modest goals, the Italian campaign soon took on a nightmarish quality, reminiscent of World War I, as Allied troops were forced into frontal assaults against well-fortified positions.

The U.S. 7th Army, led by General George S. Patton, Jr., and the British 8th, commanded by Montgomery, landed on the western and eastern coasts of Cape Passero, respectively. These forces then deliberately worked their way throughout Sicily until Patton reached Messina on 15 August—a day ahead of Montgomery. By that time the remaining German forces had escaped across the Strait of Messina, and the Italian government, having just overthrown Mussolini, began the process of complete capitulation to the Allies.

Thinking the end of fascist Italy would mean a softer campaign, the Allies proceeded to invade the mainland part of the country. Little did the Allied leadership realize what lay ahead of their forces—instead of an easy campaign, a desperate slugfest ensued. Several Allied landings took place in the early fall of 1942: a diversionary British force at the toe of Italy, the Americans at Salerno, and another British force at Taranto.[48] By the time the new Italian government officially joined the Allies on 13 October, British and American forces held a solid position across Italy from Termoli on the Adriatic and Naples on the Tyrrhenian Sea. Heavy fighting continued along the Gustav Line (a series of German defensive positions northwest of Naples) throughout the remainder of the year.

At the end of December 1943, Eisenhower and Montgomery departed the Italian Theater to prepare for the Normandy invasion, leaving overall command of Allied forces to General Harold Alexander (with General Mark Clark in charge of the American troops). During the beginning of January 1944, Alexander directed several offensive operations to kick-start the stalled Italian campaign. While an amphibious assault was carried out at Anzio on 20 January, other Allied forces assaulted German strongholds at Monte Cassino and San Pietro, positions that blocked passage up the Liri Valley to Rome. Not only did the Anzio landing fail to break out of its beachhead, but Clark's forces at Monte Cassino were being repulsed as well. It was not until 23 May, when both the Anzio and Monte Cassino positions were able to converge, potentially trapping the ensnared 10th German Army, that the Allied forces were able to make a significant breakthrough. However, because General Clark wanted the Americans to receive the publicity of rescuing the first capital city from the Nazis, he diverted from his original plan and got his picture taken on the jubilant streets of Rome instead. By allowing the Germans to fight again another day, Clark's decision prolonged the Italian campaign and increased the American casualties. The Allies in Italy were still engaged in combat when Germany surrendered.

D-DAY (THE NORMANDY INVASION)

Operation Overlord, the great Allied invasion of the European continent known as D-Day, was the greatest single amphibious assault of the war. Even the code name of the landing itself, Neptune based on the Roman god of the sea, suggested something of mythical importance. If any legacy of this war will be commemorated by a future Homer, it will be from what occurred on 6 June 1944 on the beaches of Normandy.

The operation began in darkness when 23,400 American and British paratroopers were dropped over France to cover the flanks of the five beach landings, which were code-named Utah, Omaha, Gold, Juno, and Sword. By early morning, almost 7,000 Allied naval vessels and landing craft were assembled off the shore of northern France to protect and unload the 75,215 British and Canadian forces and the 57,500 U.S. soldiers who tried, one way or another, to find their way ashore on that day. By the end of the Neptune phase of the operation, ending on 30 June, 850,279 men, 148,803 vehicles, and 570,505 tons of supplies and ammunition had come ashore.[49]

Although the deadly calculus of warfare was no more evident than it was in World War II, the fighting at Normandy in particular was more than about mere statistics, it truly was about individuals. For the initial landing party, it was a nightmare on those beaches; but as more Allies kept coming ashore, their numbers eventually overwhelmed the German defensive forces positioned there against them. By that midnight, 155,000 Allied soldiers had made it to land. Only at the American beachhead, Omaha, had the Allies encountered prolonged difficulties.

On Omaha, the U.S. 1st Infantry Division was engaged in a frantic battle for survival as they faced the German 352nd Division, "the best German formation in coastal positions on 6 June."[50] The steep cliffs also aided the defenders, as well as the U.S. troops' difficulty in getting their floating armor ashore. Without the supporting firepower that American tanks would have provided, the unlucky U.S. infantrymen who were first on the beach were either killed or pinned down until reinforcements arrived. Because they controlled the high ground, the Germans were able to direct an enormous amount of lethal fire onto the beach. Omaha beach was thus the scene of the worst casualties on D-Day. Fortunately for the Allies, the other beaches did not receive as much resistance as the D-Day planners originally expected.

Once again, German forces were misled by Hitler. Even after the Allied forces were ashore, Hitler believed the real invasion would come elsewhere, so he withheld reinforcements until it was too late.[51] The crucial opportunity to defeat the Allies on the beaches quickly dissipated. By 8 June, the British and Americans were linked at Colleville-sur-Mer, securing a united Allied beachhead, and it was only a matter of time before the Germans were pushed back from the French coast in retreat. Despite their secure foothold in coastal northern France, the Allies soon found it difficult to push the Germans out of the thick hedgerows planted by ancient Celtics 2,000 years earlier. John Keegan describes the predicament that the hedgerows provided:

To the Germans they offered almost impregnable defensive lines at intervals of 100 or 200 yards. To the attacking American infantry they were death traps. Before them green American infantry lost heart, forcing Bradley, the First Army commander, to call too often on the overtired parachutists to lead the assault. The "All American" and "Screaming Eagles" never flinched from the task; but the cumulative effect of losses in their ranks threatened these superb formations with dissolution.[52]

On 29 June, final German resistance in the port of Cherbourg stopped, and on 18 July, the Allies initiated Operation Goodwood, an offensive to push the Germans completely away from the Normandy beachhead.[53] By 27 July, the Americans were rolling southward out of the Cherbourg peninsula. During the month of August, the Allies consolidated their gains.

By the beginning of September, the Germans were in full retreat across France. The Allies had already liberated Paris on 23 August. The essential port of Antwerp fell to the Allies on 4 September, but still they were not able to exploit fully their numerical advantage over the Germans. The Allied offensive thus momentarily stalled, and the Germans took the opportunity to stabilize their forces. Replacement troops were being organized, including the 1st Parachute Army cobbled together by Hermann Goering and assigned to a new front in southern Holland. Two SS armored divisions were stationed near Arnhem in the Netherlands. Skillful German counterattacks, defensive maneuvers, and a shortened supply line kept the Allies out of Germany until 1945, despite the enormous Allied success at Normandy.

MARKET-GARDEN

Although the number of combatants involved in the Market-Garden offensive was relatively insignificant compared to that of other campaigns, the combination of (what was then) high-tech warfare and age-old human drama made this event one of the most compelling stories in the war and warrants it an extensive discussion here. This offensive to outflank the formidable West Wall of Germany and gain easy access to the industrial Ruhr River valley— the essential manufacturing region of the Nazi war machine—was the most daring large-scale airborne operation attempted by the Allies in Europe.

Market-Garden involved a very complex operation of both airborne (Market) and armored (Garden) forces. The plan called for the American 101st Airborne Division, commanded by Major General Maxwell D. Taylor, to hold the southernmost part of the battlefield, the corridor between Eindhoven and Veghel in central Holland. His men would have to capture and hold two major canal crossings and at least nine highway and railroad bridges. Taylor decided that he would have most of his men land right in the middle of the territory he had to hold and then have them spread out; the rest of the units he would drop closer to other important bridges they had to secure for the armored forces driving up from Belgium.

The mission for the 82nd Airborne division that Brigadier General James Gavin commanded was even more complicated. Gavin had a ten-mile area to control, which was wider than the 101st's sector. The 82nd had to seize the large 1500-foot-long Maas River bridge at Grave and one of the four smaller railroad and road bridges that crossed the Maas-Waal Canal. However, the main objective for this unit was to capture the bridge over the Waal River in downtown Nijmegen. For the operation to be fully successful, Gavin's men had to control the Groesbeek Heights southwest of Nijmegan and the Reichwalds, a forested area on the German border. Like Taylor, Gavin was also determined to have his men drop right down on their targets.

The most treacherous of all the missions fell to Major General Robert Urquhart's British 1st Airborne Division and the attached Polish Brigade. Their primary objective, "the prize of Market-Garden,"[54] was the highway bridge that spanned the Lower Rhine at Arnhem. Two other objectives for this unit were to capture a floating pontoon bridge and a double-tracked railway crossing, two and a half miles west of town. This mission was primarily complicated because not only had the Germans been fortifying the local area with anti-aircraft weapons, they also had been grouping units near the bridge itself. Since the area near the bridge was hostile to parachute landing, Urquhart and his men had to land miles from the bridge and march their way in.

The success of the Garden half of the plan required that the British armored units, led by Lieutenant General Brian Horrocks,

The Waal River Bridge at Nijmegen, the Netherlands.

sweep northward up Holland virtually unopposed. Starting on the Meuse-Escaut Canal in Belgium, the 30th Corps had to cover the 59-mile trip to Arnhem in three days and relieve the vulnerable British airborne forces there. Spearheading the armored attack for the British were the Irish Guards, commanded by Lieutenant Colonel Joe Vandeleur.[55]

Opposing the British was a hodge-podge of the German troops that had survived the Allied breakout after D-Day and retreated out of both Belgium and France. Despite the fact many of the Germans had recently been in a full-fledged rout, they quickly rallied behind their leadership and the other forces that had been sent into Holland to reorganize themselves—particularly the forces led by Generaloberst Kurt Student, Supreme Commander of the Fallschirmjaeger (German paratroopers). After the return of Antwerp, Belgium, to the Allies, the German High Command sent Student on a moment's notice to form a force to defend the Albert Canal and the entrance to the Netherlands.

At the time of Market-Garden, Field Marshall Gerd von Rundstedt had just replaced the man, Field Marshall Walther Model, who had recently replaced the man who originally replaced von

Rundstedt as commander of the German Army in the West. This confusing game of musical chairs among the German military leadership demonstrated the increasingly erratic behavior of Hitler, who was making all of these decisions himself. Since the D-Day invasion of Europe, the status of commander of all German forces on the Western Front had been chaotic at best. Model's demotion meant that he now was the overall commander of German Army Group B forces that were bivouacked in Holland. On the day of the air drop, Model was residing at the Tafelberg Hotel in Oosterbeek, very near where the British airborne forces would land. After recovering from the shock of seeing a large airborne army drop almost right on top of him, Model quickly organized his forces to counter the attack, a feat that proved to be key to the battle's final outcome.

In planning their offensive, the Allied thinking was that because their airborne troops had largely been underused since the D-Day invasion, they were fresh and therefore would be able to keep pressure on the German forces until the next phase of the European campaign could begin. Setting up a bridgehead in Arnhem, they thought, would be an effective head start on the invasion of Germany itself.

Despite the bravado of the men who backed the Allies' intricate plans, a generous amount of good luck was required for their operation to succeed. And almost immediately the British forces around Arnhem, the men who would need the best fortune just to survive, seemed to have no luck at all. Not only did Urquhart's forces lose a significant number of troops on the way over and through German air defenses, but they also experienced an immediate malfunction of their radio equipment. An insufficient number of vehicles also failed to arrive, compounding their problems. Most would have to walk, and since these paratroopers had landed so far away from their target and were spread out, these particular maladies could not be any worse. Bad luck, however, was not the only answer as to why the Allies were not able to maintain control over the Arnhem bridge; the Germans' ability to react to the developing situation the Allied forces had created right on top of them was also significant.

By 20 September, the Allied forces at Nijmegen and around Veghel managed to achieve most of their objectives. (The only failure for these forces was the inability to capture one minor, but key, highway bridge intact, a failure that slowed the 30th's advance up "Hell's Highway" to relieve Arnhem.) The British forces in Arnhem had not accomplished any of their objectives. In fact, the situation there could not have been worse. Despite the fact that Lieutenant Colonel Frost and his men were able to capture one end of the Arnhem Bridge over the Lower Rhine, they were eventually destroyed by persistent German counterattacks. The German forces around Arnhem subsequently encircled the Allied troops in Oosterbeek, forcing them off the battlefield, while other Allied ground forces were stopped just north of Nijmegan and kept from relieving their comrades in Arnhem. In the end, the Allies were unable to stop the Germans from completely destroying not only the British 1st Airborne Division but the main bridge at Arnhem as well.

Ultimately, the Market-Garden operation could only be considered at best a tactical draw because without the bridge at Arnhem, the other bridges were strategically worthless. Also, considering the condition of the German forces and where they were just a few weeks before the engagement began, a draw was almost a complete victory for the Wehrmacht because it further delayed the Allies from marching through the fatherland.

The final cost of this tactical draw, however, can only be understood after the Battle of the Bulge that occurred several months later. Had the Allies won Market-Garden decisively, very little would have kept them from driving on through the Ruhr Valley. Instead, the Allied offensive stalled along the Siegfried Line in western Germany, suffering a huge number of casualties. If the Allies had captured the bridge at Arnhem, the war in Europe would have been over quickly.

After the failure to succeed in the Market-Garden operation, Eisenhower decided to pursue a broad-front strategy that resulted in a costly stalemate. In his autobiography, General J. Lawton "Lightning Joe" Collins writes about his experience along the Siegfried Line. He argues that despite the heavy price that the Allies paid, the stalemate ultimately took a greater toll on the Germans:

> Costly as was the Aachen-Stolberg-Hürtgen battle to the First Army in casualties, ammunition, and equipment, it cost the Germans far more, and forced Rundstedt to employ divisions, tanks, and gasoline intended for the Ardennes counteroffensive, weakening that supreme German effort and subsequent defense of the Rhine.[56]

This hotel at Oosterbeek was used as headquarters by the British 1st Airborne during the Arnhem offensive.

Despite what Collins argues here, the stalemate and piecemeal
campaign against the Germans negated the overwhelming numerical superiority of the Allies, thereby leveling the battlefield.

THE BULGE

Hilter exploited the strategic stupor of the Allies by organizing
a last-ditch offensive on the Western Front, a bold gamble to divide
his enemies and recapture Antwerp, the essential supply port for

the Allied effort. The battle, which was actually a month-long campaign, took place in the Ardennes of Belgium, beginning on 16 December with a massive artillery barrage and attack by the German 6th Panzer Army. The newly created 6th Panzer Army was led by General Sepp Dietrich, a trusted friend of Hitler who had distinguished himself in command of the I SS Panzer Corps on the Eastern Front. Dietrich was given the primary mission of the campaign—to drive through the Allies and retake Antwerp. A ruthless commander, Dietrich was later sentenced to twenty-five years in prison by the Allies for the murder of eighty-six American prisoners at Malmédy.[57]

In *Hitler's Last Gamble*, Trevor N. Dupuy writes:

> The German Army had concentrated a total of twenty divisions—with nearly 410,000 men, more than 2,600 artillery pieces and multiple-rocket launchers, and about 1,400 tanks and assault guns—on a 110-kilometer front facing the U.S. First Army. That this concentration was completed almost without the Allies noticing is one of the most troubling aspects of the Ardennes campaign. The Allies had near-complete air superiority, their signal intelligence was of the highest order, and they built up an accurate accounting of the disturbing resurgence of strength in the German armed forces since their crushing defeats of the previous summer.[58]

Although the reasons for the Allied mistake in not foreseeing the German buildup have never been fully explained, the results of this error were more than evident. Nonetheless, in the end the battle hastened Germany's final capitulation because Hitler continued his offensive long after it was prudent to do so, although it was also the most costly battle for the Americans in the entire European Theater of Operations. Drained of all its reserves, the Wehrmacht was a shell of an army after the Bulge.

In *A Time for Trumpets: The Untold Story of the Battle of the Bulge*, Charles B. MacDonald notes that among

> 600,000 Americans eventually involved in the fighting—including 29 divisions, 6 mechanized cavalry groups, and the equivalent of 3 separate regiments—casualties totaled 81,000 of which 15,000 were captured and 19,000 killed. Among 55,000 British—2 divisions and 3 brigades—casualties totaled 1,400, of which just over 200 were killed. The Germans, employing close to 500,000 men—including

28 divisions and 3 brigades—lost at least 100,000 killed, wounded, and captured.[59]

Aided by bad weather, which grounded Allied aircraft and neutralized their air superiority, the German offensive initially experienced great success against the U.S. 1st Army, led by Lieutenant General Courtney Hicks Hodges. By 24 December, the German forces had created a fifty- to sixty-mile bulge in the Allied position—which is how the battle got its name—but this point was as far as the Germans would ever advance, only a third of the way to their objective. After Dietrich's drive to Antwerp was stopped, his forces were committed to defeating the Americans surrounded in Bastogne. On 22 December, the skies cleared and the Allies regained their air advantage, destroying the already fragile German supply system.[60] Despite a desperate New Year's Day attempt by the Luftwaffe to combat the Allied air forces, the Germans never could overcome their disadvantage in the sky.

Meanwhile, Eisenhower finally awakened from his leadership slumber and directed General George S. Patton's 3rd Army to attack northward. These forces eventually relieved the embattled American forces in Bastogne as well as Hodges' other forces throughout the Ardennes. Hitler was now forced to extricate what was left of the 6th Panzer Army. On 18 January, Patton began a drive along the base of the bulge around the German border, and by 26 January 1945 only a scattering of German troops remained in Belgium; 28 January is the official date of the end of the Ardennes campaign.

In the end, the German soldiers, despite their eventual defeat, once again proved their resilience and adaptability; but it was the American soldiers, despite their initial reversal, who subsequently demonstrated their worth as world-class combatants. MacDonald observes that except for a few isolated instances,

> the front-line American soldier stood his ground. Surprised, stunned, unbelieving, incredulous, not understanding what was hitting him, he nevertheless held fast until his commanders ordered withdrawal or until he was overwhelmed. . . . His was a story to be told to the sound of trumpets.[61]

With the last threat of a German offensive destroyed, not much was left to stop the Allies and the Soviets from crushing the remaining Wehrmacht. By 18 January, the Allies and the Soviets retook six of the capital cities that the Germans had conquered since September 1939: Warsaw, Paris, Brussels, Belgrade, Athens, and Budapest.[62] On 1 February, the Soviets were within fifty miles of Berlin and hammering the German forces with artillery and bombers, but the Wehrmacht still refused to surrender. After the Bulge, American forces soon overran the stubborn Siegfried Line and made their way to the Rhine River, first crossing it on 7 March at the town of Remagen. Unable to blow up the Remagen Bridge as planned, the Germans attempted to shell it into rubble, but the Americans were able to get enough forces across to form an eastern beachhead.[63] By the time of Roosevelt's death on 12 April, the German leadership was almost completely surrounded in Berlin; Leipzig and Nuremberg fell to the Allies on 19 and 20 April, and on 21 April, 325,000 Germans in the Ruhr pocket surrendered. In the early spring of 1945, the end was very near.

THE PACIFIC THEATER

After recovering from the initial shock and devastation of the Japanese surprise attack at Pearl Harbor and the loss of the Philippines—forces on the Bataan Peninsula surrendered on 9 April 1942 and the soldiers on Corregidor, 6 May—the U.S. military began preparing for the long conflict to defeat and destroy the Imperial Japanese military. The U.S. forces in the Pacific were divided into two theaters and lead by two stellar officers: General Douglas MacArthur and Admiral Chester Nimitz.[64]

By May 1942, U.S. forces were hard at work. After intercepting and decoding Japanese communications, the Americans confronted a Japanese carrier force first in the Coral Sea and then at Midway Island (see Chapter 3 about code breaking). The 4 June 1942 victory at Midway was the turning point in the Pacific Theater because the Japanese were never able to recover from such a devastating loss (the Japanese lost four large aircraft carriers in one day!).

A string of island-hopping operations soon followed the Midway victory as American forces took one Japanese stronghold after another. Such exotic places as Guadalcanal, where the existence of a U.S. airfield was a major blow to Japanese operations in the South Pacific; New Guinea; the Marshall Islands; Bouganville; Peleliu, in the Palau Islands; the Marianas, islands from where the American B-29 bombers could bomb mainland Japan; Iwo Jima; and finally, Okinawa became places of legendary conflicts. However, as the Americans moved closer to Japan, the Japanese fought with almost primordial ferocity. The human cost to push the Japanese back to their homeland was significant.

Fulfilling his promise to liberate the Philippine people from the Japanese occupation, MacArthur began that invasion on 20 October 1944 with a massive artillery barrage and a landing of troops on Leyte Island. The decision to regain the Philippines had been controversial because these islands could easily have been bypassed on the way to an invasion of Japan, but MacArthur insisted that the Allies were morally obliged to liberate the Filipinos since the United States had neglected them militarily before the war.

Following his success in taking the entire island of Leyte, Mac-Arthur sent invasion forces to other islands in the Philippine archipelago on his way to Manila. The Japanese, determined to inflict as much destruction as they could, defended Manila street by street. By 17 February, after days of unimaginable atrocity, the last Japanese soldier was either killed, wounded, or captured. However, despite these victories, fighting in the Philippines continued until the last day of the war.

This campaign to retake the entire Philippine Islands was complicated because the Japanese gave up ground contentiously, as they had done throughout the war. For 67 days American forces battled the 80,000 Japanese on the island, and in the end 55,344 Japanese soldiers died in the campaign.[65] On 23 October, the largest naval battle in history began in the Leyte Gulf. By the end of this engagement, which lasted three days, 36 Japanese warships (equal to 300,000 tons) had been sunk; the Americans lost only 6 ships (or 37,000 tons). This battle was also noteworthy because it initiated the Japanese Kamikaze attacks. These suicide attacks into American vessels proved to be a terror that was particularly difficult to defend.

On 19 February, the U.S. Marines landed on the beaches of Iwo Jima, an eight-mile-square volcanic-rock island, and three days later an American flag was raised on top of Mount Suribachi. From the airstrip on that island, U.S. B-29s soon began their bombing runs to the Japanese mainland, and the citizens of Tokyo began feeling the full weight of American airpower. On 1 April, American forces landed unopposed on the beach of Okinawa. Waiting until the 50,000 U.S. soldiers were on shore, the Japanese counterattacked, and 82 days later, after some of the most intense, brutal fighting of the war, Okinawa was completely in American hands. With the mainland only 360 miles away, the Japanese fought to the last man: 107,500 of their soldiers were killed, whereas the United States lost 7,613. Gilbert notes that before the battle was finished, over 250,000 people died in the vicinity of Okinawa. It is no wonder the American leadership was so deeply concerned about the human cost that an invasion of the Japanese mainland would incur.

V-E DAY

Adolf Hitler, who had remained in his bunker for days while the battle for Berlin raged over him, committed suicide with one shot in his mouth on 30 April 1945. His partner in crime, Mussolini, had been shot by Italian partisans two days earlier near the village of Dongo. The bodies of Mussolini and his mistress were taken to Milan and hanged upside down in public display. Afraid of meeting a similar fate, Hitler had given explicit orders for the preparation of his body. Immediately after his death, the bodies of Hitler and Eva Braun (his long-time girlfriend, who he married the day before their suicides) were burned beyond recognition as his orders had stipulated. By the end of that day, the Soviets had complete control of the city.

On 7 May, General Alfred Jodl signed the German instrument of surrender, which was witnessed by General François Sevez of France. General Bedell Smith, representing the Allied Expeditionary Force, and General Ivan Susloparow, a member of the Soviet High Command, also signed the document, thereby formally accepting Germany's unconditional surrender. On 8 May 1945, the war in Europe ceased.

V-J DAY

The war in the Pacific, however, did not end for several more cruel months. Finally, on 6 August, a U.S. B-29 dropped an atomic bomb on the inhabitants of Hiroshima; on 9 August, another atomic bomb was dropped on Nagasaki. It is estimated that over

200,000 people perished in the bomb blasts over both cities combined.

Accepting the inevitable, the Japanese government, in consultation with Emperor Hirohito, agreed to unconditional surrender, which was formally signed on board the USS *Missouri*, Admiral Nimitz's flagship. With the signatures of the Japanese delegation World War II came to an end, but not before consuming the lives of over 46 million people.[66]

NOTES

1. I. C. B. Dear and M. R. D. Foot, *The Oxford Companion to World War II* (New York: Oxford University Press, 1995), 279.

2. Matthew Cooper, *The German Army: 1933–1945* (Lanham, MD: Scarborough House, 1978), 102.

3. Dear and Foot, *Oxford Companion*, 279–280.

4. Ibid., 891.

5. Brigadier Peter Young, ed., *The World Almanac of World War II: The Complete and Comprehensive Documentary of World War II* (New York: World Almanac, 1986), 36.

6. Martin Gilbert, *The Second World War: A Complete History* (New York: Henry Holt, 1989), 9.

7. Cooper, *German Army*, 169.

8. Dear and Foot, *Oxford Companion*, 891.

9. Gilbert, *Second World War*, 1

10. Dear and Foot, *Oxford Companion*, 527.

11. Gilbert, *Second World War*, 1–4.

12. Dear and Foot, *Oxford Companion*, 892–893.

13. Gilbert, *Second World War*, 14.

14. John Ellis, *World War II: A Statistical Survey* (New York: Facts on File, 1993), 253.

15. Dear and Foot, *Oxford Companion*, 515.

16. Gilbert, *Second World War*, 61.

17. Dear and Foot, *Oxford Companion*, 709.

18. Gilbert, *Second World War*, 65.

19. Dear and Foot, *Oxford Companion*, 968.

20. Young, *World Almanac*, 53.

21. Gilbert, *Second World War*, 68.

22. Young, *World Almanac*, 59.

23. Dear and Foot, *Oxford Companion*, 312.

24. Gilbert, *Second World War*, 85.

25. Young, *World Almanac*, 62.

26. Dear and Foot, *Oxford Companion*, 391.

27. Ibid., 163.

28. Ibid., 138–140.

29. Ellis, *World War II*, 236.

30. Ibid., 138.

31. Ibid., 249.

32. Stephen E. Ambrose, *D-Day: The Climactic Battle of World War II* (New York: Simon & Schuster, 1994), 92.

33. Dear and Foot, *Oxford Companion*, 984.

34. Ibid., 1073–1076.

35. Jack Delano, Ronald E. Ostman, and Royal D. Colle, *Superfortress over Japan* (Osceola, WI: Motobooks, 1996), 50.

36. Ellis, *World War II*, 233–234.

37. Ibid., 235.

38. Dear and Foot, *Oxford Companion*, 109.

39. Cooper, *German Army*, 285.

40. Dear and Foot, *Oxford Companion*, 110.

41. Ellis, *World War II*, 259.

42. John Keegan, *Who's Who in World War II* (New York: Oxford University Press, 1995), 178.

43. Dear and Foot, *Oxford Companion*, 870.

44. Ibid., 871.

45. Ibid., 872.

46. Ibid., 818.

47. Ellis, *World War II*, 255.

48. John Keegan, *The Times Atlas of the Second World War* (New York: Harper and Row, 1989), 130–132.

49. Dear and Foot, *Oxford Companion*, 853.

50. John Keegan, *The Second World War* (New York: Penguin, 1989), 387.

51. Gilbert, *Second World War*, 534.

52. Keegan, *Second World War*, 390.

53. Gilbert, *Second World War*, 534.

54. Cornelius Ryan, *A Bridge Too Far* (New York: Touchstone, 1974), 134–138.

55. Ibid., 246.

56. General J. Lawton Collins, *Lightning Joe: An Autobiography* (Novato, CA: Presidio, ([1979] 1994), 279.

57. Keegan, *Who's Who*, 43.

58. Trevor N. Depuy, David L. Bongard, and Richard C. Anderson, *Hitler's Last Gamble: The Battle of the Bulge, December 1944–January 1945* (New York: HarperPerennial, 1994), 35.

59. Charles B. MacDonald, *A Time for Trumpets: The Untold Story of the Battle of the Bulge* (New York: Quill, 1985), 618.

60. Dear and Foot, *Oxford Companion*, 52.

61. MacDonald, *Time for Trumpets*, 619.

62. Gilbert, *Second World War*, 630.

63. Ibid., 648.

64. Dear and Foot, *Oxford Companion*, 857.

65. Gilbert, *Second World War*, 606.

66. Ibid., 1.

CONVERSATIONS WITH JOSEPH HELLER

Joseph Heller, born in Coney Island, New York, in 1923, is the author of six novels. *Something Happened* and *Catch-22*, indisputably modern classics, are among the best in contemporary fiction. In his most recent novel, *Closing Time* (1994), Heller brings the reader up to date on the life of Yossarian, the impetuous protagonist of *Catch-22*. At the opening of *Closing Time*, Sammy Singer, who readers discover had been a gunner on Yossarian's B-25 during the war, describes World War II and the members of his generation who fought it:

> When people our age speak of the war it is not of Vietnam but of the one that broke out more than half a century ago and swept in almost all the world. It was raging more than two years before we even got into it. More than twenty million Russians, they say, had perished by the time we invaded at Normandy. The tide had already been turned at Stalingrad before we set foot on the Continent, and the Battle of Britain had already been won. Yet a million Americans were casualties of battle before it was over—three hundred thousand of us were killed in combat. Some twenty-three hundred alone died at Pearl Harbor on that single day of infamy almost a half a century back—more than twenty-five hundred others were wounded—a greater number of military casualties on just that single day than the total in all but the longest, bloodiest engagements in the Pacific, more than on D-Day in France.
>
> No wonder we finally went in.
>
> Thank God for the atom bomb, I rejoiced with the rest of the civilized Western world, almost half a century ago, when I read the banner newspaper headlines and learned it had exploded.[1]

Heller himself flew sixty missions aboard the B-25 during the war in the Italian Theater off the coast of Corsica.

Now living on Long Island with his wife, Valerie, Heller continues to work and enjoy his family and many friends. His memoirs, *Now and Then: From Coney Island to Here*, was published in February 1998. His comic vision and literary imagination, the genesis of which he reveals in this reverie, have made him one of the most celebrated writers of our time. Despite his celebrity, however, Heller has always been generous with his time: two of his most enlightening interviews are recorded in this book.

The first conversation transcribed here occurred among Heller and a group of undergraduates at the United States Air Force Academy, Colorado Springs, Colorado, in 1986, during a commemoration of the twenty-fifth anniversary of *Catch-22*'s publication. The second conversation was between Heller and Kathi Vosevich in New York City, December 1997, with James Hughes Meredith recording.

FROM A CONVERSATION WITH JOSEPH HELLER AT THE UNITED STATES AIR FORCE ACADEMY

(Department of English, USAFA, "Yossarian at the United States Air Force Academy" [a conference held in 1986 to celebrate the twenty-fifth anniversary of the publication of Joseph Heller's *Catch-22*])

MODERATOR: The Department of English and the United States Air Force Academy are honored to have with us this weekend the world-renowned author Joseph Heller. In 1961, Mr. Heller published *Catch-22*, so this year we celebrate the silver anniversary of the first publication of the novel. . . . Mr. Heller, it is truly a pleasure to welcome you here today. Let's begin.

STUDENT #1: You served as a bombardier on a B-25 during World War II. I was wondering how much of your personal experiences come through in the character Captain Yossarian.

HELLER: Nothing of my personal experience comes through in the character of Captain Yossarian. I think he's a much better person than I was when I was a bombardier in World War II. He's older. Yossarian was, I believe, 28 in the book—I was 21 or 22. That part of my experience I did use in the novel had to do with the mechanics of missions by B-25 bomb groups stationed in Corsica in that particular war, so I knew the procedures. . . . [P]resenting my own experiences was not at all the purpose of anything in *Catch-22*.

STUDENT #2: Mr. Heller, in view of the war presented in *Catch-22* and especially the less-than-positive perspective of your Yossarian, how do you feel that we, as members of the armed services, should feel toward our duty to defend this country?

HELLER: When it comes to duty to defend the country, I think you should feel no different than I did or Yossarian does in the novel—if the issue is as specific as that and as recognizable as that, and I believe it was in World War II. I believe World War II was a clear-cut issue between this country and Fascism, represented by Germany and Japan. This country was not in the war until the attack on Pearl Harbor, and after that attack, I believe . . . all respectful opposition to this country's participation in this war disappeared, and there was no controversy about it. In *Catch-22*, unless I miss my guess, there is never an objection raised to the involvement of this country in World War II, and there's never a protest raised on Yossarian's part, and perhaps on anyone else's part, on the legitimacy of being involved in that war. The conflicts that I try to present had to do with individuals in conflict with each other, about individuals underneath the authority of leaders who were either neglecting or were indifferent to their responsibility, or who were maybe not up to that responsibility. I tried very hard to set the fictional conflict in *Catch-22* at that point in the war when Germany was virtually defeated. I do remember this line in the book when Yossarian says very truthfully, "The country is not in danger any more, but I am."

STUDENT #3: Mr. Heller, I was wondering if you consider *Catch-22* a satirical novel.

HELLER: I consider *Catch-22* to be a novel that employs satire to a considerable degree. . . . I personally think of *Catch-22* as being a very serious novel, using humorous satire and irony as part of the techniques in making the novel effective. It was not intended to be a comic novel, although I was aware at the time I was making very much use of comedy in it. It is an irreverent novel; it is disrespectful; it is iconoclastic. It is also, I like to think, unopinionated because there are so many questions raised I can see both sides to and to which I have no answer. . . . But certainly there is nothing funny about death; there is nothing funny about the death of a young man, and the fact I often in *Catch-22* present the death of somebody in a flippant or disrespectful way was not only intended to have almost a contrapuntal effect—to avoid sentimentality—but also to make it perhaps more effective by dismissing the seriousness of death briefly as well. I think of all the people dying in *Catch-22* the only one whose death I described in detail is a character who is really unknown, Snowden. . . . Rather than dwell on the death of Nately (which I personally regarded as particularly painful to me in conceiving), it is dismissed the second two planes collide—almost as an aside. . . . In writing *Catch-22*, I was mainly interested in writing an effective novel, and I thought it would be more interesting to deal in detail with the death of somebody who was an absolute stranger to both the reader and to the people there as well. Even in describing the death of Snowden, there's a line I believe from "God's Plenty," and from *King Lear* ("ripeness is all" used in a different context)—those are flippancies on my part, but those notes of irony are put in not to diminish the effect of Snowden's death, but perhaps to make it more effective.

STUDENT #4: Mr. Heller, you used a lot of déjà vu in your book. I was wondering if you could explain why you used it so extensively and how you were able to keep track of all the events.

HELLER: Keeping track is the hard part, and I didn't succeed entirely because I still get letters from people who point out certain things as impossible in the book. There's a chart that I made, which used to be my desk blotter, in an effort to keep track of the events and of what the characters were doing. . . . There were several reasons for using déjà vu. . . . It is the suggestion that things that are happening have happened before and will happen again, unless somebody—an individual or society—makes some effort to break that chain of events. And the event that happened or was happening and has happened is a war. The idea of déjà vu in the novel was intended to broaden the circle—to circumference what was happening—to go beyond the specific event, the specific month, the specific year. It was a fictional intent rather than a philosophical one.

STUDENT #5: Mr. Heller, in your book, a lack of communication seems to play a prominent role in many events, such as the mission when Captain Yossarian kept yelling, "I'm wounded, help me." But all Aarfy could say in response was "I can't hear you" or "I still can't hear you." I was wondering about the meaning, if any, of the seeming lack of communication.

HELLER: The meaning in the book is that the people of different characters or different sensibilities do not talk to each other, do not understand each other. . . . Yossarian is there bleeding, and it's not just Aarfy saying "I can't hear you," because if Aarfy had any sense at all, he could look down and see Yossarian was wounded. So the lack of communication there is not only verbal. . . . Aarfy is also deaf to the bombs exploding all around him. So the man is completely unaware, although he's educated. . . . Other parts of *Catch-22* I wrote consciously and deliberately with what might be called the perversion of language or the manipulation of language in different ways in which phrases can be interpreted by people who want to use them that way. . . . Language is being manipulated, misused to the advantage of the person; it is very much what I was working on very consciously in *Catch-22*.

STUDENT #6: Mr. Heller, I noticed you used the word "crazy" a lot, and I wondered if you used that word in particular so repeatedly to emphasize actual insanity, or if it was meant to condition us in understanding to be crazy really meant a kind of sanity.

HELLER: You noticed something very few people have, which is undoubtedly there. From the very beginning, I would deliberately use the idiomatic word "crazy," which was used to say you're wrong or you're impractical. In a less literal way, I was trying to raise one of the several questions about behavior in a certain situation: Are you crazy to obey orders you know are irrational, or are you crazy to disobey them? At one point in the novel, Yossarian asks, "You mean to say I'm to let Colonel Cathcart decide when and where I'll be killed?" The Colonel's point of view would be that we're in a war, and if it were up to every individual to make such a decision, more lives would be lost. I think from both points of view they're right—it's one of those situations in which I do not have the answer. Other dialogues I think might show it is unmistakable of whose side I am on. I do think so much that goes on in the world is crazy, but I'm using "crazy" not in a critical sense, which is the reason it is used very, very often.

STUDENT #7: From your own experience during the war, was the environment as chaotic and insane as you portrayed it in *Catch-22*?

HELLER: No, my own experience in World War II was, I'm ashamed to say, extremely beneficial—from the time I enlisted to the time I was discharged with the exception of a few months toward the end of my tour of duty when I was scared. It was very orderly, very beneficial. I also think for most of the Americans—except those who were wounded, killed, or taken prisoner—for most of them, it was one of the most meaningful, delightful experiences in their life. . . . I was not aware of anything on my level, as an enlisted man or as a low-level officer, of anything corresponding to *Catch-22*. . . . Yossarian's protest and indignation at the choices presented to him came to me as part of the American era that followed World War II. It brought up what I think was the awful, ugly, dangerous Cold War period that followed. I can remember that I was thinking of this country—this society—being in the state of civil war, except it was not a shooting war, and the sensibility in *Catch-22*—the questions raised—came out of the post-war period rather than of the war itself.

STUDENT #8: There seems to be only one element of hope throughout the book, and that's Yossarian. Are you, as the author, expressing your own disappointment in human nature?

HELLER: I would say that everything expressed in the book would be my own view, so to the extent there's disappointment in human nature, that's certainly there because I would say about half of the characters I disapprove of, and the readers tend to disapprove of, would be individuals who would be reprehensible for one reason or another. Whether if it's my view of all mankind—of all American civilization—I really don't know. I haven't thought about that. I will say this about *Catch-22* and about every other book of mine, as much as I like to fool around and exaggerate and deal with fantasy, I cannot see myself ever professing an attitude that I myself did not genuinely feel. . . .

STUDENT #9: Who was your favorite character?

HELLER: My favorite character in *Catch-22*? It would have to be Yossarian because he is a central character, and he is also not a person I approve of uncritically. When he moves the bomb line, and he sees the planes coming back—he is conscience stricken about that. When Nately's whore is trying to kill him, she represents many things. One thing is his own awareness he has been less than perfect. . . . I did think that the Chaplain would be much more interesting and sympathetic to readers than he has been. When I started reading papers or hearing conversations on *Catch-22*, Milo Minderbinder was the person they would speak of most often, even more than Yossarian. The Chaplain is almost never mentioned. . . .

STUDENT #10: One recurring theme in *Catch-22* is the questioning of the existence and nature of God. . . . [W]ere you really trying to develop the story or were you trying to express your own personal doubts and questions about whether there is a God?

HELLER: I was trying to express my own personal doubts about the existence of God and also, in a way, to dilute the arguments of those who feel more dogmatically about it than I do and than other people do. I'm kind of surprised more people haven't picked up on that, the religious aspect. There is a tremendous amount of skepticism on my part. I am an agnostic. I tend to resent people who are dogmatic about religion; I tend to resent people who are dogmatic about anything. The discussion between Yossarian and Yossarian's nurse does have the intention to raise that question and to treat it almost as an absurdity. I, on the other hand, take the Chaplain seriously; he is a sympathetic character. I have my own private joke—although it's public once it's published—that the Chaplain begins to doubt the existence of God. As he looks around him, he finds his faith restored by this vision of this naked man in the tree, and he never finds out that the naked man is Yossarian, although the reader knows it's Yossarian. Of course, there are sections dealing with the manipulation of the concept of God for private gain or private ambition: for example, when Colonel Cathcart calls the Chaplain and wants him to say prayers only so he can get his picture in *Life* magazine.

STUDENT #11: What was your purpose in repeating the scene of Snowden's death?

HELLER: That is an artistic purpose. I thought rather than having somebody die and describe the death in its entirety when it's taking place, I thought there would be a more powerful, more perplexing, more mystifying literary effect in having Snowden die throughout the book. So earlier in the book, you know Snowden is dead and has died and that Yossarian took care of him. I thought the image of this man dying the way he does throughout the period of ten months—the time span of the book—would be more effective. . . .

STUDENT #12: Why did you name the novel *Catch-22*?

HELLER: Well, the novel was called *Catch-18* for the eight years it was being written and edited. The first chapter was published in 1955 under the title "Catch-18." The number had no significance to me whatsoever. Then, the title was changed the same year a novel by a much better known novelist at the time was being published called *Mila 18*, and publishers felt readers would not want to buy two novels with the number 18 in the title in the same year. Given the choice, they would choose his. So, it was changed to 22. I can justify 22 in the repetitious patterns of *Catch-22*, but the choice of that number was really circumstantial based on the events I just told you about.

MODERATOR: I especially thank you, Mr. Heller; you have added a great deal to our understanding of the novel. Thank you very much for joining us this afternoon.

HELLER: The questions made me think about one of my very favorite novels.

FROM KATHI VOSEVICH AND JAMES HUGHES MEREDITH,
"CONVERSATIONS WITH JOSEPH HELLER"
(*War, Literature & the Arts: An International Journal of the
Humanities* 11, no. 2 [Fall/Winter 1999])

HELLER: You can ask me anything you want. I'll answer as honestly and thoroughly as I can. Go ahead.

INTERVIEWER: OK. The first question I hope you take as a compliment. My students always said that they could tell *Catch-22* was very carefully written. In fact, they used to say, "You can't read it fast," and I took that not as a complaint, but as evidence of their admiration. Was the book hard to write? What was your method of composition?

HELLER: Everything I write is hard to write, including factual material. The method of composition was first to conceive the book, which happened very quickly. The idea of the book really, truly came to me overnight, and I wrote the first chapter the next morning. At that time and to this day, I write in longhand. And now I'm resigned to the fact that when I write in longhand, I can write for only one hour or two, and I hope to get the equivalent of one typewritten page down at the first pass. I work on a lined pad, not legal-sized, letter-sized, and I try to get three handwritten pages done. I rewrite sentences. Then when I have a batch of these pages, for fear of losing them in a fire, I put them on the word processor, and I rewrite that. Then when I have a chapter done, I rewrite that chapter on the word processor, then I rewrite it again. It's very slow and tedious. I used to get infuriated with myself and *Catch-22* because I would work only evenings—I had other jobs and no time to write—but it was still the same thing. I would only write two or three pages a night. I would try to speed it up, and then write ten pages a week, then I wouldn't like it. I would have to rewrite, so it averaged to a page a night. Then when the book was done, *Catch-22* was about 60 or 80 pages too long, and I had to cut it.

INTERVIEWER: I think it was in a *Playboy* interview you said you cut about 100 pages. And the interviewer said of what, and you said, "adjectives and adverbs."

HELLER: Yeah, almost no incidents. There were two chapters that were cut—each of them was first published in *Playboy*. Neither one was a significant incident. The cutting was done at the suggestion of an editor. They interrupted—they were merely funny or satirical and not contributing to any flow of the action.

INTERVIEWER: Do you write every day?

HELLER: When I'm writing, I like to write every day. I've never had a compulsion to write. I'm easily distracted. I can stop to go out to dinner or go to the movies. That's always been true. What's happened since the second novel, *Something Happened*, I haven't had to work at anything, and I have days free. I am happiest when I'm writing, and I have something to focus on.

INTERVIEWER: Are you working on the sequel to *Now and Then* [his memoirs published in February 1998]?

HELLER: [*laughing*] That's misleading. The reference to a sequel [in the memoirs] was intended to be jocular. I don't know what else to write that's worth writing about myself.

INTERVIEWER: You said that writing isn't a compulsion or obsession for you (like it was for Hemingway, who seemed obsessed by writing). Is it more of a business?

HELLER: Well, I wanted to write this memoir. I had something to write about, I felt. I can't think of much I left out. . . . I've not had an adventurous life, and certainly not since World War II, but that's known. There are very few adventurous experiences I've had. In my memoirs, I tried to deal with my experiences that are unknown and with my closest friendships.

INTERVIEWER: Your friendships do come out in the book. Besides yourself, they are the stars of the book.

HELLER: Yes, the fact that a lot of my friends are big celebrities, like Mel Brooks, isn't all that significant to me because they are great friends and that's all that matters.

INTERVIEWER: I haven't seen you answer this question anywhere. Which writers do you think have been most influenced by you, and which use you as their model?

HELLER: I would not say that about any writer I know of. What did happen with *Catch-22* was a movement, in this country and in Europe, to change the traditional form of the novel. These writers were acting simultaneously, those in this group, without having contact with each other. Thomas Pynchon, who was writing *V* at the time, was one of those writers. Although we had the same editor, he did not know about me, and I did not know about him until after that book was published. Ken Kesey was another. I'm not sure I would influence anyone. The effect that *Catch-22* had was to make publishers bolder in bringing out unorthodox novels.

INTERVIEWER: Did your teaching during your early professional years in Pennsylvania help or hinder your writing?

HELLER: It neither helped nor hindered my writing. It was work. It was a job. I had to do something. I didn't write much when I was teaching. I wrote one short story in those days.

INTERVIEWER: The next questions are more specific to *Catch-22*. One question my students ask constantly is what really happened to Dunbar?

HELLER: I don't know.

INTERVIEWER: You don't know?

HELLER: I don't know, and I never thought about it. He's disappeared. People do disappear in the novel. Major de Coverly disappears. There was that theme of people just going out of existence.

INTERVIEWER: In a 1986 interview at the United States Air Force Academy, you said you consider Milo Minderbinder an innocent that embodies the Puritan work ethic. Do you still consider him as such today?

HELLER: Yes, of course. He's like so many other big business people today. We have models for him today, like Ted Turner and Bill Gates. He's not consciously evil. He may create bad things as a by-product of what he does, but he is unaware of it. He's not a show-off; he's not greedy. What is good for Milo often is good for the country. The troops did get fresh eggs.

INTERVIEWER: Do you consider *Catch-22* to be an anti-war novel?

HELLER: It is more anti–traditional establishment than anti-war. To say it's anti-war doesn't say much to differentiate it from other stories about the war. I used the military organization as a construct, as a metaphor for business relationships and institutional structures. Of course, it was anti-war. I can't think of any good American fiction that is not anti-war. But I don't think anyone in *Catch-22* raises the question whether we should be fighting the war.

INTERVIEWER: A lot of the criticism on *Catch-22* is divided on whether Yossarian is a hero or anti-hero. In your view, which is he?

HELLER: I'd say yes to both. Yossarian has heroic qualities, but he acts anti-heroically as well. I don't know if I say it in the book or if I've ever said in any other interviews, but military heroes of antiquity are kind of oafish—Samson in the Bible, even Don Quixote. By a lucky coincidence of timing, when I published the book, much intellectual thought was coming around to share the views I expressed in *Catch-22*. It has been often called a novel of the '60s, but it is really a novel of the '50s because I wrote it between 1953 and 1960. I've been anti every war ever since World War II. Conceivably, I could be an isolationist—conceivably.

INTERVIEWER: Most of my students think Yossarian is amoral and that his move toward responsibility at the end of the novel—to help Nately's whore's little sister—is too little too late. Do you agree and if not, how would you counter this argument?

HELLER: I would never think of him as amoral. . . . It seems to me it would have been immoral to think any other way than the way he does then. He has done all the 70 missions otherwise required during the war, and he thinks that's enough.

NOTE

1. Joseph Heller, *Closing Time* (New York: Scribners, 1994), 11.

A GI'S PERSPECTIVE: AN INTERVIEW WITH
ROBERT B. ELLIS, AUTHOR OF *SEE NAPLES*
AND DIE

A child of missionaries who served in Iran, Robert B. Ellis survived his World War II experiences with the U.S. Army's 10th Mountain Division in the rugged Italian campaign to serve for twenty-eight years as a researcher for the CIA until his retirement in 1979 to a bay across Puget Sound from Seattle. He has since devoted his energies to battling developers and local government over environmental issues, to protecting wildlife habitats, and to preventing the pollution of local wetlands. Because of his work protecting the nesting habitats of the great blue heron in his home state, Ellis was given the 1993 "Earth Defenders Award" from the National Audubon Society.

Ellis' book about his combat experiences is one of the most extensively researched memoirs of World War II. In the Preface, Ellis writes:

> I entered the military service of my country full of optimism and gullibility. I left it embittered in many ways and ambivalent about the army and whether the horror we experienced and the losses undergone—whatever the iniquities of the Hitler and Japanese regimes—were worth the price paid. The advent of nuclear weapons has only increased this doubt.[1]

FROM AN INTERVIEW WITH ROBERT B. ELLIS
(James Meredith performed the following interview with Robert Ellis through e-mail on 22 August 1997 and 7 September 1997.)

INTERVIEWER: Your memoir is so literate and your education seems so complete. What were some of the books you read before you went to war that might have helped you form a preconception about combat? Also, what was your parents' attitude about the "education" you were acquiring in the military?

ELLIS: It is difficult for me to remember what books I was reading before World War II that did not have to do with my prep school and college courses. Because my early years encompassed life in Iran and frequent foreign travel, as well as the opportunity to observe such things as the League of Nations debates in Geneva when Italy invaded Ethiopia, my interest in international politics developed very early. Both of my parents encouraged this. Shortly after I arrived to stay in the United States at age 12, my mother wrote my father, who was still in Iran, that she found me sitting on my bed one night, very wide awake. In the letter she wrote:

> We launched into the greatest conversation. He wanted to read to me from a book written by some Korean missionary about the cruel and inhuman way the Japanese have treated the Koreans. Then we got to talking about the way Italy had treated Ethiopia and so on. Next he got on the subject of how he might help right these wrongs, asking, "How does one go at it anyway?"

I am quite certain I read some World War I memoirs by British war veterans sometime before I went into service, and I also believe I read Stephen Crane's *The Red Badge of Courage*, but I may be mixing it up with the movie of the same name. In another letter that I wrote home at age 14 in September 1939 from my prep school, I reported I had dropped Latin and was taking World History. "The teacher keeps us informed on Hitler and all the recent happenings and the causes for this war. All this war stuff is what I am interested in, and that is what this course teaches."

In a 1941 letter written to my mother from the University of North Carolina, I asked her to send me John Gunther's *Inside Latin America*. I know I read Erich Maria Remarque's *All Quiet on the Western Front*, and Ernest Hemingway's *For Whom the Bell Tolls*. I also have a very distinct memory of repeatedly attending at age 14 the play Robert Sheriff's *Journey's End*, in 1938. My brother Paul had a role in the play, and I remember being appalled by the depressing view the play depicted of the First World War and life in the trenches.

Despite fairly catholic reading interests, in retrospect it is obvious I was terribly naive about the reality of combat and the prospects for surviving the conflict. Had I not been rejected because of color blindness when at age 17 I tried to become a fighter pilot, and then rejected for the same reason by the Marines, it is unlikely I would have escaped being killed or wounded had I gone into combat that early in the war.

As for my parents' concern about women and alcohol, you must remember it was exaggerated in any case because of the missionary background from which I came. In addition, both of my parents had seen the effects of alcohol on pioneer communities in the Utah and Montana territories, where their parents served as home missionaries, and I had been urged to stay away from any form of liquor long before I went into military service. The warning against prostitutes was new, but they were rightly aware that the unnatural isolation of soldiers from the opposite sex is bound to encourage acts of behavior they would never have pursued in civilian life.

Much of my optimism and gullibility about military service was attributable to the protected environment from which I came, and my youth and lack of understanding of the inevitable cruelties, stupidity, and hypocrisy of a large organization, especially when operating under the stress of a sudden wartime mobilization. Similarly, without actually experiencing it, it is impossible for the uninitiated to fully appreciate the mayhem and carnage of ground combat. On rare occasions, television and films have shown some of its true horrors, and are the media best qualified to do so, but too often the images are sanitized for political or other reasons. My state of mind before experiencing battle reflected the naiveté expressed by others in a number of letters I've received from World War II participants who never experienced combat. Until they read my account of what front-line life was really like, quite a few have said they never realized how lucky they had been.

The Army, of course, could better prepare its soldiers for what actually happens in battle. As I tried to make clear in *See Naples and Die*, I found much of the Army's World War II training and operational practices to be without merit when it came to fighting the enemy. These included: the overemphasis on close-order drilling; the strict separation of enlisted ranks from officers; the frequent separation of friends and associates as a result of their transfer to different units, inevitably damaging morale and unit cohesion; the excessive use of soldiers on mind-numbing, make-work tasks, such as picking rocks off a drill field; the failure to use any emotional stimuli, such as the flag, bugles, or even a rebel yell, to encourage troops to advance across deadly ground it ordered to undertake an unavoidable attack; the forced return of the previously wounded to combat, and the failure to put any limit on the combat life of infantrymen, guaranteeing that they would ultimately be killed or wounded if the war lasted long enough (a defect finally corrected in the Korean War); the inadequate introduction of replacements to the men of the units to which they've been assigned; and the improper ratio of noncombatants to front-line troops. Continuing examples of this wasted training include the hazing by drill sergeants and other nonsensical practices television shows us being imposed on cadets at the VMI [Virginia Military Academy] and The Citadel, to supposedly prepare them for combat as disciplined soldiers. General S. L. A. Marshall, the military historian whom I was fond of quoting in my book, criticized much of this training dogma more than 50 years ago, yet the military have remained reluctant to re-examine their own training doctrines or to test new approaches which might upset their long-held beliefs.

INTERVIEWER: What literature have you read recently that you find informed and interesting about World War II? And what do you think about

David Guterson's *Snow Falling on Cedars*, which is set in the Pacific Northwest?

ELLIS: I've read a great many books about World War II, beginning shortly after the war when I was initially fascinated by reading the many accounts of escapes from prisoner-of-war camps. More recently, I've been most impressed by such books as William Manchester's *Goodbye Darkness: A Memoir of the Pacific War*; Farley Mowat's *And No Birds Sang* and *My Father's Son: Memories of War and Peace*; Paul Fussell's *Doing Battle: The Making of a Cynic* and *Wartime: Understanding and Behavior in the Second World War*; (editor) David Nichols' *Ernie's War: The Best of Ernie Pyle's World War II Dispatches*; and Studs Terkel's *The Good War*. What I've found particularly moving have been the collections of soldiers' letters such as (editor) Annette Topert's *Lines of Battle: Letters from American Servicemen, 1941–45*, and especially (editor) Bernard Edelman's *Dear America: Letters from Vietnam*. The latter often brought me close to tears, and I found little to distinguish the feelings expressed about that conflict from those written about the war in which I participated.

Even some of the best-written memoirs, however, have made me suspicious on occasions about their honesty. Mowat's accounts of his Canadian infantry experiences in Italy, for example, while demonstrating his exceptional writing talent and rapier wit, struck me as including much that had to be fictional. As for such memoirs as *The Men of Company K: The Autobiography of a World War II Rifle Company*, by Harold Leinbaugh and John Campbell, where the authors have gone back to their fellow soldiers some 40 to 50 years after the event and asked them to recall their actions, I am highly distrustful of their accuracy unless they can point to documentary evidence (letters, diaries, or other records) backing up their claims. Inevitably, I've found, such recollections are embellished and are only occasionally accurate.

While I rarely read novels, I found David Guterson's prose in *Snow Falling on Cedars* to be remarkably well crafted, rich, and lush. One of his particular strengths is description. While I found some of his descriptions to be a little too detailed, and it took me a while to really get into the book, Guterson's handling of the multiple story lines eventually becomes absorbing and captures your interest the rest of the way. An unusually talented writer, I was also impressed by the extraordinary amount of research he had obviously done on such subjects as fishing practices, the legal niceties of a murder trial, the work of a coroner, the Japanese-American culture, internment camps, strawberry farming, and the wildlife and vegetation characteristic of islands in Puget Sound. All of it struck me as remarkably accurate, and when coupled with the gripping multiple plots—including the emotional love story—made for a powerful novel, entirely deserving of the praise it has received.

INTERVIEWER: As a surviving veteran of the Italian campaign, what do you now think of General Mark Clark's leadership?

ELLIS: In my opinion General Mark Clark was an uninspired figure, lacking daring, imagination, and any real talent for commanding sizable forces in battle. Our impression was that he simply ordered men forward in repeated sacrificial assaults, and counted on overwhelming numbers, aerial bombardment, and artillery firepower to win the day. Since we had seen too often that the enemy was able to survive these kinds of cannonades, and still be in place when we attacked, we had little respect for him as a field commander. Moreover, his actions earlier in the war when he drove for Rome rather than trying to cut off the retreating German forces after the Anzio breakout—forces who then escaped to impose terrible losses on the Allied armies all the way up the Italian peninsula—led us to believe his principal interest was in fame and self-promotion.

INTERVIEWER: Much has been discussed about the effects of Post-Traumatic Stress Syndrome on Vietnam veterans. Did you ever experience anything like this syndrome? Or did you know of any World War II veteran who did?

ELLIS: My recollection is that during World War II, both the GIs and our battalion surgeons used the expression "battle fatigue" for what is now called Post-Traumatic Stress Syndrome. I didn't personally run into any obvious cases of such a condition in my company or platoon, but that's probably because we weren't in combat that long (only about 2½ months). Once we learned what to anticipate in the way of casualties, and that there was no way out for the infantryman unless you were killed, wounded, or the war came to an end, most of us concluded we could not help but break down if the fighting went on long enough.

While I didn't observe anyone showing obvious signs of mental illness, I did see a few—and heard of others—who were so overcome by fear that they shamed themselves in one way or another. Wetting one's pants or losing control of one's bowels was one. Another was shooting oneself in the foot or some other body part in a way that wouldn't prove fatal. Still another was the disappearance of a comrade in the course of an attack who explained his absence and lack of any observable injury by saying he lost contact with his fellow soldiers from a shell or grenade, which rendered him senseless for a time.

One member of my platoon, when ordered under heavy shell fire to escort some prisoners back to a collection point, proceeded to kill all before reaching his destination. This, too, I attribute in large part to fear.

Only a few weeks ago I was told about a lieutenant in the 10th who commanded a platoon whose mission I won't identify, but it was more dangerous than the average. One of the members of his platoon, whom I have never met but who read my article in *The Nation* exposing Bob Dole's exaggerated war record, called me to talk about the article. In the course of the conversation, he suddenly started talking about this lieutenant, saying: "He claims now to have won two Bronze Stars, but I know how he acted near the end of the war. He couldn't handle it so he went to the rear at [name omitted] and then spent a year afterwards going around to every guy in the platoon apologizing. . . . At our first platoon reunion, he cried and told me . . . [the caller never finished the sentence]. It's a terrible thing and he's lived with it, and I sympathize and understand it, but . . ."

Clearly, this was a case of battle fatigue or fear finally rendering the officer incapable of performing his duties. I never reached that state during or after the war, but in my memoir I tried to describe my varying emotions and the impact they had on my actions while in combat.

INTERVIEWER: Did you have any emotional aftereffects of your combat experience? Do you feel that the experience of the World War II veteran was much different than the Vietnam one?

ELLIS: For a time the impact of the war most obvious to me, my fiancée, and a few others was my startled reaction to any sudden noises that reminded me of incoming shell fire. This was accompanied by nightmares about the war, but both aftereffects gradually diminished and eventually disappeared. The loss of so many close friends, however, had the continuing effect of making me less eager to establish and maintain close relationships with others. As a result, I have been less affected by the ending of these relationships because of death, geographic separation, or other reasons.

As for how we World War II veterans may have differed (if at all) from our Vietnam counterparts, our relative non-involvement in drugs, other than alcohol, must be an important reason why we were better able to handle the adjustment back to civilian life. In neither war did the home front or the newly trained recruit have any real appreciation of what the front-line combat soldier must go through and the looks and smells of real war. Television and more honest journalism helped somewhat in the case of Vietnam, but the horrors of battle remain largely foreign to the civilian observer. Still, World War II was a popular undertaking throughout the years of our involvement, and we were admired and respected when we returned home. (Not that we dwelt on it that much. Most of us were eager to forget the whole thing and get on with our interrupted lives.) This clearly was not the case in the Vietnam War, and it had to have a profound effect on the returning veterans.

INTERVIEWER: Do you have any explanations for the absolute evil Hitler represents? Is a Hitler possible today?

ELLIS: Hitler was the product of many complex forces, some of the principal ones being: the harsh conditions imposed on Germany by the Versailles treaty in particular, and on all the Central Powers by the Treaty of Paris; the disregard the Allied peacemakers showed for about half of [Woodrow] Wilson's Fourteen Points [the U.S. government's stated goals for peace after World War I]; the failure of the U.S. Congress to let the United States join the League of Nations; the weakness of the League in dealing with the crises which developed; and the onset of the worst economic depression in history. Hitler simply used the human inclination to find a scapegoat for one's troubles and took advantage of the German attraction to authority to establish a dictatorial regime. (A friend, whose first diplomatic assignment in 1952 was that of a vice-consul in Germany, told me that when he made his first speech to a German audience, and asked if some of them would mind coming forward to fill some of the empty seats in front, the entire assemblage rose as one and did as they were asked.)

There is good and evil in all of us, and if we are placed under stress and properly manipulated by a clever propagandist—whether it be a politician (e.g., Mussolini or Joe McCarthy), theologian (e.g., Father Coughlin or Pat Robertson), popular hero/expert (e.g., Lindbergh), or zealot of any stripe—we can be influenced to commit terrible acts. Hitler was unique only in the scale and efficiency with which his evil instructions were carried out. The recent examples of Pol Pot, Radovan Karadzic, and the genocidal killings in Rwanda and Burundi are in some ways more horrific than the crimes of the Hitler regime, and demonstrate how ordinary people, given the opportunity, can undertake despicable acts of equal ferocity.

INTERVIEWER: As we are now creeping toward a new millenium, are you now optimistic or pessimistic about the future of humanity?

ELLIS: I'm afraid I do not believe that human nature has changed very much over the millennia. In developed countries, given a combination of reasonably satisfactory economic conditions and democratic governments, civilized institutions can flourish and there is less opportunity for extremists to come to power or for conflicts, whether domestic or international, to be undertaken. Even there, however, religious, racial, class, and nationalistic rivalries can develop with serious consequences.

The continued destruction of our natural environment, even including the species to which we are most closely related; technological advances which facilitate the undertaking and destructive power of terrorist acts; our seeming inability or unwillingness to limit population growth; and the growing inequalities that exist in our country and elsewhere in the world between the haves and the have-nots—to name but a few of mankind's problems—make me less and less optimistic about the future. Like the writer Farley Mowat, I too have come to the reluctant conclusion that we are a bad species, that we probably don't have much time left on this planet, and that it will likely be better off once we've left the stage.

NOTE

1. Robert B. Ellis, *See Naples and Die: A World War II Memoir of a United States Army Ski Trooper in the Mountains of Italy* (Jefferson, NC: MacFarland, 1996), 3.

A POET'S PERSPECTIVE OF COMBAT:
RICHARD WILBUR

A former poet laureate of the United States—the second one chosen after Robert Penn Warren—Richard Wilbur is one of the eminent authors of the twentieth century and by most accounts the premier poet of the century's latter half. A native of New York City who grew up in North Caldwell, New Jersey, Wilbur enlisted in the U.S. Army after his graduation from Amherst College and served in World War II from 1943 to 1945, reaching the rank of staff sergeant. During the war he served in southern France, along the Siegfried Line, and at Cassino and Anzio in Italy. Upon his return, he attended Harvard on the GI Bill and completed his M.A. degree, published his first book of poetry, *The Beautiful Changes and Other Poems* (1947), and embarked on a career of writing and teaching English at Wellesley, Harvard, Wesleyan, and Smith.

His work is wide ranging. Among his ten books of poetry are *Things of this World: Poems* (1956), for which he won his first Pulitzer Prize and the National Book Award, *Walking to Sleep: New Poems and Translations* (1969), which won the Bollingen Prize, and his most recent *New and Collected Poems* (1989), which won a second Pulitzer Prize. He has also won the Bollingen Prize for his translation of Molière's *Tartuffe*, edited the poems of William Shakespeare and Edgar Allan Poe, written a number of critical commentaries including an essay examining the poetry of Emily Dickinson, and composed (with Lillian Hellman) the lyrics for the comic opera *Candide*. His translations include a number of dramatic works by Racine and Molière, many of which have been performed on Broadway and in the English-speaking world generally.

This interview took place at Wilbur's summer residence in Cummington, Massachusetts, in October 1997 and was conducted by Colonel Joseph T. Cox of the United States Military Academy. Wilbur talked about his World War II experiences and their influence on his poetry.

FROM JOSEPH COX, "AN INTERVIEW WITH RICHARD WILBUR"
(*War, Literature & the Arts: An International Journal of the Humanities* 10, no. 1 [Spring/Summer 1998])

INTERVIEWER: I believe your graceful rage for order and your vision of the world are, in part, a legacy of your World War II experience. To explore that thesis, I begin with a question about your comments to Stanley Kunitz that "it was not until World War II took me to Cassino, Anzio, and the Siegfried Line that I began to versify in earnest. One does not use poetry for its major purposes, as a means of organizing oneself and the world, until one's world somehow gets out of hand." How had your world gotten "out of hand"?

WILBUR: Well, as it became more and more likely America would be involved in World War II, I resisted the draft for various reasons. I was inclined toward pacifism, for religious reasons, and had the cause been more dubious I might have ended as a C.O. [conscientious objector]. Some of my teachers and much of my reading had also made me a potential war resister on political grounds. Add to these things the fact that I was clever with words and enjoyed making a stir, and it may be clear why, in my editorials for the *Amherst Student*, I was a sort of America-Firster until Pearl Harbor put an end to all smart-ass debate. When it was clear the American involvement was necessary and just, and I was going to be in it, I didn't think of getting into some 90-day-wonder program, because I had a romantic preference for being a common soldier and because, never having been much of a team player, I was not drawn to being a leader of men. If I had to go to war, it would be as a specialist. At some point—I can't say just when—I took a course in cryptography from the U.S. government, and that was one specialty I knew a bit about. In June of '42 I took a telegraph key on my honeymoon, and my new wife and I practiced Morse Code together, in a pleasant cabin on the Maine coast. After six months of training in all aspects of radio communications, I then reported for duty, and you know the rest of my story.

I've told you all this in order to answer your question about how, with World War II, my world had gotten "out of hand." No doubt war is disturbing and disorienting for everyone, civilians included; it cancels one's plans and alters the playing-field; it calls for sacrifice and for degrees of discipline and physical courage less required in peacetime. It also puts the future of one's country and civilization in doubt. Some people, however, come into their own in time of war, and I was not one of those. To find myself in the Army was a shock to my anti-war youth, my anti-militarism, my dislike of regimentation; and once I was in a combat unit, the war challenged my sanguine suppositions about human nature and the goodness of God's world. On the positive side, I learned a lot about loyalty, mutual dependence and (something I had never expected to experience) esprit de corps.

INTERVIEWER: Much has been written about the embittering process that is war. Many memoirists, poets, and writers of fiction say the military destroyed their idealism. You seem to draw contrary conclusions. What was the difference in your experience from others?

WILBUR: My uncle Fred's letters from the trenches, in World War I, were full of the sort of zeal and noble conviction that can lead to disillusion— though that didn't happen to him. My generation went into World War II in a more realistic and less crusading spirit, resolved to do what plainly had to be done; and so there was less damage to our expectations. It may be that the literature of World War I, which told of so much beastliness and stupid waste of lives, prepared us to be not altogether surprised.

INTERVIEWER: What do you mean by the phrase "versify in earnest"? How did your war experiences transform your attitude toward poetry? How did the chaos of war affect your poetics?

WILBUR: Poetry seems to me a serious game in which one tries to be fully articulate about self and world. If both have been shaken up, one's old vocabulary will not suffice; one needs to find new and risky words with which to express one's confusion, and thus begin to order it. That's what "versifying in earnest" (a mock-pompous expression) amounts to, and "Mined Country" or "First Snow in Alsace" would represent that sort of seriousness. I could also explain the expression "versifying in earnest" in terms of concentration; poetry, as many soldiers discovered during World War II, was the art which could most readily be practiced under the circumstances. You can't set up an easel in a foxhole. With a pencil and a piece of paper, poetry could help you at once to escape the situation and to master it. If you wanted to order and express the life you were living, you were likely to concentrate earnestly on poetry.

In regard to technique and structure, I was not inclined to fall into "the fallacy of imitative form" and write chaotically about chaos. The war didn't change my sense of what a good poem was or what forms might be adequate to the matter at hand. My adjustments had to do with the inclusion of words and of kinds of experience.

INTERVIEWER: Is there any poetry you wrote before your war experiences you would dare share with today's audience?

WILBUR: Before World War II made me focus fervently on poetry, I had practiced a variety of arts. I had written most kinds of journalism and expected to make a career of that; it was in our family tradition on my mother's side. I'd done political cartooning, in the veins of Kirby and Fitzpatrick and Art Young, and rather fancy color cartoons in the manner of the old *Vanity Fair*, and comic strips, too, which had some of the quality of *Krazy Kat*. I had a guitar and was an artless folk singer who knew 60-odd verses of "Frankie and Albert." As for poems, I had written them since my earliest years, because I was a wordy kid and a reader, influenced from the beginning by Mother Goose, by a volume called *Poems of American Patriotism*, by Lear and Belloc, and in adolescence by Hart Crane, Robert Frost, and many others. But it was just one of the things I did, growing up in the house of a painter where any sort of art was encouraged. Many of my early poems have been lost, and I'm not inclined to share those which have survived, because they belong to the time before I wrote poems "in earnest" and was on my way to outgrowing my influences.

INTERVIEWER: What poems did you write during the war? How did you write them? With whom did you share them? Were there other poets or soldiers in the ranks who appreciated your verse?

WILBUR: Of course, I wrote many poems during the war which didn't seem good enough to include in my first book. Looking through that book, I'd say that the following were written during my time in the army. "Cicadas" (originally "Cigales"); "Water Walker" (prompted, I think, by a life of St. Paul that I read while in the service); "Tywater," which concerns a corporal in my company who was killed on the Anzio beachhead, shortly after delivering me at our front line; "Mined Country"; "Potato"; "First Snow in Alsace"; "On the Eyes of an SS Officer"; "Place Pigalle"; "June Light"; "Lightness"; "Caserta Garden."

During the war, I composed poems with a pencil and any available bit of paper, as I still do; when our code room—sometimes an actual room, sometimes a cellar, sometimes a 6 × 6 truck—was idle, I'd type them up on a code machine. I sent all my poems home to my wife by V-mail, and sometimes sent them to an old friend from college, or to one of my Amherst teachers. I very seldom entertained the thought of publication. One poem of mine was published in the *Saturday Evening Post* because my wife's school friend, Betsy List, was working for the magazine. At some time, I sent "Potato" to the English magazine *Horizon*, and it was graciously declined.

I almost never showed a "serious" poem of mine to my fellow soldiers in the 36th; one of them, a Jewish fellow from New Jersey, once handed a poem back to me, saying, "I'm sorry, Dick, but my attitude is Poetry, Schmoetry." The other guys knew, of course, that I wrote highbrow poetry and carried Gerard Manley Hopkins in my musette bag, but that didn't make me *very* different, in their eyes, from the thousands of other soldiers who appeared in the "Puptent Poets" column of the *Stars & Stripes*. The other guys *did* like my light verse and my cartoon illustrations, therefore, and I had warm and amusing relationships with almost everyone, partly because, being mostly country Texans, they were enjoyers of words—good storytellers and inventive cussers.

INTERVIEWER: How did the war affect your appreciation of nature? How did it affect your heightened sense of the sacred in the everyday?

WILBUR: I am not philosophic enough, or self-conscious enough, to be able to trace the development of my ideas and attitudes; I don't so much put them into poems as look and see what comes out—what notions have managed to emerge from the pressure-cooker of a poem. But, of course, the war did make me aware of the violence and perversity of man and nature, and made it a necessity to acknowledge those things while looking to reaffirm the sacramental in the world.

INTERVIEWER: How did the war affect your imagination and art after the war was over? Were there specific events or experiences in the war that found their way into specific poems? Is, for example, a poem such as "The Death of a Toad" informed by the kind of stoicism that you saw in men dying during the war? Are there poems that on the surface don't appear to be "war poems" but in fact are?

WILBUR: In the poems of my second book, I see "The Pardon" as resolving not to evade death, and "Marché aux Oiseaux" as resolving not to deny the darker side of love itself, and I think I could find many poems throughout my writing life which, though I finally tend to affirm, acknowledge the worst and are thus continuous with my war experience and are "war poems" regardless of subject.

INTERVIEWER: When did you first see yourself as a poet? How did the war help define you in that role? Would you have pursued a career as a poet had you not served in World War II? What kind of poet would you have been had you never served overseas during World War II?

WILBUR: Robert Frost once answered the frequently asked question "When do you know that you're a poet?" by saying, "It's when somebody sends you a ten-dollar check for a poem." That no doubt sounded cynical to some people, but I think we must not look down on that ten-dollar check; it says that your work has given pleasure to an editor and may be of some emotional or imaginative value to the readers of some magazine. The unexpected acceptance of my first batch of poems by the publishing house of Reynal & Hitchcock made me think that poetry might be my calling, and since then I have been confirmed in that belief by every out-of-the-blue letter which has told me a poem has been used at a wedding, or at a burial, or at the bedtime of some lonely person—I have been of use. The war challenged me to organize a disordered sense of things, and so prepared me to write a poetry of maximum awareness and acknowledgment, but of course I can't say how I'd have written had I never gone to war. No doubt there are other fruitfully disordering experiences.

INTERVIEWER: What was the transformation like from military to civilian life? Were you starving for art when you were discharged?

WILBUR: With my mustering-out pay of $441.11, and with the promise of monthly GI Bill checks, my wife and I went straight to Harvard and its graduate school. Like the many other returning veterans there, I plunged into literary studies and worked my head off—not to forget the war, but because I was spoiling to make full use of my specific talents. I have never since known an academic atmosphere in which there was so much high-spirited avidity for art and knowledge.

INTERVIEWER: Do you think there was anything special about your generation of soldiers that made them different from Vietnam veterans?

WILBUR: Movies about World War II often made much of the socially varied composition of an infantry patrol, and I think it was true of all of our armed forces that they drew upon every group and class. My impression is the dreadful Vietnam War was largely fought by the unprivileged, while those with educational deferments made anti-war protest an excuse for every kind of self-righteous self-indulgence.

INTERVIEWER: Looking back on your war experience, can you point to any work of literature that helped you cope? How did it prepare you for the nature of war? Was there any book or poem that you read as a youth that totally had it wrong? Have you written anything that would help someone who might have to endure war?

WILBUR: I don't think that the laudations of martial courage in *Poems of American Patriotism* gave me false expectations of war or of myself, or that such novels as Dos Passos' *Three Soldiers*, or the poems of Owen and Sassoon, were a practical preparation for our rather different world war. But I think *all* literature—what I'd read of it, anyway—had somewhat prepared me to cope with war experience as it came. One needs words and concepts to take the measure of things and achieve some clearness and balance, and not be mutely overwhelmed.

INTERVIEWER: What do you think about what is now called Post-Traumatic Stress Syndrome (what the military establishment called "battle fatigue" during World War II)? Did it occur? Did you know any soldiers who suffered "battle fatigue"? Did you experience anything like it?

WILBUR: I believe that there came a day, during the Battle of the Bulge, when some of our exhausted line company soldiers had to be begged to get out of their foxholes. I couldn't possibly blame them. Is that what "battle fatigue" means? Our signal company didn't have it as hard as the line losses. It is difficult—stressful—to do a technical job like wire-laying or radio transmission or the encoding of messages in close proximity to a firefight. The man I replaced, just before Cassino, had gone home with a "Section Eight," and I confess that I once found myself banging my head against an iron safe. But that's as close as I came to the edge.

INTERVIEWER: You served in World War II with the 36th Infantry Division, a unit that was known as a "hard luck" outfit that suffered especially heavy casualties in the Italian campaign. Ernest Hemingway in his World War II novel *Across the River and Into the Trees* makes a brief allusion to the 36th's difficulty at the Rapido River. Did you ever hear any of your fellow soldiers in the division talk about the failed Rapido River crossing? If any fellow soldiers talked about that battle, did they feel betrayed by their leadership or did they take that defeat personally? What do you think of General Mark Clark's leadership?

WILBUR: The Division had lost a great many troops at Salerno and San Pietro before I ever joined it; on top of that, the losses at the Rapido were staggering. But I never heard anyone say at the time that a difficult crossing had been ill planned by the divisional command or that an *impossible* crossing had been ordered by Mark Clark, in deference to higher-ups who felt there would be psychological advantages to taking Rome before such and such a date. I never heard those conflicting views—and others—until after the war. I suspect ordinary soldiers don't usually know, in a broad strategic sense, what the hell is going on, and so don't do a lot of informed criticizing. One thing we all thought we knew, by the way, was the Germans were violating the Geneva Convention by using the monastery tower as an OP [observation post]. But apparently that wasn't so; I was told as much at a luncheon in Cambridge by a trustworthy German who had been up on that hill when I was down in the valley.

INTERVIEWER: Having lived through World War II, the dropping of the atomic bomb, and the Cold War, are you optimistic or pessimistic about the development of world civilization? Where does art go from here?

WILBUR: I guess that I am optimistic because I am helplessly optimistic; it is my nature to be so. I am perfectly aware that we could do ourselves in very easily given the number of warheads that are still there in Russia and are far more vulnerable to misuse than they were before. And I suppose the Russians are not the only potential villains in that matter. Still, I hope that we have enough sense to survive the invention of the atomic bomb.

Art will go on to have all of the functions it has always had. It seems to me art does not commence in a nuclear age to have a different character and use than it had before. I suppose it's true that as civilization has developed art has become less and less obviously functional. One thinks of the way poetry initially was simply integrated into the lives of the tribal people and was meant to remind them of their histories, of their myths, and of their values. I think poetry nowadays, in our supposedly advanced society, does that sort of thing still but less obviously and with more variation and uncertainty. It is still the main part of the job of poetry to celebrate our collective values as far as that can be done and to tell us stories about how we got here.

VOICES OF THE WAR

THE SEEDS OF WAR

On 1 April 1924, Adolf Hitler began his prison term for the attempted putsch (governmental overthrow) at Munich in November 1923, and soon he began dictating to his protégé and fellow convict, Rudolph Hess, what eventually became *Mein Kampf*. The first volume was published in 1925, and a second volume in 1926; in 1930 the two volumes combined to form the standard edition. An estimated 10 million copies of *Mein Kampf* were sold during Hitler's lifetime.[1]

In *Mein Kampf*, Adolf Hitler, a gassed and wounded veteran of World War I, writes a pathological response to his war experiences and the defeat of Germany. Without being overly psychoanalytic, it is easy to see his obsessive self-absorption and extraordinary fixation on nationalism in this description of why he got involved in politics. The most noticeable aspect of Hitler's style is the overblown sophistry and sentiment. Although at times the writing is barely coherent, its message of hatred and violence is distinct.

FROM ADOLF HITLER, *MEIN KAMPF* (1923)
(Trans. Ralph Manheim; Boston: Houghton Mifflin, 1971)

Since the day when I had stood at my mother's grave, I had not wept. When in my youth Fate seized me with merciless hardiness, my defiance mounted. When in the long war years Death snatched so many a dear comrade and friend from our ranks, it would have seemed to me almost a sin to complain—after all, were they not dying for Germany? And when at length the creeping gas—in the last days of the dreadful struggle—attacked me, too, and began to gnaw at my eyes, and beneath the fear of going blind forever, I nearly lost heart for a moment, the voice of my conscience thundered at me: Miserable wretch, are you going to cry when thousands are a hundred times worse off than you! And so I bore my lot in dull silence. But now I could not help it. Only now did I see how all personal suffering vanishes in comparison with the misfortune of the fatherland.

• • •

I could not help but laugh at the thought of my own future which only
a short time before had given me such bitter concern. Was it not ridic-
ulous to expect to build houses on such ground? At last it became clear
to me that what had happened was what I had so often feared but had
never been able to believe with my emotions.

Kaiser William II was the first German Emperor to hold out a concili-
atory hand to the leaders of Marxism, without suspecting that scoundrels
have no honor. While they still held the imperial hand in theirs, their
other hand was reaching for the dagger.

There is no making pacts with Jews; there can only be the hard; either-
or.

I, for my part, decided to go into politics. (204–206)

PEARL HARBOR

The Japanese surprise attack on Pearl Harbor shocked the American people. The following *Time* magazine reporting of the events
following the attack depicts the mood of the country and President
Roosevelt's preparation for addressing Congress to request a declaration of war.

FROM *TIME*, DECEMBER 15, 1941

National Ordeal

The Government and People of the United States declared war on the
Japanese Empire at 4:10 P.M. Monday, Dec. 8, 1941.

At dawn the day before, the Japanese had attacked savagely all along
the whole great U.S. island-bridge which stretches to the Orient.

It was premeditated murder masked by a toothy smile. The Nation had
taken a heavy blow. The casualties crept from rumor into uglier-rumor:
hundreds on hundreds of Americans had died bomb-quick, or were dying, bed-slow.

But the war came as a great relief, like a reverse earthquake, that in
one terrible jerk shook everything disjointed, distorted, askew back into
place. Japanese bombs had finally brought national unity to the U.S.

Alarm

Instantly on the news from Pearl harbor, President Roosevelt ordered
the Army and the Navy: "Fight Back!" The U.S., after 22 years and 25
days of peace, was at war.

All news from scenes of action was routed immediately to the White

House, issued at once in bulletins to the press. The War Council was telephoned. The President called a Cabinet meeting for 8:30 P.M., a session with Congressional leaders for 9 P.M.

He had already finished the first draft of his war message. In the second-floor red-room study, he talked to the Cabinet, then brought in the Congressional leaders—among them, on his first visit to the White House in many a moon, aging croak-voiced Senator Hiram Johnson of California, oldest of the Isolationists. The President was deadly serious. There was no smile. The lines in his face were deeper.

When his visitors had gone, the President went back to work. In the small hours, he went to bed, slept for five hours. (18)

STALINGRAD

Although the American involvement in the war meant the inevitable defeat of the Axis Powers, the true turning point in the war was the complete defeat and surrender of the German 6th Army at Stalingrad by the Soviets. Joachim Wieder was a veteran of the Wehrmacht's devastating defeat and wrote about his experiences in *Stalingrad: Memories and Reassessments* (1993).

FROM JOACHIM WIEDER AND HEINRICH GRAF VON EINSIEDEL,
STALINGRAD: MEMORIES AND REASSESSMENTS (1962)
(Trans. Helmut Bogler; London: Arms and Armour, 1993)

While our staff in the ravine near Gorodishche was still trying to lead out increasingly dissolving corps and prepare the perimeter defense, the ruins of the beaten forces were flowing in an unending march of misery on the road of retreat via Gumrak air base toward the northern and western suburbs of Stalingrad.

In freezing cold and wild snow flurries I rode across the desolate battlefield on a motorcycle together with a sergeant of the military police. We soon reached the road of catastrophe arising dark grey against the backdrop of the snow-bound steppe, marked by all kinds of abandoned rubbish, half-covered cadavers of horses and wrecked vehicles, scattered pieces of equipment, crates, destroyed weapons.

In the zone of horror at Gumrak, dead chimneys, walls, and stumps of buildings rose eerily from the snow. In the grounds of the railway station stood the long, wide rows of box-cars that I knew to be filled to overflowing, as were the neighboring cellars, holes and bunkers, with wounded, sick, and dying. These were the places where suffering, misery, wounded, and desperation were horribly concentrated. And over all this misery lay a heavy artillery and mortar bombardment that had dirtily stained the snow-covered earth all around. (94–95)

THE ITALIAN CAMPAIGN

The most celebrated American World War II correspondent was Ernie Pyle, who wrote about the war from a GI's viewpoint until he was killed in 1945 covering the Pacific Theater. The following excerpt is part of a dispatch he wrote on 25 April 1944 from the Anzio beachhead.

FROM ERNIE PYLE, *ERNIE'S WAR: THE BEST OF ERNIE PYLE'S
WORLD WAR II DISPATCHES*
(Ed. David Nichols; New York: Touchstone, 1986)

The cemetery is neat and its rows of wooden crosses are very white— and it is very big. All the American dead of the beachhead are buried in one cemetery.

Trucks bring the bodies in daily. Italian civilians and American soldiers dig the graves. They try to keep ahead by fifty graves or so. Only once or twice have they been swamped. Each man is buried in a white mattress cover.

The graves are five feet deep and close together. A little separate section is for the Germans, and there are more than three hundred in it. We have only a few American dead who are unidentified. Meticulous records are kept on everything.

• • •

Even the dead are not safe on the beachhead, nor the living who care for the dead. Many times German shells have landed in the cemetery. Men have been wounded as they dug graves. Once a body was uprooted and had to be reburied.

The inevitable pet dog barks and scampers around the area, not realizing where he is. The soldiers say at times he has kept them from going nuts. (266)

With all the many aspects about the Italian campaign that proved to be controversial, the one that was *not* was the uncommon bravery of the common Allied soldiers. In the Italian campaign much of what was once considered extraordinary in combat became, regrettably, almost too ordinary as the limits of human endurance were once again tested.

Time magazine's coverage of the fall of Rome underscores not only the significance of the recapture of the first European capital, but also the fact that much more work was yet to be done. Although this certainly was a noteworthy achievement, it was backpage news to the coverage of the Normandy invasion in the same issue.

FROM *TIME*, JUNE 12, 1944

From Rome to . . .

Rome was taken, and Rome was barely scarred. To most of the world these were the important facts about the capture of the first European capital retaken from the Germans. But General Sir Harold R. L. G. Alexander and his conquering troops were busy with another, further fact: Kesselring's army, battered, tired and in retreat, could still be destroyed. Alexander's troops surged through and around Rome and pressed the pursuit northward.

Beyond Rome the three main highways leading north were clogged with German motor equipment. Alexander's tactical air force tore savagely into them with guns and bombs. In the hills and fields, German foot soldiers backed northward, fighting stubbornly while the main bodies sped away from trouble. Allied units pressed closely. At one point they lost contact entirely with the retreating enemy, closed up fast to regain it.

It was no time to stop and throw hats in the air, as the populace in Rome was doing. For military men there was a parallel in the fall of Richmond in 1865. Lee had pulled out and swung away from the city when his resistance faltered. Grant followed, drove him to the end at Appomattox. Thus Harold Alexander hoped to finish off his foe. (22)

D-DAY (NORMANDY BEACH)

In his book about this epic battle, Stephen Ambrose voices the many different experiences of the soldiers who fought there. One such experience is representative of the horror that occurred on those beaches.

FROM STEPHEN AMBROSE, *D-DAY, JUNE 6, 1944: THE CLIMACTIC*
BATTLE OF WORLD WAR II
(New York: Simon & Schuster, 1994)

F Company, 116th, supposed to come in at Dog Red, landed near its target, astride the boundary between Dog Red and Easy Green. But G Company, supposed to be to the right of F at Dog White, drifted far left, so the two companies came in together, directly opposite the heavy fortifications at Les Moulins. There was a kilometer or so gap to each side of the intermixed companies, which allowed the German defenders to concentrate their fire.

For the men of F and G companies, the 200 meters or more journey from the Higgins boats to the shingle was the longest and most hazardous trip they had ever experienced, or ever would. The lieutenant commanding the assault team on Sgt. Harry Bare's boat was killed as the ramp went down. "As ranking noncom," Bare related, "I tried to get my mind off the boat and make it somehow to get under the seawall. We waded to the sand and threw ourselves down and the men were frozen, unable to move. My radioman had his head blown off three yards from me. The beach was covered with bodies, men with no legs, no arms—God it was awful." (331)

MARKET-GARDEN

In *A Bridge Too Far*, Cornelius Ryan describes the dramatic opening movement of the Market-Garden campaign.

FROM CORNELIUS RYAN, *A BRIDGE TOO FAR* (1974)
(New York: Touchstone, 1995)

Shortly after 10 A.M. on Sunday, September 17, 1944, from airfields all over southern England the greatest armada of troop-carrying aircraft ever assembled for a single operation took to the air. In this, the 263rd week of World War II, the Supreme Allied Commander, General Dwight Eisenhower, unleashed Market-Garden, one of the most daring and imaginative operations of the war. Surprisingly Market-Garden, a combined airborne and ground offensive, was authored by one of the most cautious of all Allied commanders, Field Marshal Bernard Law Montgomery.

Market, the airborne phase of the operation, was monumental: it involved almost five thousand fighters, bombers, transports and more than 2,500 gliders. That Sunday afternoon, at exactly 1:30 P.M., in an unprecedented daylight assault, an entire Allied airborne army, complete with vehicles and equipment, began dropping behind the German lines. The target for this bold and historic invasion from the sky: Nazi-occupied Holland. (11)

Although Robert J. Kershaw was not an eyewitness reporter of the Market-Garden operation, in *"It Never Snows in September,"* he describes the German perspective of the engagement by relying extensively on the archives of the Wehrmacht. In this passage, Kershaw describes the situation of both the Allies and the German Army just prior to the opening of the Market-Garden offensive.

FROM ROBERT J. KERSHAW, *"IT NEVER SNOWS IN SEPTEMBER":*
THE GERMAN VIEW OF MARKET-GARDEN AND THE BATTLE OF
ARNHEM, SEPTEMBER 1944
(New York: Sarpedon, 1996)

Both at the front and in the rear, effective leadership and initiative, supported by a staff system geared to the needs of the combat soldier, steadily and persistently began to organize order from the chaos. Unbeknown to the Germans, the Allied armies in the west had all but outrun their logistic support. "Mad Tuesday," 5 September, following the fall of Antwerp, marked the climax of the panic-stricken flight; an appropriate term accorded by Dutch historians. A breathing space was to emerge unexpectedly. As the exhausted Allies replenished and debated whether a "broad front" or "single thrust" was required to finish off the Reich, German commanders frantically improvised and exploited any means at their disposal to blunt it. A crust began to form. (22)

THE PACIFIC THEATER

The defeat of the Imperial Japanese Army followed a difficult and painful campaign, requiring a complex tactical and logistical plan of operations. But like the campaigns in Europe and North Africa, the campaign in the Pacific demanded the unwavering courage of the soldiers. The following excerpts come from the writings of two men who witnessed or participated in the combat leading to the ultimate defeat of Japan.

FROM JOHN LARDNER, "D DAY, IWO JIMA"
(The New Yorker Book of War Pieces; New York: Schocken, 1947)

The nature of the Iwo Jima battle did not change much in the days that immediately followed [the initial invasion]. The Marines made slow and costly gains in ground as they fought northward—gains that struck me then, and still do, as very little short of miraculous. A week or so after D-Day, in a little scrub grove halfway across the island, I recognized, behind his whiskers, a staff officer in our transport group who used to surprise me a little by the passion and complete engrossment with which he could discuss for two or three hours at a time such a question as whether or not certain items of battalion equipment should be distributed divisionally, or whether a brother officer of his named Logan, thirty-five hundred miles away, stood eighty-sixth or eighty-seventh on the promotion list. It now seemed to me that such preoccupations were useful indeed if they contributed to the professional doggedness with which this man and the troops of his unit moved forward against such overpowering intimations of mortality. "I hear that the mortar fire is easing up on the beaches," he said seriously. "That's good. There's no reason why everybody on the island should get killed." (471)

In the introduction to E. B. Sledge's *With the Old Breed: At Peleliu and Okinawa*, Paul Fussell writes that "[t]oday, almost fifty years later, Sledge still has nightmares about the bloody muddy month of May on Okinawa, when the artillery fire from both sides was so heavy and unremitting that he had a constant headache."[2]

FROM E. B. SLEDGE, *WITH THE OLD BREED: AT PELELIU AND OKINAWA* (1981)
(Oxford: Oxford University Press, 1990)

It was an appalling chaos. I was terribly afraid. Fear was obvious on the faces of my comrades, too, as we raced to the low slope and began to dig in rapidly. It was such a jolt to leave the quiet, beautiful countryside that morning, and plunge into a thunderous, deadly storm of steel that afternoon. Going onto the beach to assault Peleliu and attacking across the airfield there, we had braced ourselves for the blows that fell. But the shock and shells of 1 May at Okinawa, after the reprieve of a pleasant April, caught us off balance.

Fear has many facets, and I do not minimize my fear and terror during that day. But it was different. I was a combat veteran of Peleliu. With terror's first constriction over, I knew what to expect. I felt dreadful fear but not near-panic. Experience had taught me what to expect from the enemy guns. More importantly, I knew I could control my fear. The terrible dread that I might panic was gone. I knew that all anyone could do under shellfire was to hug the deck and pray—and curse the Japanese. (206)

NOTES

1. I. C. B. Dear and M. R. D. Foot, *The Oxford Companion to World War II* (New York: Oxford University Press, 1995), 737.

2. E. B. Sledge, *With the Old Breed: At Peleliu and Okinawa* (Oxford: Oxford University Press, [1981] 1990), xvii.

UNCONDITIONAL SURRENDER

After the United States joined the war effort, there was no question that the Allies were now strong enough to force complete Axis capitulation. From that time on, it was not a matter of *if*, but *when*, the Allies would win the war and at what cost. The unconditional surrender concept, first openly discussed by President Roosevelt in January 1943, eventually became official Allied policy for the repatriation of Germany and Japan. What other type of surrender could the Allies think of, in view of the evil that they were facing? Moreover, the negotiated Treaty of Versailles had exacerbated the problems leading up to World War II, and the Allies did not want to make a similar mistake again.[1]

Considering the complex political and military activity that represented the largest war and global merger of national power in the history of mankind, the two unconditional surrender documents are quite simple. These documents are important because they demonstrate the clarity of the Allied aim: to rid the world of unbridled fascism and imperialism.

[THE GERMAN INSTRUMENT OF SURRENDER]
(http://www.yale.edu/lawweb/avalon/avalon.htm)

Only this text in English is authoritative

1. We the undersigned, acting by authority of the German High Command, hereby surrender unconditionally to the Supreme Commander, Allied Expeditionary Force and simultaneously to the Soviet High Command, all forces on land, sea, and in the air who are at this date under German control.

2. The German High Command will at once issue orders to all German military, naval, and air authorities and to all forces under German control to cease active operations at 2301 hours Central European time on 8 May to remain in the position occupied at the time. No ship, vessel, or aircraft is to be scuttled, or any damage done to their hull, machinery or equipment.

3. The German High Command will at once issue to the appropriate commander, and ensure the carrying out of any further orders issued by the Supreme Commander, Allied Expeditionary Force and by the Soviet High Command.

4. This act of military surrender is without prejudice to, and will be superseded by any general instrument of surrender imposed by, or on behalf of the United Nations and applicable to Germany and the German Armed forces as a whole.

5. In the event of the German High Command or any of the forces under its control failing to act in accordance with this act of surrender, the Supreme Commander, Allied Expeditionary Force and the Soviet High Command will take such punitive or other action as they deem appropriate.

Signed at Rheims at 0241 on the 7th day of May, 1945
On behalf of the German High Command
[Jodl]

In the Presence of
On behalf of the
Supreme Commander,

On behalf of the
Soviet High Command
[Sousloparov]

Allied Expeditionary Force
[Smith]

Major General, French Army
(Witness)
[Sevez]

[THE JAPANESE INSTRUMENT OF SURRENDER]
(http://www.yalc.cdu/lawweb/avalon/avalon.htm)

We, acting by command of and on behalf of the Emperor of Japan, the Japanese Government and the Japanese Imperial General Headquarters, hereby accept the provisions set forth in the declaration issued by the heads of the Government of the United States, China and Great Britain on 26 July 1945 at Potsdam, and subsequently adhered to by the Union of Soviet Socialist Republics, which four powers are hereafter referred to as the Allied Powers.

We hereby proclaim the unconditional surrender to the Allied Powers of the Japanese Imperial General Headquarters and all Japanese armed forces and all armed forces under Japanese control wherever situated.

We hereby command all Japanese forces wherever situated and the Japanese people to cease hostilities forthwith, to preserve and save from damage all ships, aircrafts, and military and civil property and to comply with all requirements which may be imposed by the Supreme Commander for the Allied Powers or by agencies of the Japanese Government at his direction.

We hereby command the Japanese Imperial General Headquarters to issue at once orders to the Commanders of all Japanese forces and all forces under Japanese control wherever situated to surrender unconditionally themselves and all forces under their control.

We hereby command all civil, military and naval officials to obey and enforce all proclamations, orders and directives deemed by the Supreme Commander for the Allied Powers to be proper to effectuate this surrender and issued by him or under his authority and we direct all such officials to remain at their posts and to continue to perform their non-combatant duties unless specifically relieved by him or under his authority.

We hereby undertake for the Emperor, the Japanese Government and their successors to carry out the provisions of the Potsdam Declaration in good faith, and to issue whatever orders and take whatever action may be required by the Supreme Commander for the Allied Powers or by any other designated representative of the Allied Powers for the purposes of giving effect to that Declaration.

We hereby command the Japanese Imperial Government and the Japanese Imperial General Headquarters at once to liberate all Allied prisoners of war and civilian internees now under Japanese control and to provide for their protection, care, maintenance and immediate transportation to places as directed.

The authority of the Emperor and the Japanese government to rule the state shall be subject to the Supreme Commander for the Allied Powers who will take such steps as he deems proper to effectuate these terms of surrender.

[Signed by Japanese Foreign Minister Mamoru Shigemitsu and General Yoshijiro Umezu and General Douglas MacArthur, Commander in the Southwest Pacific and Supreme Commander for the Allied Powers. USS *Missouri*, 2 September 1945, 0904 hours.]

NOTE

1. I. C. B. Dear and M. R. D. Foot, *The Oxford Companion to World War II* (New York: Oxford University Press, 1995), 1174–1176.

TOPICS FOR WRITTEN AND ORAL DISCUSSION

1. Do you know any veterans of World War II in your family or community? If not, contact a local chapter of the Veterans of Foreign Wars. Interview this veteran and find out about his or her particular experience during that conflict. Bring a camera and take a picture, and ask him or her to bring a picture of himself or herself during the war. Write an essay about the interview.

2. All too often we drive right by a monument without paying it a bit of attention. Visit a local museum or monument commemorating some aspect of World War II. Then research the history of the event, unit, or equipment being commemorated. Write an essay not only about your research but also about your own connection to the topic. Do you have some new attachment to what is being commemorated?

3. Debate the pros and cons of strategic bombing. In terms of the outcome of World War II, was it militarily worth the significant costs in civilian lives, social infrastructure, and culture?

4. In your opinion, how does American culture romanticize war? Compare the very unromantic view of war provided by the authors presented here with the image of combat presented today in the mass media. How is the development of 24-hour news coverage changing the cultural message about war?

5. Write or outline a short story that uses a war veteran as its protagonist. Exchange your story with another student. Compare the circumstances of each story. Is the setting before, during, or after an engagement? What do the differing circumstances of the combat say about each story? Examine the perspectives of stories written by other students.

SUGGESTIONS FOR FURTHER READING

Ambrose, Stephen E. *Citizen Soldiers: The U.S. Army from the Normandy Beaches to the Bulge to the Surrender of Germany*. New York: Simon & Schuster, 1997.

———. *D-Day, June 6, 1944: The Climactic Battle of World War II*. New York: Simon & Schuster, 1994.

Clark, Alan. *Barbarosa: The Russian-German Conflict, 1941–1945*. New York: Quill, 1965.

Collins, J. Lawton, General, U.S. Army. *Lightning Joe: An Autobiography*. Novato, CA: Presido, 1979.

Dupuy, Trevor N. *Hitler's Last Gamble: The Battle of the Bulge, December 1944–January 1945*. New York: HarperPerennial, 1994.

Ellis, Robert B. *See Naples and Die: A World War II Memoir of a United States Army Ski Trooper in the Mountains of Italy*. Jefferson, NC: MacFarland, 1996.

Flower, Desmond, and James Reeves, eds. *The War: 1939–1945*. New York: De Capo Press, 1997.

Gabel, Kurt. *The Making of a Paratrooper: Airborne Training and Combat in World War II*. Ed. William C. Mitchell. Lawrence: University of Kansas Press, 1990.

Gaijdusek, Robert E. *Resurrection: A War Journey*. Notre Dame, IN: University of Notre Dame, 1997.

Heller, Joseph. *Now and Then: From Coney Island to Here*. New York: Knopf, 1998.

Hemingway, Ernest. *Across the River and into the Trees*. New York: Scribners, 1950.

Jones, James. *Whistle*. New York: Delacorte, 1978.

————. *WWII: A Chronicle of Soldiering*. New York: Ballantine, 1975.

Keegan, John. *The Battle for History: Re-Fighting World War II*. New York: Vintage, 1995.

————. *Six Armies in Normandy: From D-Day to the Liberation of Paris*. New York: Penguin, 1982.

————, ed. *The Times Atlas of the Second World War*. New York: Harper and Row, 1989.

Miller, Edward G. *A Dark and Bloody Ground: The Huertgen and the Roer River Dams, 1944–1945*. College Station: Texas A&M University, 1995.

Overy, Richard. *Why the Allies Won*. New York: Norton, 1995.

Prange, Gordon W. *At Dawn We Slept: The Untold Story of Pearl Harbor*. New York: Penguin, 1981.

Pyle, Ernie. *Ernie's War: The Best of Ernie Pyle's World War II Dispatches*. Ed. David Nichols. New York: Touchstone, 1986.

Ryan, Cornelius. *A Bridge Too Far*. New York: Touchstone, (1974) 1995.

————. *The Longest Day: June 6, 1944*. New York: Touchstone, (1959) 1994.

Wieder, Joachim, and Heinrich Graf von Einsiedel. *Stalingrad: Memories and Reassessments*. Trans. Helmut Bogler. London: Arms and Armour, (1962) 1993.

2 ———————————————

The Home Front

An Analysis of Bette Greene's *Summer of My German Soldier* and David Guterson's *Snow Falling on Cedars*

LITERARY ANALYSIS

During and after World War II, life changed. It would never be the same as it had been before the war. Although remarkable alterations in the social fabric were taking place in England, France, Germany, Russia, the Netherlands, Japan, and Italy, as well as in other countries involved in the global conflict, this chapter primarily concentrates on changes that occurred in the United States. Both novels analyzed in this chapter address a few of the dramatic, if not tragic, changes in American society brought on by World War II.

SUMMER OF MY GERMAN SOLDIER

Primarily written for a young audience, this book (published in 1973) offers an interesting look at changes occasioned by the arrival of a large group of German POWs in small-town Jenkinsville, Arkansas, during World War II. The story is told from the first-person perspective of Patty, a precocious Jewish girl whose family owns Bergen Department Store. Not only does the book explore the relationship between a young Jewish-American girl and a

German POW, it also gives glimpses of ordinary life on the home front. The reader finds such typical World War II–era occurrences as obituary notices about local GIs killed in action, Victory gardens, and automobiles that make more noise than usual because quieter, new ones are rationed. In a much different vein, the reader also discovers a community more paranoid than usual.

Like most adolescents, Patty finds growing up to be a complicated and difficult process, but more so because her family is Jewish in a predominantly Baptist town. About her feeling out of place, Patty observes:

> My geography problem is in being a Jewish girl where it's a really peculiar thing to be. Even when I went to Jewish Sunday school in Memphis the geography thing was still there. I would come in on a cold Sunday morning wearing short-sleeved, short-legged union suits under my sash-tied dresses, while the other girls looked as though they were born into this world wearing matching sweater and skirt outfits.[1]

Adding to her difficulties is the fragile emotional condition of her family. They seem to be suffering an inordinate amount of strain—especially her father, an angry, bitter man lacking sufficient affection for his daughter.

Further compounding Patty's problem is the fact that one of the newly arrived German POWs, Anton Reiker, escapes and hides for a while in her secret clubhouse, the empty rooms over the family's garage. Patty soon becomes infatuated with him. During his brief stay in the clubhouse Patty provides food and new clothing for Anton, and they become good friends. Anton, the descendent of a past president of the university in Gottingen, has been a reluctant German soldier; an educated young man, he understands the dishonesty and cruelty of Hitler. Nevertheless, being a soldier of the Wehrmacht, Anton also understands the irony of his being helped by a Jewish girl. This irony bonds the two together:

> "It's extraordinary," he said. "Who would believe it? 'Jewish girl risks all for German soldier.' Tell me, Patty Bergen"—his voice became soft, but with a trace of hoarseness—"why are you doing this for me?"
>
> It wasn't complicated. Why didn't he know? There was really only one word for it. A simple little word that in itself is reason enough.

> "The reason I'm doing this for you," I started off, "is only that I
> wouldn't want anything bad to happen to you." (83)

The simplicity of Patty's reasoning, while underscoring the purity
of her heart, belies the complexity of her complicity in Anton's
remaining a fugitive. Whether she realizes it or not, she is committing a serious crime in wartime America.

Of course, as news gets out that a German POW is on the loose,
the townspeople become frightened, especially since Anton's escape comes on the heels of a foiled espionage attempt by German
agents. The town is further excited when FBI agents converge on
Jenkinsville. Because Patty previously had an encounter with Anton
in her father's store, the FBI questions her; for the time being, she
keeps her secret about Anton's whereabouts.

However, a series of events—starting with her father's painful
whipping of Patty and Anton's aborted attempt to rescue her—
forces Anton to leave his hiding place. Before he leaves, he gives
Patty a ring once belonging to his great-grandfather bearing the
seal of his office as university president. Anton is eventually found
and killed while trying to avoid capture, and it is then discovered
that he is wearing a fine shirt with the monogram "HB" on it—
the initials of Patty's father. Patty is questioned again. Unable to
provide the authorities with an alternative story, she confesses her
connivance with an enemy of the people.

The whole community is now whipped up into a hysterical
frenzy. How dare this Jew help this Nazi! Patty is tried, convicted,
and sentenced to reform school in Arkansas "for a period of not
more than six months nor less than four months" (174); she barely
misses being tried under the Treason Act, which likely would have
resulted in her execution. Unable to understand the enormity of
her actions, Patty begins her sentence by imagining a better time
to come:

> The vision was still there waiting for me, soft and appealing. I let it
> in. It's six years from now. I'm eighteen. The war is over. With my
> thousand-dollar bond, I have money enough to take a train to New
> York and from there a ship to Germany. Another train ride and I'm
> in Gottingen. (181)

Alone in the reform school, her only visitor is Ruth, Patty's African
American nanny. Besides Ruth, all she has for comfort is a hope
for a better future. Patty is truly paying for her act of humanity.

Although Jenkinsville, Arkansas, is about as far way from the battlefield as it could possibly be, the inhumanity of war finds its way there anyway. This novel demonstrates just how pervasive the tragedy of war can be. Patty, an innocent, is forced to face the moral implications of a global war on a very local level. As in the stories concerning actual combatants, Patty learns that an individual's greatest threat may come from those who are closest—even from someone's own family. The story is written with deceptive simplicity and thereby challenges the assumptions that the U.S. home front was safe and unequivocally unified.

SNOW FALLING ON CEDARS

Winner of the 1996 American Booksellers Book of the Year award, this novel is about the dramatic changes that occurred in Amity Harbor, a small community on San Piedro Island in the Pacific Northwest, when America entered the war. After the Japanese surprise attack at Pearl Harbor, the citizens on San Piedro Island, like most Americans, are whipped into a frenzy of fear concerning their Japanese American neighbors. The most dramatic manifestation of this fear is the incarceration of Japanese Americans in relocation camps, an action that changed the people on San Piedro long after the war's end.

The novel opens in 1954, about nine years after V-E Day, with accused murderer Kabuo Miyamoto, a Japanese American, on trial for the death of Carl Heine, a local fisherman. It is winter, and snow is falling on the community with an energy fueled by the sea wind. As the courtroom proceedings develop over the course of the novel, it is not only Kabuo who seems to be on trial but the entire community as well. Despite the importance of the deliberations on the accused, the trial becomes a means to review all the tragic misunderstandings and bitterness of San Piedro's ethnic division. The death of Heine and the arrest of Kabuo reopen many festering wounds between the American and Japanese American citizens of the island.

One such wound that has not healed concerns the youthful love affair between Ishmael Chambers (named for the melancholic narrator of Herman Melville's *Moby-Dick*) and Hatsue Miyamoto, the wife of the accused murderer. While covering the trial for his local newspaper, Ishmael, as melancholy as his namesake, is brought back to the memories of his forbidden relationship with Hatsue. Adding to Ishmael's discontent is a wound he incurred during his combat duty in the Pacific against the Japanese. "He had only one arm, the left having been amputated ten inches below the shoulder joint, so that he wore the sleeve of his coat pinned up with the cuff fastened to the elbow."[2] At the trial he confronts his former lover, whom he has never gotten over. The snow, falling in seeming defiance of the human conflicts, pushes Ishmael into bittersweet reminiscences of his youth. "He hoped it would snow recklessly and bring to the island the impossible winter purity, so rare and precious, he remembered fondly from his youth" (8).

At the heart of this story is the treatment of the Japanese American community during the early stages of U.S. involvement in World War II, right after the Japanese surprise attack on Pearl Harbor. Heine's father had previously agreed to sell a portion of his land to the family of the accused murderer. In court during the murder trial, Carl's mother (Etta) explains that

> [the deal] included a five-hundred-dollar down payment and an eight-year "lease-to-own" contract. Carl [the father] to collect two hundred and fifty dollars every six months, June 30 and December 31, with six and a half percent interest annually. Papers to be held by Carl, another set by Zenhichi, a third set for any inspector [who] wanted to see them. The Miyamotos—this was back in '34, said Etta—couldn't really own land anyway. They were from Japan, both of them *born* there, and there was this law on the books prevented them. (121)

Mrs. Heine explains that because the law would only allow Japanese Americans born in the United States who were at least twenty years of age to own property, the land could only revert to the oldest son, Kabuo, after the end of the eight-year lease in 1942. However, according to Etta, the Miyamotos were not able to make the last two of sixteen payments (actually, they were only one payment away from satisfying the loan) because they had been incarcerated in relocation camps; unable to work to make money, they were unable to pay off the loan. The Miyamotos had only been given eight days to take care of their business before being sent to the relocation camp.

When her husband dies in 1944, Mrs. Heine sells the property to another member of the community, Ole Jurgensen, and moves into town, sending the Miyamotos' equity to them in their California relocation camp. Etta also relates that despite her dissent, Carl Jr. and Kabuo had been best friends as boys, but all of that was before the war and before the bitterness of Mrs. Heine's cold-hearted refusal to allow the Miyamotos to possess their land. When Kabuo returns from serving his country in 1945, himself a veteran of the Italian campaign, he asks Etta to return his family's land to them, but she refuses even to discuss the matter.

This disagreement over ownership of that land is what the prosecution theorizes is Kabuo's motive for murdering Carl Jr., especially since Jurgensen eventually agrees to resell the land to Carl right before the murder. The prosecution theorizes that Kabuo murdered Carl out of revenge for taking his family's land again. Carl had beaten Kabuo to the property only by a few hours; Jurgensen had not even had time to take down the For Sale sign. After all, the prosecution asserts, three different fishermen reported seeing Kabuo's boat near Carl's boat on the night of the murder. Kabuo had to have done it. In the end, however, the facts of the matter prove that Carl's death had indeed been an accident—it turns out that on the day of the murder he and Kabuo had agreed to return the property to the Miyamoto family.

Another element in the story concerning the relocation of the Japanese Americans in this community is the separation of Hatsue and Ishmael—the star-crossed lovers. The bitterness of their breakup (initiated by Hatsue's family, who forbade her to continue the relationship) darkens Ishmael's entire life. He can neither forget nor forgive her; his heart has turned cold like the snow. However, because the trial has thrown them back together, he is eventually able to reconcile his bitter experience and his loss. Ironically, it is Ishmael who saves Hatsue's husband from conviction by proving that Carl's death was accidental—the result of his boat being swamped by the wake of a much larger boat. It turns out that Carl's boat had lost electrical power due to a weak battery and that Kabuo had stopped to help him. (This is when the two men agreed to the return of the property.) After Kabuo loaned Carl a spare battery, Carl recklessly attempted to save the old, rusted lantern lashed to his ship's mast, which was about to be destroyed by the wake of an approaching ship. His head was crushed from the fall when the wake hit before he could climb down safely from the mast. Ironically, this act of parsimony on Carl's part, a trait inherited from his mother, dooms him to death. Ishmael reports his evidence to the trial judge, and the case is dismissed.

Because it forces him to exorcise his bitterness over his lost love, Ishmael's saving of Hatsue's husband also ends up saving himself as well. Although he withholds the evidence of Kabuo's innocence for several days while he wrestles with his conscience, he eventually does the right thing. Ishmael's action to save the man who separates him from his true love propels him out of the moral inertia he has maintained since the breakup of his relationship with Hatsue many years earlier.

The accidental death of Carl not only put an innocent man on trial, it also put Ishmael and the entire community on trial for its past transgression. Ironically, Carl's death, as sad as it was for his family, is the catalyst for the reconciliation of past wrongs, an act of atonement for the sins of the community that sent the Japanese Americans to relocation camps. The book ends with Ishmael writing the final report of the story for the newspaper. Although he has not extrinsically gained anything in the novel, Ishmael seems reconciled to his fate, finally devoid of the bitterness that was so prevalent in the beginning:

> Well, thought Ishmael, bending over his typewriter, his fingertips poised just above the keys: the palpitations of Kabuo Miyamoto's heart were unknowable finally. And Hatsue's heart wasn't knowable, either, nor was Carl Heine's. The heart of *any* other, because it had a will, would remain forever mysterious.
>
> Ishmael gave himself to the writing of it, and as he did so he understood this, too: that accident ruled every corner of the universe except the chambers of the human heart. (460)

Although the novel ends like it begins with Ishmael alone, he has at least learned that the human heart is just as capable of doing good as doing evil. In this knowledge he discovers that he has no one to blame, no one to hate, for his losses. Ishmael regains his humanity.

This well-crafted novel illustrates the tragic consequences of the wartime treatment of the Japanese Americans by the U.S. government. The relocation of these citizens not only deprived them of their homes and livelihoods but permanently damaged their lives.

This story is just one example of what happened to innocent people during the time when Americans, temporally overcome by fear, acted contrary to the principles of freedom and fairness. But as the novel's title suggests, the power of nature endures in spite of the foibles of flawed humanity. Snows will fall on cedars forever.

Like Greene's *Summer of My German Soldier*, Guterson's evocative novel demonstrates that during World War II the dangers abounded for individuals no matter where they happened to live.

NOTES

1. Bette Green, *Summer of My German Soldier* (New York: Bantam, 1973), 106–107. All subsequent quotations of this text come from this source.

2. David Guterson, *Snow Falling on Cedars* (New York: Vintage, 1995), 7. All subsequent quotations of this text come from this source.

HISTORICAL CONTEXT

THE U.S. POW CONCENTRATION SYSTEM

Beginning with the Declaration of Paris in 1856, the major military powers have periodically convened to formulate rules for a more humane conduct of war. The outcome of these various conventions (or conferences) has been a series of agreements that have continually shaped the laws of war. By updating and improving the agreement signed at the 1907 Hague Conference, the 1929 Geneva Convention established the proper treatment of prisoners of war. The United States, along with forty-one other nations, signed that treaty. Among other things, this treaty stipulated that prisoners be quickly and safely removed from the battlefield, and that whereas officers and non-commissioned officers could only perform supervisory duties, all other prisoners could be put to work. America, a place safely removed from the European battlefield and also in need of farm labor, eventually became the destination for German POWs during World War II.

Germany lost over 4,500,000 soldiers[1] as POWs, and 380,000 ended up in the United States.[2] These POWs were dispersed among 155 base camps or 500 branch camps scattered all over America. (There were seventeen camps in Arkansas alone.) In *We Were Each Other's Prisoners: An Oral History of World War II American and German Prisoners of War*, Lewis H. Carlson observes that the first significant group of Germans to come over were from Rommel's Africa Corps—dedicated, disciplined soldiers who had been hardened by tough fighting.[3] These soldiers remained committed to the Nazi war effort. The next group to arrive were the survivors of the Sicilian and Italian campaigns; these men were also still committed to Hitler, although they had been in almost constant combat for over five years. The last group of POWs, soldiers captured after D-Day when the German High Command was trying to stop the Allied advance, were a demoralized lot—many were teenagers "who had been rushed into the front lines without adequate training."[4]

Carlson writes about the mutual experiences of American and German POWs:

American and German World War II prisoners shared much in common. All were lonely, bored, and no longer capable of controlling their individual destinies; most indulged in introspective examinations of self; all suffered indignities, but many experienced an incident or two that reinforced their belief in human decency; all had to learn patience and a degree of tolerance; some became very self-confident after realizing they could handle extreme adversity; others suffered what has become known as post-traumatic stress disorder (PTSD). Almost all agree that their imprisonment, along with the war itself, was the central experience of their lives.[5]

Whereas most experts argue that the American POWs experienced significant deprivation of food, medical care, adequate shelter, and clothing, and some received overt abuse by their captors, there is very little disagreement that German POWs "were reasonably well treated; after all, they looked like the majority of Americans, and they shared a common heritage with many of their captors."[6] If ordinary German POWs encountered any trouble, it probably was from the hands of their more fanatical Nazi comrades. After the war, the United States executed fourteen Nazi POWs convicted of murdering other Germans.[7]

THE INCARCERATION OF JAPANESE AMERICANS

Although the pressures of war can bring out the best in people, they can also bring out the worst. As will be discussed in subsequent chapters, the Nazis were responsible for murdering at least 6 million Jews, and the Japanese committed countless atrocities against innocent civilians in occupied China. Even America was not without some blame in its treatment of innocent civilians. The U.S. government's treatment of second-generation Japanese Americans, called Nisei, is among the more troubling events in U.S. history.

Even before World War II, the United States was not very hospitable to Japanese Americans. For example, the Japanese Exclusion Act of 1924 limited certain rights of Japanese Americans. During World War II, the U.S. government singled out these citizens for relocation into camps that excluded them from the larger American culture. The main reason these citizens were relocated was that the U.S. government feared that Japanese Americans would commit espionage on behalf of their ancestral home. Few of the other American ethnic groups representing the Axis Powers were ever affected. It did not matter if any of these individuals were American citizens or resident aliens; they were all sent to relocation camps for one reason alone—because they were of Japanese ancestry.[8] Especially affected by this policy were the 125,000 Nisei living on the West Coast.[9] Interestingly, the 150,000 Nisei living on Hawaii, where the Japanese surprise attack took place, were hardly affected by U.S. policy.[10]

By 1944, American society seemed to have recovered its balance and the relocation program was revoked; the Supreme Court declared the incarceration of any citizen whose loyalty was unchallenged to be unconstitutional.[11] But a lot of damage had already occurred. The discriminatory treatment of Japanese American citizens is a disappointing, cautionary episode in U.S. history, a warning about what can happen when a society becomes caught up in hysteria.

RATIONING, WAR BONDS, AND VICTORY GARDENS

The U.S. government instituted many initiatives to rally the American people around the war effort. Three particular programs—rationing, war bonds, and Victory gardens—excited the imagination of the American people and made a lasting impression on the historical consciousness of the nation. They have become symbols of a society united under a single purpose, even if those memories are more the stuff of romanticized nostalgia than reality.

Americans still had vivid memories of the hard times during the Great Depression, when rationing of scarce products was instituted throughout the country. The American consumers had been hardened by these times and were more used to governmental control than at any time in U.S. history, but that did not mean they liked it. Leon Henderson, head of the Office of Price Administration (OPA), had the enormous responsibility of organizing and controlling the rationing program; he also became the focal point of criticism when favorite commodities such as sugar, shoes, coffee, and especially gasoline (already a substance Americans would fight for) became rationed. As in many programs under governmental control, inequities and abuses soon surfaced. It did not take long to discover hundreds of congressmen with "X" cards that allowed them the same no-limit gasoline rationing reserved primarily for service providers such as doctors, policemen, and firemen.[12] With these and other problems, Henderson had his hands full:

> Rationing radiated, and shortages spread. Radios for the civilian market sputtered out of production. Spare parts and tubes were all but unobtainable. Soon families had to rely on the good nature of neighbors with functioning sets. . . .
>
> An undeniable shortage of a commodity generally taken for granted—paper and paper products—stemmed in part from the robbing of the lumber camps' manpower. . . . Stores urged customers to "bring your own paper bag"—a humble item that nonetheless accounted for some two and a half million tons of paper a year in peacetime.[13]

Even diapers, made of cotton, a fiber essential in making uniforms, had to be rationed; but as Hoehling notes, that did not stop more than 10 million babies (a record) from being born during the war years.[14] Even the discomforts of scarcity and rationing failed to stop the power of romance.

Despite the call for patriotism, black (illegal) markets became prevalent soon after rationing was implemented, and angry criticism of rationing and the control of scarce products by the OPA remained unabated. America, the land of the free as well as the home of the brave, never got completely used to being restricted in terms of what to buy and the bureaucracy that went along with it.

Associated with the problem of rationing, Victory gardens were promoted to overcome food shortages, but more important, to revive a sense of self-reliance. In 1942 alone the nationwide 4-H club, with a membership at the time of 1.5 million boys and girls, grew 3 million bushels of vegetables, canned 14 million jars of food, and raised 6.5 million chickens, 300,000 hogs, and 65,000 cows.[15]

To finance the huge amount of capital required to manufacture weapons to defeat the Axis Powers, the U.S. government began a campaign to sell war bonds. The Treasury department marketed the purchase of war bonds not only as a financially wise decision but as a patriotic one as well. Everyone was encouraged to do their duty for the country and the boys overseas. Even Hollywood celebrities such as Carole Lombard did their part, traveling all over the country making guest appearances promoting war bonds. Lombard, in the first major war bond rally in Indianapolis, Indiana, helped sell a record $2.5 million worth of bonds.[16] Even the notoriously stingy Jack Benny sold his beloved $75 violin at a War Bond rally held in Gimbel's, the landmark New York department store, for $1 million!

But even on the home front, the war effort could exact the ultimate cost: Lombard was killed, along with the other twenty-one passengers on board, when the Douglas DC-3 "Sky Club" airplane she was traveling in crashed on the way back to Los Angeles from the Indianapolis rally.

WOMEN GO TO WORK

Before America joined the Allies against the Axis Powers, women constituted only 25 percent of the work force.[17] But by 1944, the year of highest female employment during the war, women would constitute 36 percent of the work force.[18] A. A. Hoehling notes that although the minimum wage for women had been increased from 44.5 cents an hour to the male minimum of 70.5 cents to attract more workers, the supply of women with the requisite skills still remained tight.[19] Hoehling writes:

> The aviation industry was the first to lower the so-called sex barrier to permit women to fill almost any job hitherto guarded greedily by the male as his own. The delicate, exact, and tedious work associated so closely with aircraft manufacture could be accomplished much better, it was discovered, by the female. In fact, one aircraft manufacturer so much better liked the feminine way of doing things, together with the lower absenteeism rate of women, that a permanent place was reserved for them in postwar blueprints.[20]

It was in the aviation industry—in companies such as Lockheed, Boeing, North America, and Consolidated—that the infamous "Rosie the Riveter" became the cultural symbol of female toughness. This image was plastered on propaganda posters throughout the country.

In an oral history of her wartime work experience, Sybil Lewis describes her job as a riveter:

The women worked in pairs. I was the riveter, and this big strong white girl from a cotton farm in Arkansas worked as the bucker. The riveter used a gun to shoot rivets through the metal and fasten it together. The bucker used a bucking bar on the other side of the metal to smooth out the rivets. Bucking was harder than shooting rivets; it required more muscle. Riveting required more skill.[21]

Hardened not only by the social changes they faced but by physical labor as well, women contributed significantly to the progress of the war.

Women also contributed to their own liberation, but not without difficulties. Some men resented the changes, but their attitudes were overwhelmed by the necessity to hire women. Interestingly, Hoehling observes that the most difficult troubles came from women

who would not bid adieu to high heels, who were reluctant to switch skirts for slacks, or who persisted in the prevalent peek-a-boo hairdo of actress Veronica Lake. Although a long swatch of tresses drooping over one eye and down almost to the shoulder might be fetching under the moonlight or in the boudoir, appalling things happened when hair became snagged in a whirring chunk of machinery.[22]

Like anyone new to the industrial labor force, women had to adapt to a radically new environment, and the success of their adaptation changed American culture. Once they had adapted to a new life-style, women were not eager to revert back to their pre-war way of life. According to 1944 Labor department figures, 80 percent of the women who were interviewed expressed a desire to continue their work after the war.[23]

THE JIM CROW ARMY

World War II brought about changes in the treatment of minorities as well. After the Civil War, much of America systematically discriminated against African Americans through a program of Jim Crow practices. Jim Crowism (from a nineteenth-century term of derogation against black American citizens) was even evident in the U.S. Army. In his introduction to *Taps for a Jim Crow Army: Letters from Black Soldiers in World War II*, Phillip McGuire describes the slow and painful progress of African Americans' quest for equality in the armed forces. According to McGuire, the War department and U.S. politicians claimed that they did not want to turn the military into a social experiment; therefore African Americans found very little change in attitudes despite their willingness to fight a common enemy. Like the American society at large, African American GIs were completely segregated from white soldiers.[24] The segregation and degradation of African American soldiers during World War II, citizens who proudly served and died for their country, remains a shameful irony of American society during the war period.

One group of African Americans who particularly distinguished themselves were the Tuskegee Airmen. Under pressure from African American leadership to be included in the war effort, the War department on 21 March 1941 activated the 99th Pursuit Squadron, and by July 1941 construction began on the Tuskegee Airfield in Alabama.[25] One year later five young men were the first to graduate into the U.S. Army Air Force. Charles E. Francis describes the 99th's first taste of combat:

> The pilots assigned to make the first combat missions were Lt. Charles B. Hall, William A. Campbell, Clarence C. Jamison and James R. Wiley. . . .
>
> The morning of June 2 was one of the most important days for the squadron, for it was on this morning that Lieutenants Hall and Campbell received the necessary briefing for the first combat mission. After the briefing, Hall and Campbell were taken to the dispersal area in a jeep. On arrival at the area, they jumped out of the jeep and walked swiftly towards their planes. When they reached their planes and, with the aid of their crew chiefs, they then adjusted their equipment. This completed, the crew chiefs stepped down off the wings of the planes. The two pilots then started the engines and taxied up the runway for the takeoff. Hall led and Campbell followed closely behind. As they reached the edge of the runway, they stopped their planes and raced their engines. The roar of the two planes sounded unusually loud, but, to the jubilant members of the squadron, who had assembled to watch the takeoff, there was indescribable beauty in this roar.[26]

Proving themselves equal to any soldier, the Tuskegee Airmen accomplished great achievements during the war. For example,

The Tuskegee Airman monument at the United States Air Force
Academy, Colorado.

they flew a grand total of 15,533 sorties, receiving 918 decorations
for service to their country. Despite the remarkable achievements
of these airmen and other African American servicemen in World
War II, racial prejudice continued after the war. President Truman,
however, removed the biggest obstacle to the recognition of African American contributions when he signed two executive orders
on 26 July 1948 ending segregation and official discrimination in
the armed forces.[27]

NOTES

1. I. C. B. Dear and M. R. D. Foot, *The Oxford Companion to World
War II* (New York: Oxford University Press, 1995), 913.

2. Lewis H. Carlson, *We Were Each Other's Prisoners: An Oral History
of World War II American and German Prisoners of War* (New York:
Basic Books, 1997), xix.

3. Ibid., xix–xx.

4. Ibid., xx.

5. Ibid., viii.

6. Ibid., viii–ix.

7. Ibid., ix.

8. Dear and Foot, *Oxford Companion*, 632.

9. A. A. Hoehling, *Home Front, USA* (New York: Thomas Y. Crowell, 1966), 32.

10. Dear and Foot, *Oxford Companion*, 632.

11. Ibid., 70.

12. Ibid., 634.

13. Hoehling, *Home Front*, 65–67.

14. Dear and Foot, *Oxford Companion*, 70.

15. Ibid., 71.

16. Ibid., 13.

17. Mark Jonathan Harris, Franklin D. Mitchell, and Steven J. Schechter, eds., *The Homefront: America during World War II* (New York: G. P. Putnam's Sons, 1984), 115.

18. Ibid.

19. Hoehling, *Home Front*, 58.

20. Ibid.

21. Hoehling, *Home Front*, 59.

22. Harris et al., *Homefront*, 119.

23. Ibid., 118.

24. Phillip McGuire, ed.,*Taps for a Jim Crow Army: Letters from Black Soldiers in World War II* (Lexington: University of Kentucky Press, 1983), xxi.

25. Charles E. Francis, *The Tuskegee Airmen: The Men Who Changed a Nation* (Boston: Branden Publishing, 1993), 16.

26. Ibid., 57.

27. Ibid., 256.

PRESIDENT FRANKLIN DELANO ROOSEVELT
(1882–1945)

Elected to the U.S. presidency in 1932, Roosevelt was not only commander in chief of the powerful U.S. Army during the war, he also was the leader of the home front. Until the United States entered the war after Pearl Harbor, Roosevelt had concentrated his efforts largely on reviving the depressed American economy. While serving an unprecedented fourth term during the war, FDR died in Warm Springs, Georgia, on 12 April 1945, just months before the conclusion of the war that had exhausted his strength. And the free world mourned.

The editors of *FDR's Fireside Chats*, Russell D. Buhite and David W. Levy, write that among all the qualities constituting Roosevelt's political character,

> none was more important to him or put to better service than his unique ability to communicate to the American people. Roosevelt had a gift for effective language, for anecdote and metaphor and witticism. He seemed to recognize this gift and genuinely to enjoy addressing the public one way or another. . . .
>
> The Fireside Chats were normally delivered from a room on the first floor of the White House, the president sitting behind a desk loaded with microphones. Almost all of the speeches were given in the evening and more than a third of them on a Sunday.[1]

FDR's communication skills and his willingness to share them with the American people during a time of historic difficulties boosted the nation's morale, helping to win the war on the home front. What follows are two Fireside Chats delivered by FDR during the war period.

FROM THE ADDRESS OF THE PRESIDENT, 9 DECEMBER 1941,
AT 10:00 P.M.
(http://www.rnhrcc.org/fdrlchat1a.html)

My Fellow Americans: The sudden criminal attacks perpetrated by the Japanese in the Pacific provide the climax of a decade of international immorality.

Powerful and resourceful gangsters have banded together to make war upon the whole human race. Their challenge has now bccn flung at the United States of America. The Japanese have treacherously violated the long-standing peace between us. Many American soldiers and sailors have been killed by enemy action. American ships have been sunk; American airplanes have been destroyed.

The Congress and the people of the United States have accepted that challenge.

Together with other free peoples, we are now fighting to maintain our right to live among our world neighbors in freedom, in common decency, without fear of assault.

I have prepared the full record of our past relations with Japan, and it will be submitted to the Congress. It begins with the visit of Commodore Perry to Japan eighty-eight years ago. It ends with the visit of two Japanese emissaries to the Secretary of State last Sunday, an hour after Japanese forces had loosed their bombs and machine guns against our flag, our forces and our citizens.

I can say with utmost confidence that no Americans, today or a thousand years hence, need feel anything but pride in our patience and in our efforts through all the years toward achieving a peace in the Pacific which would be fair and honorable to every nation, large or small. And no honest person, today or a thousand years hence, will be able to suppress a sense of indignation and horror at the treachery committed by the military dictators of Japan, under the very shadow of the flag of peace borne by their special envoys in our midst.

The course that Japan has followed for the past ten years in Asia has paralleled the course of Hitler and Mussolini in Europe and in Africa. Today, it has become far more than a parallel. It is actual collaboration so well calculated that all the continents of the world, and all the oceans, are now considered by the Axis strategists as one gigantic battlefield.

In 1931, ten years ago, Japan invaded Manchukuo—without warning.

• • •

We are now in this war. We are all in it—all the way. Every single man, woman and child is a partner in the most tremendous undertaking of our American history. We must share together the bad news and the good news, the defeats and the victories—the changing fortunes of war.

So far, the news has been all bad. We have suffered a serious setback in Hawaii. Our forces in the Philippines, which include the brave people of that Commonwealth, are taking punishment, but are defending themselves vigorously. The reports from Guam and Wake and Midway Islands are still confused, but we must be prepared for the announcement that all these three outposts have been seized.

• • •

This Government will put its trust in the stamina of the American people, and will give the facts to the public just as soon as two conditions have been fulfilled: first, that the information has been definitely and officially confirmed; and, second, that the release of the information at the time it is received will not prove valuable to the enemy directly or indirectly.

• • •

Many rumors and reports which we now hear originate, of course, with enemy sources. For instance, today the Japanese are claiming that as a result of their one action against Hawaii they have gained naval supremacy in the Pacific. This is an old trick of propaganda which has been used innumerable times by the Nazis. The purposes of such fantastic claims are, of course, to spread fear and confusion among us, and to goad us into revealing military information which our enemies are desperately anxious to obtain.

Our Government will not be caught in this obvious trap—and neither will the people of the United States.

It must be remembered by each and every one of us that our free and rapid communication these days must be greatly restricted in wartime. It is not possible to receive full and speedy and accurate reports from distant areas of combat. This is particularly true where naval operations are concerned. For in these days of the marvels of the radio it is often impossible for the Commanders of various units to report their activities by radio at all, for the very simple reason that this information would become available to the enemy and would disclose their position and their plan of defense or attack.

Of necessity there will be delays in officially confirming or denying reports of operations, but we will not hide facts from the country if we know the facts and if the enemy will not be aided by their disclosure.

To all newspapers and radio stations—all those who reach the eyes and ears of the American people—I say this: You have a most grave responsibility to the nation now and for the duration of this war.

If you feel that your Government is not disclosing enough of the truth, you have every right to say so. But in the absence of all the facts, as revealed by official sources, you have no right in the ethics of patriotism to deal out unconfirmed reports in such a way as to make people believe that they are gospel truth.

Every citizen, in every walk of life, shares this same responsibility. The lives of our soldiers and sailors—the whole future of this nation—depend upon the manner in which each and every one of us fulfills his obligation to our country.

• • •

Precious months were gained by sending vast quantities of our war material to the nations of the world still able to resist Axis aggression. Our policy rested on the fundamental truth that the defense of any country resisting Hitler or Japan was in the long run the defense of our own country. That policy has been justified. It has given us time, invaluable time, to build our American assembly lines of production.

Assembly lines are now in operation. Others are being rushed to completion. A steady stream of tanks and planes, of guns and ships and shells and equipment—that is what these eighteen months have given us.

But it is all only a beginning of what still has to be done. We must be set to face a long war against crafty and powerful bandits. The attack at Pearl Harbor can be repeated at any one of many points, points in both oceans and along both our coast lines and against all the rest of the hemisphere.

It will not only be a long war, it will be a hard war. That is the basis on which we now lay all our plans. That is the yardstick by which we measure what we shall need and demand; money, materials, doubled and quadrupled production—ever-increasing. The production must be not only for our own army and navy and air forces. It must reinforce the other armies and navies and air forces fighting the Nazis and the war lords of Japan throughout the Americas and throughout the world.

• • •

Over the hard road of the past months, we have at times met obstacles and difficulties, divisions and disputes, indifference and callousness. That is now all past—and, I am sure, forgotten.

The fact is that the country now has an organization in Washington built around men and women who are recognized experts in their own fields. I think the country knows that the people who are actually responsible in each and every one of these many fields are pulling together with a teamwork that has never before been excelled.

On the road ahead there lies hard work—grueling work—day and night, every hour and every time.

I was about to add that ahead there lies sacrifice for all of us.

But it is not correct to use that word. The United States does not consider it a sacrifice to do all one can, to give one's best to our nation, when the nation is fighting for its existence and its future life.

It is not a sacrifice for any man, old or young, to be in the Army or the Navy of the United States. Rather it is a privilege.

It is not a sacrifice for the industrialist or the wage earner, the farmer or the shopkeeper, the trainman or the doctor, to pay more taxes, to buy more bonds, to forego extra profits, to work longer or harder at the task for which he is best fitted. Rather it is a privilege.

It is not a sacrifice to do without many things to which we are accustomed if the national defense calls for doing without it.

A review this morning leads me to the conclusion that at present we shall not have to curtail the normal use of articles of food. There is enough food today for all of us and enough left over to send to those who are fighting on the same side with us.

But there will be a clear and definite shortage of metals for many kinds of civilian use, for the very good reason that in our increased program we shall need for war purposes more than half of that portion of the principal metals which during the past year have gone into articles for civilian use. Yes, we shall have to give up many things entirely.

And I am sure that the people in every part of the nation are prepared in their individual living to win this war. I am sure that they will cheerfully help to pay a large part of its financial cost while it goes on. I am sure they will cheerfully give up those material things that they are asked to give up.

• • •

I repeat that the United States can accept no result save victory, final and complete. Not only must the shame of Japanese treachery be wiped out, but the sources of international brutality, wherever they exist, must be absolutely and finally broken.

• • •

We may acknowledge that our enemies have performed a brilliant feat of deception, perfectly timed and executed with great skill. It was a thoroughly dishonorable deed, but we must face the fact that modern warfare as conducted in the Nazi manner is a dirty business. We don't like it— we didn't want to get in it—but we are in it and we're going to fight it with everything we've got.

• • •

The true goal we seek is far above and beyond the ugly field of battle. When we resort to force, as now we must, we are determined that this force shall be directed toward ultimate good as well as against immediate evil. We Americans are not destroyers—we are builders.

We are now in the midst of a war, not for conquest, not for vengeance, but for a world in which this nation, and all that this nation represents, will be safe for our children. We expect to eliminate the danger from Japan, but it would serve us ill if we accomplished that and found that the rest of the world was dominated by Hitler and Mussolini.

So we are going to win the war and we are going to in the peace that follows.

And in the difficult hours of this day—through dark days that may be yet to come—we will know that the vast majority of the members of the human race are on our side. Many of them are fighting with us. All of them are praying for us. But, in representing our cause, we represent theirs as well—our hope and their hope for liberty under God.

FROM THE LABOR DAY RADIO ADDRESS OF THE PRESIDENT,
7 SEPTEMBER 1942, AT 9:30 P.M.
(http://www.rnhrcc.org/fdrlchat22.html)

MY FRIENDS: I wish that all Americans could read all the citations for various medals recommended for our soldiers and sailors and marines. I am picking out one of these citations which tells of the accomplishments of Lieutenant John James Powers, United States Navy, during three days of the battles with Japanese forces in the Coral Sea.

During the first two days, Lieutenant Powers, flying a dive-bomber in the face of blasting enemy anti-aircraft fire, demolished one large enemy gunboat, put another gunboat out of commission, severely damaged an aircraft tender and a twenty-thousand-ton transport, and scored a direct hit on an aircraft carrier which burst into flames and sank soon after.

The official citation then describes the morning of the third day of battle. As the pilots of his squadron left the ready room to man their planes, Lieutenant Powers said to them, "Remember, the folks back home are counting on us. I am going to get a hit if I have to lay it on their flight deck."

He led his section down to the target from an altitude of 18,000 feet, through a wall of bursting anti-aircraft shells and swarms of enemy planes. He dived almost to the very deck of the enemy carrier, and did not release his bomb until he was sure of a direct hit. He was last seen attempting recovery from his dive at the extremely low altitude of two hundred feet, amid a terrific barrage of shell and bomb fragments, and smoke and flame and debris from the stricken vessel. His own plane was destroyed by the explosion of his own bomb. But he had made good his promise to "lay it on the flight deck."

I have received a recommendation from the Secretary of the Navy that Lieutenant John James Powers of New York City, missing in action, be awarded the Medal of Honor. I hereby and now make this award.

You and I are "the folks back home" for whose protection Lieutenant Powers fought and repeatedly risked his life. He said that we counted on him and his men. We did not count in vain. But have not those men a right to be counting on us? How are we playing our part "back home" in winning this war?

The answer is that we are not doing enough.

Today I sent a message to the Congress, pointing out the overwhelming urgency of the serious domestic economic crisis with which we are threatened. Some call it "inflation," which is a vague sort of term, and others call it a "rise in the cost of living," which is much more easily understood by most families.

That phrase, "the cost of living," means essentially what a dollar can buy.

• • •

Our experience with the control of other prices during the past few months has brought out one important fact—the rising cost of living can be controlled, providing that all elements making up the cost of living are controlled at the same time. I think that also is an essential justice and a practical necessity. We know that parity prices for farm products not now controlled will not put up the cost of living more than a very small amount; but we also know that if we must go up to an average of 116 percent of parity for food and other farm products—which is necessary at present under the Emergency Price Control Act before we can control all farm prices—the cost of living will get well out of hand. We are face to face with this danger today. Let us meet it and remove it.

I realize that it may seem out of proportion to you to be over-stressing these economic problems at a time like this, when we are all deeply concerned about the news from far distant fields of battle. But I give you the solemn assurance that failure to solve this problem here at home— and to solve it now—will make more difficult the winning of this war.

If the vicious spiral of inflation ever gets under way, the whole economic system will stagger. Prices and wages will go up so rapidly that the entire production program will be endangered. The cost of the war, paid by taxpayers, will jump beyond all present calculations. It will mean an uncontrollable rise in prices and in wages, which can result in raising the overall cost of living as high as another 20 percent soon. That would mean that the purchasing power of every dollar that you have in your pay envelope, or in the bank, or included in your insurance policy or your pension, would be reduced to about eighty cents worth. I need not tell you that this would have a demoralizing effect on our people, soldiers and civilians alike.

Overall stabilization of prices, and salaries, and wages and profits is necessary to the continued increasing production of planes and tanks and ships and guns.

• • •

Therefore, I have asked the Congress to pass legislation under which the President would be specifically authorized to stabilize the cost of living, including the price of all farm commodities. The purpose should be to hold farm prices at parity, or at levels of a recent date, whichever is higher. The purpose should also be to keep wages at a point stabilized with today's cost of living. Both must be regulated at the same time; and neither one of them can or should be regulated without the other.

At the same time that farm prices are stabilized, I will stabilize wages.

That is plain justice—and plain common sense.

And so I have asked the Congress to take this action by the first of October. We must now act with the dispatch which the stern necessities of war require.

• • •

The responsibilities of the President in wartime to protect the Nation are very grave. This total war, with our fighting fronts all over the world, makes the use of the executive power far more essential than in any previous war.

If we were invaded, the people of this country would expect the President to use any and all means to repel the invader.

Now the Revolution and the War Between the States were fought on our own soil, but today this war will be won or lost on other continents and in remote seas. I cannot tell what powers may have to be exercised in order to win this war.

The American people can be sure that I will use my powers with a full sense of responsibility to the Constitution and to my country. The American people can also be sure that I shall not hesitate to use every power vested in me to accomplish the defeat of our enemies in any part of the world where our own safety demands such defeat.

And when the war is won, the powers under which I act will automatically revert to the people of the United States—to the people to whom those powers belong.

• • •

The nation must have more money to run the War. People must stop spending for luxuries. Our country needs a far greater share of our incomes.

For this is a global war, and it will cost this nation nearly one hundred billion dollars in 1943.

In that global war there are now four main areas of combat; and I should like to speak briefly of them, not in the order of their importance, for all of them are vital and all of them are interrelated.

1. The Russian front. Here the Germans are still unable to gain the smashing victory which, almost a year ago, Hitler announced he had already

achieved. Germany has been able to capture important Russian territory. Nevertheless, Hitler has been unable to destroy a single Russian Army; and this, you may be sure, has been, and still is, his main objective. Millions of German troops seem doomed to spend another cruel and bitter winter on the Russian front. Yes, the Russians are killing more Nazis, and destroying more airplanes and tanks than are being smashed on any other front. They are fighting not only bravely but brilliantly. In spite of any setbacks Russia will hold out, and with the help of her Allies will ultimately drive every Nazi from her soil.

2. The Pacific Ocean area. This area must be grouped together as a whole— every part of it, land and sea. We have stopped one major Japanese offensive; and we have inflicted heavy losses on their fleet. But they still possess great strength; they seek to keep the initiative; and they will undoubtedly strike hard again. We must not over-rate the importance of our successes in the Solomon Islands, though we may be proud of the skill with which these local operations were conducted. At the same time, we need not under-rate the significance of our victory at Midway. There we stopped the major Japanese offensive.

3. In the Mediterranean and the Middle East area the British, together with the South Africans, Australians, New Zealanders, Indian troops and others of the United Nations, including ourselves, are fighting a desperate battle with the Germans and Italians. The Axis powers are fighting to gain control of that area, dominate the Mediterranean and the Indian Ocean, and gain contact with the Japanese Navy. The battle in the Middle East is now joined. We are well aware of our danger, but we are hopeful of the outcome.

4. The European area. Here the aim is an offensive against Germany. There are at least a dozen different points at which attacks can be launched. You, of course, do not expect me to give details of future plans, but you can rest assured that preparations are being made here and in Britain toward this purpose. The power of Germany must be broken on the battlefields of Europe.

Various people urge that we concentrate our forces on one or another of these four areas, although no one suggests that any one of the four areas should be abandoned. Certainly, it could not be seriously urged that we abandon aid to Russia, or that we surrender all of the Pacific to Japan, or the Mediterranean and Middle East to Germany, or give up an offensive against Germany. The American people may be sure that we shall neglect none of the four great theaters of war.

Certain vital military decisions have been made. In due time you will know what these decisions are—and so will our enemies. I can say now that all of these decisions are directed toward taking the offensive.

Today, exactly nine months after Pearl Harbor, we have sent overseas three times more men than we transported to France in the first nine months of the First World War. We have done this in spite of greater danger and fewer ships. And every week sees a gain in the actual number of American men and weapons in the fighting areas. These reinforcements in men and munitions are continuing, and will continue to go forward.

This war will finally be won by the coordination of all the armies, navies and air forces of all of the United Nations operating in unison against our enemies.

This will require vast assemblies of weapons and men at all the vital points of attack. We and our allies have worked for years to achieve superiority in weapons. We have no doubts about the superiority of our men. We glory in the individual exploits of our soldiers, our sailors, our marines, and our merchant seamen. Lieutenant John James Powers was one of these—and there are thousands of others in the forces of the United Nations.

Several thousand Americans have met death in battle. Other thousands will lose their lives. But many millions stand ready to step into their places—to engage in a struggle to the very death. For they know that the enemy is determined to destroy us, our homes and our institutions—that in this war it is kill or be killed.

Battles are not won by soldiers or sailors who think first of their own personal safety. And wars are not won by people who are concerned primarily with their own comfort, their own convenience, and their own pocketbooks.

We Americans of today bear the gravest of responsibilities. And all of the United Nations share them.

All of us here at home are being tested—for our fortitude, for our selfless devotion to our country and to our cause.

This is the toughest war of all time. We need not leave it to historians of the future to answer the question whether we are tough enough to meet this unprecedented challenge. We can give that answer now. The answer is "Yes."

NOTE

1. Russell D. Buhite and David W. Levy, *FDR's Fireside Chats* (Norman: University of Oklahoma Press, 1992), xii–xiii, xix.

MINORITY VOICES OF THE WAR

THE AFRICAN AMERICAN EXPERIENCE

The painful legacy of racism against African American troops during World War II is a regrettable aspect of American history. This group of American citizens was as willing and proud to serve their country as anyone else. Yet instead of being treated as patriotic Americans, they faced discrimination. Not only were African Americans segregated from other troops, they were typically used only as support (mostly as truck drivers) and treated as if they could not measure up as combat soldiers. In *Taps for a Jim Crow Army*, Phillip McGuire has collected letters from African American soldiers who served their country during World War II. They describe the pain of being treated as inferiors.

FROM *TAPS FOR A JIM CROW ARMY: LETTERS FROM BLACK SOLDIERS IN WORLD WAR II*
(Ed. Phillip McGuire; Lexington: University of Kentucky Press, 1983)

938th Quartermaster Plt.
Transportation Air Base
Fort Logan, Colorado
April 26, 1943

The Pittsburgh Courier
Dear Sirs:
   We are soldiers who are stationed in Fort Logan, Colorado. We would appreciate it to the highest if our little article was printed in your paper against discrimination.
   We are colored soldiers who have been discriminated against terribly to the extent where we just can't possible [*sic*] stand no more. We're supposed to be representing part of the Army in which we're fighting for equality, justice and humanity so as all men, no matter of race, color, or creed, can be free to worship any way that they please.
   Here on the Post we're treated like dogs. We work on different positions, sometime for 9 or 10 hours daily. In the morning we report to one particular job and at noon we are taken from the former one into a complete new one by order of the white NCOs . . . and at these jobs we

work at a very tiresome task, one that is unfit for even a dog. And yet the whites which are supposed to be a labor battalion just sit down and watch us do work.

• • •

Why can't we eat, live and be respected as the whites? We're constantly being cursed at, and mocked. But yet we too have to die as well as them, and even perhaps beside them. . . . We'd rather be carried to our graves and go home to the Lord and be saved. In fact we'd rather die on our knees as a man, than to live in this world as a slave. (64–65)

One of the most celebrated officers to come from the Tuskegee Airmen experience was Daniel "Chappie" James, Jr., the first African American four-star general in the U.S. military. He served his country as a pilot not only in World War II but in the Korean conflict and the Vietnam War as well. Just like every other African American in the segregated military, General James experienced racism firsthand.

FROM JAMES R. McGOVERN, *BLACK EAGLE: GENERAL DANIEL "CHAPPIE" JAMES, JR.*
(Tuscaloosa: University of Alabama Press, 1985)

Separate but equal, in the military as in civilian society, really meant, of course, racially unequal, as any comparison of the quality of officer's clubs, opportunities for promotion, and social freedom of black and white officers proves. This type of segregation and racial discrimination especially rankled James, who had been taught that qualified blacks were entitled to the same prerogatives as whites. He was particularly incensed because the law, despite the discriminatory practice, prohibited exclusion of black officers from officers' clubs for whites. Army Regulations 210–10 stated specifically that officers' clubs, messes, and similar social organizations must be open for full membership to all officers on duty at a post. If a post limited membership in any particular military organization, it was obliged still "to extend the right of temporary membership to all officers on duty at the post." These rules were not observed by base commanders, however, because they feared the effects of biracial socializing. As long as blacks were located on all-black bases, such as Tuskegee, no problems over inequities arose.

• • •

Lieutenant James recalled that he and his friends went into the officers' club for whites and ordered drinks, thereby forcing the bartender to close down the club. The black officers left and returned when one of their friends among the white officers called and reported the club was open again and serving. The determination of black aviators to desegregate the officers' club proved a new and baffling predicament for white commanders. . . . This temperament would inspire in 1945 a nonviolent sit-in to hasten the day of civil rights in the military, fifteen years before students at Greensboro, North Carolina, would first attempt to integrate lunch counters in civilian society. (42, 44)

THE JAPANESE AMERICAN EXPERIENCE

The incarceration of Japanese Americans during World War II was an alarmist action taken by the U.S. government and people. It seemed for just a time that American culture had come dangerously close to losing its sense of humanity and the war's moral high ground. The needless incarceration of these people was a painful disruption of their lives, and many of them never fully recovered.

FROM YOSHIKO UCHIDA, *DESERT EXILE: THE UPROOTING OF A
JAPANESE-AMERICAN FAMILY*
(Seattle: University of Washington Press, 1982)

Evacuation

Hundreds of Japanese Americans were crowded into the great hall of the church and the sound of their voices pressed close around me. Old people sat quietly, waiting with patience and resignation for whatever was to come. Mothers tried to comfort crying infants, young children ran about the room, and some teenagers tried to put up a brave front by making a social opportunity of the occasion. The women of the church were serving tea and sandwiches, but very few of us had any inclination to eat.

Before long, we were told to board buses that lined the street outside, and the people living nearby came out of their houses to watch the beginning of our strange migration. Most of them probably watched with curious and morbid fascination, some perhaps even with a little sadness. But many may have been relieved and glad to see us go.

Mama, Kay, and I climbed onto one of the buses and it began its one-way journey down familiar streets we had traveled so often in our own

car. We crossed the Bay Bridge, went on beyond San Francisco, and sped
down the Bayshore Highway. Some of the people on the bus talked nervously, one or two wept, but most sat quietly, keeping their thoughts to
themselves and their eyes on the window, as familiar landmarks slipped
away one by one.

As we rode down the highway, the grandstand of the Tanforan race-
track gradually came into view, and I could see a high barbed wire fence
surrounding the entire area, pierced at regular intervals by tall guard
towers. . . . As I looked out the window for a better view, I saw armed
guards close and bar the barbed wire gates behind us. (67–68)

FROM DAISUKE KITAGAWA, *ISSEI AND NISEI: THE INTERNMENT YEARS*
(New York: Seabury Press, 1967)

When I woke up, it must have been around 5 A.M.; the train had already
stopped. Presently we were told that we had arrived at our destination,
Tule Lake. Another processing—family number, contents of luggage, etc.,
etc. Tired, sleepy, and uninspired by that prospect, I got off the train.

•   •   •

Our camp, surrounded by sagebrush, was situated in the middle of
nowhere. The nearest town was Newell, California, a strong American
Legion town from which we later had a lot of trouble. In front of the
camp, between the gate and the hill, ran the highway connecting Klamath
Falls, Oregon, and Reno, Nevada. . . . The ground on which our camp was
built was sandy and extremely hard on shoes. The whole camp was divided into eight wards, each ward consisting of six blocks. Members of
the appointed personnel lived in barracks, better constructed than ours,
on the other side of the administration building. Their area was set apart
from ours by a fence of barbed wire. The entire camp was wire-fenced
and had armed military personnel stationed just outside the gate.
(74–76)

TOPICS FOR WRITTEN AND ORAL DISCUSSION

1. Research examples of the treatment of POWs on all sides of the conflict. By most accounts, the treatment of American POWs by the Japanese was not only worse than the American treatment of Japanese POWs but even worse than the Germans' treatment of their war prisoners. Why were there so many differences in the treatment of prisoners throughout the conflict?

2. Interview a friend or relative who was living in the United States during World War II. Have this person describe some of the different policies and attitudes that existed then. Ask them to describe their lives then. Do they sound nostalgic or realistic?

3. The treatment of Japanese Americans during World War II has somewhat been rationalized by the pressures of war. Can you think of any examples in American culture in which a group of people may have been demonized because the nation was in conflict with them or the country of their origin? Interview someone whose racial or ethnic background is different from your own. Find out what their experience in American culture has been. Write a narrative describing what they tell you.

4. America has always been known as the land of plenty, but during World War II our society had to make sacrifices in support of the war effort. If we had to make similar sacrifices today, what do you think we would have to give up? Make a list of things you now take for granted that you would least like to give up. Do you think Americans today are capable of making many sacrifices? Argue both the positive and negative sides of this question. What examples can you provide?

SUGGESTIONS FOR FURTHER READING

Buhite, Russell D., and David W. Levy, eds. *FDR's Fireside Chats*. Norman: University of Oklahoma Press, 1992.

Carlson, Lewis H. *We Were Each Other's Prisoners: An Oral History of World War II American and German Prisoners of War*. New York: Basic Books, 1997.

Francis, Charles E. *The Tuskegee Airmen: The Men Who Changed a Nation*. Boston: Branden Publishing, 1993.

Fussell, Paul. *Wartime: Understanding and Behavior in the Second World War*. New York: Oxford University Press, 1989.

Harris, Mark Jonathan, Franklin D. Mitchell, and Steven J. Schechter, eds. *The Homefront: America during World War II*. New York: G. P. Putnam's Sons, 1984.

Hoehling, A. A. *Home Front, USA*. New York: Thomas Y. Crowell, 1966.

McGuire, Phillip, ed. *Taps for a Jim Crow Army: Letters from Black Soldiers in World War II*. Lexington: University of Kentucky Press, 1983.

Occupation, Resistance, and Espionage

An Analysis of John Steinbeck's *The Moon Is Down*, Jack Higgins' *The Eagle Has Landed*, and Paul West's *The Very Rich Hours of Count von Stauffenberg* and *Rat Man of Paris*

LITERARY ANALYSIS

The four novels examined in this chapter represent a broad range of subjects and styles concerning the topics of occupation, resistance, and espionage. John Steinbeck's *The Moon Is Down* is about an imaginary village under occupation by oppressive invaders; despite the threat of harsh punishment, the village forms an organized resistance to the occupation. Jack Higgins' *The Eagle Has Landed* concerns a fictional attempt by Hitler, Himmler, and the German Abwehr (military intelligence) to kidnap or assassinate Winston Churchill. This novel recounts daring acts of espionage that will hold any reader's interest. Paul West's *The Very Rich Hours of Count von Stauffenberg* is about the man who, as a member of the German resistance movement, came the closest to assassinating Hitler—an audacious act of espionage. West's *Rat Man of Paris* shares a few characteristics with the other novels but is the most uniquely constructed of them all. Set in post-war France, it relates the inner life of the "Rat Man" as he tries to heal from the wounds of oppression. During the war the Rat Man, his family, and his village suffered greatly under Nazi occupation.

Although the four books cover a wide variety of subjects, they all share the theme of (self-) deception. The occupiers of the village in Steinbeck's novel not only deceive the villagers into believing that Corell, an agent planted years before the war, is also a villager, but they also deceive themselves into believing that what they are doing is right. Higgins' novel is crammed full of deceptions and self-deceptions. Both of West's novels have numerous examples of deceptions as well: for example, Stauffenberg deceives Hitler into allowing him into his presence, and the Rat Man entertains people on the streets through sleight-of-hand. Deception is such an essential element in understanding the experience of occupation, resistance, and espionage that it is the main theme discussed in this chapter.

THE MOON IS DOWN

At the time of America's entry into World War II, John Steinbeck had just finished a remarkable run of publications and was flush with success. His literary masterpiece, *The Grapes of Wrath* (1930), had securely pushed him to the top of the American—if not the world's—literary hierarchy; largely on the basis of his early successes, Steinbeck eventually received the Nobel Prize for Literature in 1962. Donald Coers, in *John Steinbeck as Propagandist*, writes that in

> early March 1942, a scant three months after Pearl Harbor, John Steinbeck published his play novel *The Moon Is Down*, igniting in this country the most heated literary debate of the Second World War. He had intended to celebrate the "durability of democracy" with this fablelike tale, in which a small, peace-loving country, rather like Norway, is demoralized after being invaded by a powerful fascist state, rather like Nazi Germany, but recovers to form a promising resistance movement. Steinbeck had been eager to lend his talents to the Allied war effort, and he had hoped that *The Moon Is Down* would boost morale both in his own country and in occupied Europe by proclaiming that free people are inherently stronger than the "herd people" controlled by totalitarian leaders, and that, despite the initial advantage of the military mighty dictators, the democracies would eventually win the war.[1]

A fable, as defined by the *Encyclopedia of Literature*, is a "narration intended to enforce a useful truth. . . . The Fable differs from the ordinary folktale in that it has a moral that is woven into the story and often explicitly formulated in the end."[2] Instead of trying to write a comprehensive, detailed analysis about an entire country, Steinbeck economically reduces the story to the trials and tribulations of one small community. This reduction magnifies the story's theme (its moral), which is that although oppression may win battles, democracy wins wars.

The story begins with the invasion of the unidentified country already in place: "By ten-forty-five it was all over. The town was occupied, the defenders defeated, and the war finished."[3] The twelve local troops, a militia, had been surreptitiously led away by the town's popular storekeeper, Mr. Corell, who the reader soon discovers is really an enemy agent planted by the invading force years before the war. By donating food, targets, and cartridges for a shooting competition on his property, Mr. Corell enticed the troops six miles away from the town. When they see the invading planes and the parachutes of the airborne invaders, the militia rushes back to town only to be ambushed on the way—and six men are killed, buried within minutes of their defeat. The invaders bivouac in Mr. Corell's warehouse by the pier and are given provisions from his supply shelf. Every detail has been pre-planned. The invasion and occupation of this community are a model of clockwork efficiency.

A proud, distinguished public official, Mayor Orden soon becomes the leader of the resistance. He is the town's only elected leader. In his five-room palace the mayor awaits the arrival of Colonel Lanser, the commanding officer of the invaders and the new, unelected leader of the community. In the mayor's office, waiting for both men to arrive at the appointed hour of 11 o'clock, is Doctor Winter, a man described as "so simple that only a profound man would know him as profound" (3). Although the doctor is not an elected official, he is a friend and confidant of the mayor, as well as the unofficial historian of the community. Minutes before the appointed hour, the mayor and his overly attentive wife enter the office. After having the mayor's palace searched for weapons, per regulations, the colonel's arrival is announced, and with formal courtesies he introduces himself to the small gathering. Responding to the requests of the mayor, the colonel dismisses Corell from the meeting.

The colonel informs the mayor that like this own small commu-

nity, the whole nation has now been conquered. With this declaration the mayor is powerless to refuse the colonel's request to
use the mayor's residence for his headquarters. Realizing that such
a situation could cause confusion within the citizenry, the mayor
asks a question, knowing all the while what the answer must be:
" 'Am I permitted to refuse this honor?' " (17). This question leads
to a pointed exchange:

> "I'm sorry," the colonel said. "No. These are the orders of my
> leader."
>   "The people will not like it," Orden said.
>   "Always the people! The people are disarmed. The people have
> no say."
>   Mayor Orden shook his head. "You do not know, sir." (17)

These words of the mayor prove to be prophetic; indeed, the theme
of the power of the people is repeated throughout the novel. In contrast to the tyrannical Leader (and the colonel, his more humane but
nonetheless oppressive representative), the mayor is a democrati-
cally elected representative of the people, the voice of reason and
sanity—the personification of the democratic ideals for which the
Allies are fighting.

In Chapter 2 Colonel Lanser, along with five members of his
staff (Major Hunter, Captain Bentick, Captain Loft, and Lieutenants
Prackle and Tonder), has indeed set up his headquarters in the
upstairs of Mayor Orden's palace. Major Hunter was "an engineer,
and except in case of war no one would have thought of giving
him command of men" (19). Captain Bentick "was a family man,
a lover of dogs and pink children and Christmas. He was too old
to be a captain, but a curious lack of ambition had kept him in
that rank" (19). Captain Bentick also loved to affect the manners
and clothes of a British gentleman. Whereas Captain Bentick was
lacking in military ambition, Captain Loft "was as much a captain
as one could imagine. He lived and breathed his captaincy. He had
no unmilitary moments" (20). On the other hand, Lieutenants
Prackle and Tonder were "sentimental young men, given to tears
and to furies" (20). Like the Leader, Prackle hated degenerate art
because it did not propagandize the occupiers' cause, and he even
destroyed several paintings with his own hands. Tonder was a

darkly bitter romantic poet who longed for heroic death on the battlefield.

Inexperienced in combat, each of these soldiers (except Colonel Lanser) is self-deceived about the true nature of war. Of them all, Lanser best knows the reality of war (22). A distinguished veteran, Lanser is cynical of his nation's leadership (22). Despite (or because of) Lanser's cynicism, he remains calmly in charge of his unit; although unlike the cohesive members of the oppressed community, his men, who after all are strangers in this land in spite of being the conquerors, show the strains of their differences. For example, Corell, the accomplished deceiver, continually complains that he should be playing a larger role in the post-invasion operations, but the Colonel will not hear of it and puts him off. Lanser, the proper soldier, probably distrusts Corell and his type of warfare. Ironically, it is the oppressors who are under pressure and argue among themselves. The oppressed do not.

A coal mine is the reason that this particular village is of importance to the invaders, and therefore the mine is the center of attention. At the end of Chapter 4 a miner named Alex Morden, described by his wife, Molly, as "not a murdering man" but quick tempered (44), is accused of killing Captain Bentick. Morden is summarily executed without a proper trial. The hapless Mayor Orden stands by sadly in his office when he hears the "crash of firing" from the firing squad (55). Immediately thereafter a shot is fired through the mayor's office and Lieutenant Prackle is wounded. Colonel Lanser then orders his men to search the village for weapons and to find the perpetrators of the retaliatory crime against one of his men. The oppressor must squelch the rebellion before it can get started, and Lanser is successful—but only for a while.

Chapter 5 begins after a passage of time since the execution of Morden. A semblance of routine has settled in, but it is a routine that is anything but normal. Excavation of coal from the mine has not been as successful as the invaders had anticipated. Formerly highly skilled miners have become clumsy and slow, and the equipment seems to be breaking down more frequently than usual. The railroads, the only source of transportation by which to transport the coal from the country, are continually sabotaged; and despite more retaliatory executions, the sabotage continues.

The longer the enemy stays in their community, the more the people are united in their opposition. Their experience of oppression gives them all a purpose to live for—or to die for, if they have to. Whereas the oppressed grow spiritually stronger from their ordeal, the oppressors become weaker and weaker. Away from home in a land that has grown hostile to them, Lanser's men are nervous (58)—the morale of Lanser's men sinks lower and lower, almost to the point of no return. The men begin to crack; three men even go insane and cry all day and night until they are sent back home. But this outbreak of insanity is checked when word gets out that the three soldiers who were sent home received "mercy" killings, and a mercy killing does not sound like something any of the remaining soldiers would want to have happen to them (59). The descent in the oppressors' morale presages the beginning of their eventual defeat.

This worsening in the morale of Lanser's men underscores the moral of the story that although brute force may win battles, democracy will win wars—and the theme of deception is an important element in that moral.

Illustrating a paradoxical image of the fly capturing the flypaper, Molly Morden, the wife of the executed miner, is courted by one of the occupiers, Tonder. Although she rebuffs his overture, her rejection of him is far kinder than would seem normal under the circumstances, considering he is part of a group that killed her husband. Tonder gives Molly a foolishly romantic love poem. And because Molly does not violently reject Tonder's advances, her loyalty to the resistance is questioned by her friend Anne (although her suspicions are later dismissed). When the reader later learns that Tonder is murdered by the resistance that night, it becomes obvious how Molly, the fly, was drawing Tonder, the flypaper, into a trap: in this world of occupation, it is easy to misunderstand who has captured whom.

As a man caught between fulfilling his duty as a soldier (although his homeland is being led by a madman) and honoring his sense of humanity, Lanser possesses surprisingly sympathetic characteristics. For a man who has forced people from another country into servitude, he possesses a complex sensibility that seems to be at great odds with his martial obligations. He argues with the single-minded Corell over the strategy to handle the mayor, whom Corell has correctly recognized as the key member of the resistance. Corell wants the mayor killed. Colonel Lanser, however, considers the mayor to be an essential element in keeping order in the community.

Ironically, both men are correct in their assessments. Such is the condition of these occupiers; caught in the middle of powerful human contradictions (and self-deceptions), these oppressors are unable to control the people. Corell insists that the rebellion, fueled by the emergence of dynamite, must be crushed: both Mayor Orden and Doctor Winter must be arrested and held hostage against further acts of resistance. Lanser, finally unnerved by the contradictions, succumbs to the determined Corell. Lanser orders both men arrested and puts Corell on notice that he had better be correct. He, in a sense, washes his hands of the situation.

Of course, as soon as the villagers hear of their leaders' arrest, they become more motivated than ever to resist their captors, rushing into the countryside in even greater numbers to find the dynamite. Condemned to die, Mayor Orden and Doctor Winter are left to contemplate their fate. While the two captives argue with Colonel Lanser about the inevitable collapse of the occupation, sounds of the rebellion, explosions and a warning siren from the mine, emanate throughout the village. The end is near, but not before the senseless sacrifice of the mayor is performed. Although the reader does not actually read about the mayor's execution, it is intimated in his last words, which echo the famous last words of Socrates. The mayor's martyrdom, like Socrates', signals the eventual defeat of repression in his country. In death, Orden becomes a power that he could never hope to achieve in life—a symbol of and catalyst for freedom.

THE EAGLE HAS LANDED

This action/adventure novel by Jack Higgins is very different from the other works of fiction discussed in this book. Written more for entertainment than as a serious exploration of espionage, this novel, layered with deceptions, concerns a fictional attempt by the Nazis to kidnap Winston Churchill. In the book's prologue, Higgins writes:

At precisely one o'clock on the morning of Saturday, November 6, 1943, Henrich Himmler, Reichsführer of the SS and Chief of State

Police, received a simple message: "The Eagle has landed." It meant that a small force of German paratroopers were at that moment safely in England and poised to snatch the British Prime Minister . . . from the Norfolk country house where he was spending a quiet weekend near the sea. This book is an attempt to re-create the events surrounding that astonishing exploit. At least fifty per cent of it is documented historical fact. The reader must decide for himself how much of the rest is a matter of speculation, or fiction.[4]

More than any other novel in this casebook, *The Eagle Has Landed* fits the definition of a genre popularly known as historical fiction. Although every one of the novels discussed in this book is a work of fiction set during a particular event in history, the characters in Higgins' novel are different in several fundamental ways. Any historical novel is primarily a work of fiction, but some novels are more factual than others in their reconstruction of a historical event or period. Ultimately, it matters very little if any of the events in Higgins' novel are true because this novel is less concerned about historical veracity than it is about entertainment.

As an entertaining work of fiction, the novel relies heavily on both a complicated plot and robust characterization. Higgins also wrote the novel with some considerable craft. For example, to underscore the theme of betrayal, Higgins repeats the word "judas" several times throughout the novel. He uses "judas" to mean a "one-way peep hole in a door,"[5] (as in "someone looked through the judas to spy on the unsuspecting officer"). However, the word also suggests the more obvious meaning of a person "who betrays under the appearance of friendship."[6] (It was Judas who deceived and betrayed his friend, Jesus.) The whole novel is about deceivers who are entirely different from what they appear to be, and the repetition of "judas" reinforces this theme.

To develop an illusion of authenticity and excitement, Higgins frames this story in as much historical reality as possible before he begins to develop the plot. The more real he makes it appear, the more intense the story becomes; believability leads to excitability in this case. In the prologue, Higgins inserts himself into the context of the novel to give the story the illusion of veracity.

Higgins begins the book with himself scouring the Norfolk countryside for the grave of an old sea captain, Charles Gascoigne. Snooping around a Catholic cemetery in the seaside city of Studley

Constable, Higgins accidentally discovers a hidden grave marker with a German cross at the head and an inscription that reads *Hier ruhen Oberstleutenant Kurt Steiner und 13 Deutche Fallshirma-jager gefallen am 6 November 1943*, translated as "Here lies Lieutenant-Colonel Kurt Steiner and 13 German paratroopers, killed in action on the 6th November, 1943" (10). The mysterious reaction of the locals makes Higgins curious about the fate of these German soldiers buried so far from home.

Higgins' curiosity leads him on a journey that he says consumed a full year. He explains it was a year of exhaustive research and extensive interviews, all in the hopes of discovering the history of Kurt Steiner. Despite what Higgins tries to claim, Steiner is a fiction—a deception. Although there does not seem to be any evidence of Steiner in the historical records, there is plenty of material on Otto Skorzeny, the historical man who retrieved the hapless Mussolini from his captors. By inserting this historical man into the story, in however incidental a fashion, Higgins makes the fictional Steiner seem all the more authentic.

According to historian John Keegan, Skorzeny was a lieutenant colonel in the German Army. He was

> one of Hitler's most successful irregular soldiers. He had been invalided out of the service in December 1942 and found himself appointed to organize a special commando unit. As an unknown he had been appointed by the German Army High Command to sabotage the outfit which Hitler specifically requested, but in fact, he succeeded in establishing a most successful unit. Their first coup was in September 1943 when Skorzeny and 90 soldiers landed on the plateau of the Gran Sasso in the Abruzzi mountains and succeeded in abducting Mussolini.[7]

In the case of Skorzeny, Higgins is historically accurate in having Hitler pleased with the successful rescue of the Italian dictator. Besides Skorzeny, Higgins includes other historical figures such as Admiral Wilhelm Canaris and Himmler, two intense rivals in the German intelligence community.

Keegan writes that Canaris, a U-boat commander during World War I, eventually became

> Head of the Abwehr, the Intelligence Department of the German Armed Forces High Command. Although pro-German in attitude,

Canaris and other Abwehr officers loathed some of the practices of the Nazi regime, which in many ways rendered the Abwehr and its organization somewhat less effective than it might otherwise have been.[8]

Whereas Canaris detested the Nazi control and abuses, Himmler personified it, more than anyone else besides Hitler.

It was Himmler who eventually had Canaris arrested and executed, thereby disbanding the entire Abwehr operation. Higgins not only correctly conveys this rivalry between Canaris and Himmler, but he also denotes the complex rivalries between the German High Command and the Nazis who were in control of the country. Developing the historical situation of the German High Command and their espionage agencies creates the illusion (the deception) of authenticity. The historical half of the novel intensifies the fictional half.

In the novel, Canaris is embarrassed by the success of Skorzeny's irregular unit and is forced to plan the kidnapping of Winston Churchill, an audacious operation that could allow the Abwehr to save face with Hitler and stay in operation. As a leader of the German resistance against Hitler, Canaris does not really want to kill or kidnap Churchill; but to perpetuate his own deception, he has to at least appear to be going along with the plan. He gives the job of creating a feasibility study for this operation to his trusted assistant, Colonel Max Radl. A decorated, severely wounded veteran who is not privy to this deception, Radl immediately sets out to make the operation a success.

Radl soon learns that because an extensive espionage network has been operating in England for quite a while, much of the operational scenario has already been worked out. The basic plan goes like this:

It was simple enough. The British Prime Minister, Winston Churchill, was to inspect a station of RAF Bomber Command near the Wash on the morning of Saturday 6 November. Later on the same day, he was scheduled to visit a factory near Kings Lynn and make a brief speech to the workers.

Then came the interesting part. Instead of returning to London he intended to spend the weekend at the home of Sir Henry Willoughby, Studley Grange, which was just five miles outside the village of Studley Constable. It was a purely private visit, the details supposedly secret. Certainly no one in the village was aware of the plan, but Sir Henry, a retired naval commander, had apparently been unable to resist confiding in Joanna Grey, who was it seemed, a personal friend. (31)

As it turns out, Joanna Grey (born Joanna Van Oosten, whose father was killed by the British during the Boer War) is also a secret agent for the Germans. Like Corell in Steinbeck's novel, Grey has deceived her "friends" into believing she is someone she really is not—a loyal British subject.

Almost all the plans are now complete except for determining who will actually lead the daring mission into Britain. Because the unit will be so far into enemy territory, the leader—besides being a man of daring and formidable military skill—has to speak English fluently. And the only man in Germany who fits these qualifications is Kurt Steiner. Higgins describes Steiner as the only son of a German general and an American heiress of a wealthy Bostonian wool fortune. Steiner's mother had died in an automobile accident in 1931. Educated in England before finally returning to Germany with his father, Steiner is fluent in English. He also has family in Yorkshire that he continued to visit until 1938 (52).

The young Steiner continues his education by studying art in Paris. He is supported by his father with the proviso that if he does not succeed as an artist he must join the Army—which he soon does, subsequently volunteering for parachute duty. Adept at this type of modern, daring soldiering, Steiner drops into such places as Poland, Norway, and the Albert Canal, where he is wounded during the drive for Belgium (52). Greece and Crete are next, where he receives severe wounds while fighting for the Maleme airfield (53). Then comes the nightmarish Winter War in Russia. A night drop during the battle for Leningrad gains him another wound, a Knight's Cross, and a reputation for bravery and ability. After two more daring operations Steiner receives a promotion to lieutenant colonel and Oak Leaves for his Knight's Cross.

On the way back to Germany from the Eastern Front with what is left of his troops, Steiner and his men are arrested in Warsaw by the SS for helping a Jewish girl escape from her captors. Steiner and his men are court martialed, found guilty, and sentenced to a penal colony on the group of German-held islands in the English Channel. Because Steiner and his men are assigned to the very dangerous mission of torpedoing Allied shipping in the English Channel, they are basically given a death sentence.

Steiner plays an important role in this novel; it is important to show him not only as a daring, highly competent officer but as a sensitive human being as well. After all, Steiner is a German soldier and as such, the enemy; however, he is clearly not a Nazi—which is an important distinction. Despite the fact that his mission is to kidnap one of the most important Allied leaders, Steiner is nonetheless a very sympathetic character.

Although Canaris is deceptively against this kidnapping operation, Himmler is not. Without Canaris' knowledge, Himmler takes the plans Radl has finalized and presses forward. To ensure that his deception against Canaris is secure, Himmler orders Radl not to tell Canaris anything about the plans for the operations. With so many differing deceptions taking place, especially within the German hierarchy, it is not hard to see deception as a major theme of the novel—things are never what they appear to be.

Himmler tells Radl that he has ensured Steiner would be eager to help, since the Gestapo recently arrested his father on charges of being part of a conspiracy to kill Hitler. Although Steiner's cooperation is now certain, the honorable Radl goes to the Channel Islands personally to "persuade" Steiner. With Steiner on board, the final detail is accomplished when Radl recruits an Irish Republican Army (IRA) member, Liam Devlin, to help Joanna Grey in England. The handsome and charming (but tough and resourceful) Devlin proves to be a very helpful agent not only in helping Joanna Grey but in facilitating the whole operation as well. Hardened by his hatred of the British, this veteran IRA member is ruthlessly experienced in deception and espionage.

After the pre-operation plans are in place, the mission begins. Joanna secures employment for Devlin in Norfolk, which will serve as his cover during the operation. He parachutes into Ireland, eventually ending up in England. While making the many arrangements for Steiner and his men, Devlin runs into trouble with some local petty criminals who identify him to Scotland Yard. Further complicating his situation in England, Devlin develops a love interest with a local young woman, Molly Prior. Meanwhile, the "Eagle," Steiner and his men, posing as a crack Polish Special Air

Service (SAS) unit on maneuvers, land in England despite the fact that bad weather and extremely low visibility make flying almost impossible.

The situation for Steiner and his men soon becomes complicated. One of Steiner's men, Sturm, heroically saves the life of a local child from being crushed by a water wheel after the child falls into a stream. Sturm, however, is killed. After Sturm's body is retrieved from the stream, the deception is revealed when his outer uniform is removed. Upon Himmler's insistence, Steiner's men have worn their *Fliegerbluse* under their Polish SAS uniform. When the villagers recognize the German uniform, Steiner is forced to take many of the locals as hostages.

Not only does this episode reveal their true identity as German soldiers, but it reveals the character of these men as well. By unblinkingly sacrificing his life to save an English child, the German Sturm also reveals his humanity. This revelation does not go unnoticed in the village. Sturm's sacrifice of himself to save the child destroys the English delusion (a form of self-deception) that all German soldiers are monsters (309). The English locals learn that the hated Germans may not be as bad as they thought they were.

The situation soon gets even worse for Steiner and his men. When a local U.S. Ranger unit finds out about what is going on in the village, a shoot-out ensues between them and Steiner's men. Steiner and his men win the early stages of the fight, but the Americans eventually trap the Germans in the same church where the novel began. Steiner and his men are now at risk of being executed under the rules of the Geneva Convention because they began their operation deceptively wearing Allied uniforms. Although they are now wearing their German uniforms, these men have no choice but to fight it out—continuing the battle means certain death, but it is better to die "with one's (own) boots on."

The situation seems very dire for Steiner and his men, seconds away from imminent destruction. However, the novelist, like an accomplished magician, still has many more deceptions up his sleeve. In the nick of time Molly Prior, who still loves Devlin despite her now knowing he has been deceiving her, saves the day by showing Devlin, Steiner, and his men a secret passageway out of the church. This escape allows Steiner a momentary stay from death; with the help of the priest's automobile he flees this battle, but only to continue his appointed mission.

Steiner makes a last attempt to complete the operation. Creating one deception after another, he eventually makes his way to confront Churchill; but before he can kill the prime minister, an act he still regrets having to fulfill, Steiner is shot through the heart. The stoic Churchill comments on the bravery of this fine soldier (384).

Meanwhile, Devlin has managed to escape the land that he so despises, stealing away on a German E-boat (the German equivalent of the U.S. Pt-boat). Snug in her Norfolk bed, young Molly experiences a sensation of profound relief at the exact moment Devlin exits the English coast. Luckily for the Allies and the German resistance movement, the operation to kidnap Winston Churchill ends in failure.

Ingeniously, Higgins uses the last chapter to explain why there is no official record of this episode—besides the fact that no one would want the world to know how close it came to losing Churchill. One last deception remains to be revealed: it is not the real Churchill who Steiner almost killed, but George Howard Foster, an actor whose profession it was to deceive people into believing he was someone else. Until the very end there is nothing but deceptions, deceptions, and more deceptions.

Where this novel truly succeeds, beyond being exciting to read, is in its explanation of the real accouterments of the war—such things as the British-made sten gun and the differences in the types of parachutes used by the Germans and the British. In these instances (and others, such as the rivalry between Himmler and Canaris), Higgins allows the seemingly incompatible world of fact and fiction to co-exist.

THE VERY RICH HOURS OF COUNT VON STAUFFENBERG

A brilliant stylist, Paul West is one of the most richly prolific writers in contemporary literature. With a keen interest in things historical, West has written two powerful novels about people and events of World War II: *The Very Rich Hours of Count von Stauffenberg* (1989) and *Rat Man of Paris* (1993). Both books sensitively convey the dark and complex experience brought to so many people by this tragic war.

David W. Madden, in *Understanding Paul West*, writes that the form of *The Very Rich Hours of Count von Stauffenberg* derives from medieval books of hours of prayers, which were:

> prayer books popular among the wealthy in the fourteenth and fifteenth centuries, and the laity's attempt to imitate the revered clergy, these volumes became their personal breviaries. In the broadest sense they were works designed to sanctify secular time of lay people, providing them with an opportunity for absorbing rumination and privacy. These books were prepared by a group of professionals under the direction of a master and thus were not only religious artifacts but independent artistic expressions in their own right.[9]

Even though West radically transforms this medieval genre into a modern novel, he maintains "strict structural correspondences between the two forms."[10] Staying true to the spirit of the medieval period, West portrays the aristocratic, modern, efficient German officer as a chivalrous knight—who finally wakes up to his responsibility and plots to assassinate Adolf Hitler, who is in the process of engulfing the world in war and about to destroy Germany as well. Stauffenberg, motivated by his love of Germany, pursues his quest single-mindedly.

The novel begins with Stauffenberg on duty in Tunisia, dreaming about his wife. In his dream he and his wife are in a field of wild strawberries ten years in the past, 1933. They are making jam from the crop of berries they have just picked. Soon after this dream Stauffenberg is severely wounded and lies in the hospital with an amputated right hand, as well as the third and fourth finger from his other hand. His right eye is also removed, and his left ear and knee are damaged. The wounding of Stauffenberg marks a dramatic change in his life.

The novel then transitions to "The Hour Glass" chapter in which Stauffenberg, in bed recuperating from his wounds, begins to narrate his life history mentally.[11] A man who enjoys such mental activities, Stauffenberg understands himself fully in relation to the rich history of his family—his father supervised the abdication of the king and queen of Württemberg in 1918. He especially remembers a childhood Christmas in 1922 when, after decorating the house for the holidays, the family read aloud a passage from the First Epistle to the Corinthians 13:2: " ' . . . and though I have all faith, so that I could remove mountains, and have not charity, I am nothing' " (25). In addition to this reminiscence of his childhood, courtship and marriage are prominent memories as well. Besides the love of his wife, readers learn that Stauffenberg has several other loves in his life: his horse, Jagd, and the poet Stefan George (whom Stauffenberg calls his lodestar). Although he is a complex man, Stauffenberg is made to re-examine life by his wounding and is now clearly aware of who he is and what is important to him.

Stauffenberg is now also aware of whom he does not like, and that is S'gruber, or Schicklegruber, the leader of Nazi Germany. Stauffenberg's disdain for Hitler (a name he never uses) also arises from his woundings. Stauffenberg admits that he was once more ambivalent about S'gruber when, after the death of his poet friend, George, "a certain poetic streak in us became homeless" (31). But now more fully cognizant of his feelings about the leader, Stauffenberg observes that a "genius dies and a charlatan usurped the role of god" (31). He states that "I was not duped as was a sleepwalker. Deep down I wanted a king, not a Führer, a Franconian and Swabian court, not a Star Chamber of gangsters. Easy to say; impossible to know at the time" (31). Detailed to represent his army regiment at a Nazi demonstration in Bamberg, Stauffenberg and a fellow officer are driven to leave when a Nazi speaker "railed against Jews in such revoltingly scatological language" (33). He notes that the "massed eyes of the besotted faithful watched us go, bathing us in contempt, incredulity, and here and there a flush of awe" (33). From this experience one can understand that even though Stauffenberg is a patriotic German, he cannot be a blind follower of the Nazis.

Stauffenberg then narrates the development of his service in the Wehrmacht. His military career is successful because he is comfortable in the role he has developed as the completely dependable type. (Dependability is an important trait in a military officer, especially for a military preparing for war.)

In the "Occupations" chapter Stauffenberg narrates some of his military experiences, especially his participation in the invasion of Poland. In these experiences Stauffenberg cannot help but recognize the atrocities his army has been committing, or at least allowing to happen: "The Polish campaign was a bloodbath, an orgy of impromptu atrocities that became more systematic the longer it lasted" (44). Recognizing the evil that his country is carrying out in Europe, Stauffenberg rationalizes his own involvement (48). It is only a matter of time before the honorable Stauffenberg converts his self-deception into action. He eventually discovers that he is not alone in his anxieties about the conduct of the German military and the disastrous direction in which S'gruber is taking them. As it is explained in the Historical Context discussion that follows in this casebook, Stauffenberg eventually conspires with a large group of Wehrmacht general officers to execute a coup d'état against Hitler and his henchmen. The coup will fail, and Stauffenberg, who actually plants the bomb beside Hitler, will be ordered shot by a co-conspirator, a man eager to dissociate himself from the failed coup. Since West is a careful writer and faithfully follows the biographical and historical facts of Stauffenberg's life and assassination attempt, there is very little reason to examine that part of the novel concerning the coup.

What is more important to examine is the quality of West's narrative. Besides exploring Stauffenberg's humanity—his passions; the intense love for his country, his wife and family, and his horse—West, the imaginative novelist, magically takes the consciousness of Stauffenberg beyond the grave, a place where neither biographer nor historian would dare to take him. The remains of Stauffenberg are never found, but the fictional Stauffenberg knows exactly where his body is deposed. He tells us that his body was photographed, stripped, and cremated. "What could do they with the dust?" Stauffenberg asks. "Scatter it in the open fields, as Himmler insisted" (238).

For the remainder of the novel Stauffenberg continues to explain the coup's bloody postscript, as S'gruber (Hitler) mercilessly takes vengeance on anyone even tangentially connected to the coup, including innocent members of their families. His body now completely destroyed, Stauffenberg can only imagine himself at thirty-six years of age, the age he was when he was killed. In his disembodied imagination he remembers himself as he wants to be remembered: riding his horse, playing with his children, and loving his wife. But he also wants to be remembered as he was when he faced his death: refusing the blindfold but accepting the crucifix, and regretting that he had not been the man who killed S'gruber (Hitler) (348–349).

The careful reader of this novel can see why West takes Stauffenberg's consciousness into the afterlife; as the meditative formulation of the novel, a spiritual form, indicates, this book is the (auto) biography of a soul. Thus, Stauffenberg's spirit will continue to live like "something sacred" (351).

RAT MAN OF PARIS

In this complex novel, which is stylistically similar to the works of the Nobel Prize–winning author Samuel Beckett, West writes about the life of Etienne Poulsifer, the Rat Man of Paris. The novel is told from several perspectives, including the Rat Man's own psychologically confused point of view.

Although the plot is not the most important aspect of the novel, one cannot fully appreciate the novel's style without first knowing the story. Summarizing the main plot of the novel, Madden writes:

> Poulsifer is another victim of the Nazi regime, a man whose parents were murdered in the destruction of his childhood village and who becomes an orphan to all that would appear normal and ordinary. Veteran of numerous menial and disgusting jobs, Rat Man parades the Paris streets flashing his rats and generally living on the periphery of society. During one of these "performances" he meets Sharli Bandol, a schoolteacher, who becomes his lover and virtually adopts him. When Rat Man learns that an ex-Nazi is being deported from South America to stand trial for war crimes, he believes it is the commander who engineered the destruction of his village and pledges to bring the man to justice. After he is shot by an unknown assailant, Rat Man and Sharli retreat to Nice, where she gives birth to a son.[12]

An examination of the novel's style reveals that it represents a consciousness and experience wrecked by the Nazis' repression.

Obsessed with thoughts of the Nazi who he thinks destroyed his village and family, Poulsifer can think of nothing else:

> He goes on dreaming up the hated image, glad to have pinned him down, free of all Alphonses.
> Not such a big man after all. Married with a daughter. And a son. Expert in Jewish affairs. Iron Cross, second class 1941ish. Only ever captain. *Chef du commando exterieur de la Sipo-Sd* near the Swiss frontier. He was the man who said his aides weren't tough enough.

1943, Iron Cross, first class. With sword. Pat on the back from Heinrich Himmler.

Installed at the Hotel Terminus (ironic name for many), near the
Perrache station, Lyon, he amassed a notable score: 14,311 arrested;
4,342 assassinated; 7,591 deported. Plus, Rat Man notes, tumultu-
ously, six hundred and forty-three others. Twenty-six thousand, he
says, eight hundred and eighty-seven.

Always carried a bullwhip.

Competent amateur pianist. Moonlight sonatist.[13]

As this segment of his thoughts demonstrates, Poulsifer has kept
every detail, every vital statistic, of this Nazi's butcher bill in his
head. Disturbed by his extreme experience at the hands of the
Nazis, the Rat Man does not cope well with the "normal" experiences of his post-war life. France, divided even during the war
about how to resist German occupation, is now at best ambivalent
about how to treat suspected war criminals.

It seems everyone except Poulsifer wants to get on with their
lives. Unable to think of little else, Poulsifer cannot cope with normal existence. In a post-war world that wants to get back to normalcy and forget the past, Poulsifer is an unwanted reminder. But
not only is he unable to forget the past, when he starts to dress
up like the Nazi mass murderer, he re-creates the past; he becomes
a living monument to what is best forgotten, according to the
thinking of more "normal" people.

As complex as West's literary reconstruction of Poulsifer's consciousness is, the answer to the Rat Man's emotional dilemma is
very simple—it is love. Fragmented by the pain of his past, unable
even to imagine the faces of his parents, it is the age-old power of
love that pulls together the shards of Poulsifer's personality. With
the unconditional caring love of Sharli, a sensitive schoolteacher
who gives birth to the Rat Man's child and makes a home for him,
Poulsifer can at least experience the good of humanity for a
change. In Sharli, Poulsifer (who will never again be completely
whole) recovers a semblance of his own identity by discovering
that humanity is as much capable of tremendous love as it is of
tremendous hate.

Near the very end of the novel, West describes the recovery of
Poulsifer's personality quite elegantly: "Rat Man dozes. Poussif
wakes. Baby sleeps again. Odd, he muses, how that other side of

him, the bloodthirsty boulevardier, died into Poussif the ordinary chap. The two of him are one" (176).

In his two books, West explores the terrific human cost of Nazi occupation and oppression; but more important, he also explores examples of the human spirit resisting these forces of evil. And like the moral of Steinbeck's novel, in the end free people always win the war over oppression.

NOTES

1. Donald V. Coers, *John Steinbeck as Propagandist*: The Moon Is Down *Goes to War* (Tuscaloosa and London: University of Alabama Press, 1991), xi.

2. *Encyclopedia of Literature* (Springfield, MA: Merriam-Webster, 1995), 399.

3. John Steinbeck, *The Moon Is Down* (New York: Bantam, [1942] 1966), 1. All subsequent quotations of this text come from this source.

4. Jack Higgins, *The Eagle Has Landed* (New York: Pocket Books, 1975), 1. All subsequent quotations of this text come from this source.

5. *American Heritage Dictionary* (Boston: Houghton Mifflin, 1982).

6. Ibid.

7. John Keegan, *Who's Who in World War II* (New York: Oxford University Press, 1995), 141.

8. Ibid., 25.

9. David W. Madden, *Understanding Paul West* (Columbia: University of South Carolina Press, 1993), 81–82.

10. Ibid.

11. Paul West, *The Very Rich Hours of Count von Stauffenberg* (Woodstock, NY: Overlook Press, 1989), 22. All subsequent quotations of this text come from this source.

12. Madden, *Understanding Paul West*, 119.

13. Paul West, *Rat Man of Paris* (Woodstock, NY: Overlook Press, 1993), 97. All subsequent quotations of this text come from this source.

HISTORICAL CONTEXT

ESPIONAGE AND CODE BREAKING

Many people made a profession of deception during World War II—spies, saboteurs, and practitioners of espionage and organized resistance. Espionage and state-sponsored deception was carried out extensively by all sides during the war: the British had the SOE, the Americans had the OSS, the Germans had the Abwehr and the Gestapo, and the Soviets had the Rote Kapelle, the GRU, the NKVD, the SMERSH, and the NKGB.

After forming the Special Operations Executive (SOE)—a secret organization devoted to subversive warfare in enemy-occupied territory—in July 1940, the British were the leaders in espionage. The SOE was organized by combining three independent units of the British government: a sabotage branch of M16 (the secret English intelligence bureau), Section D (a semi-secret propaganda office of the Foreign Office), and a small research branch of the war office.[1]

The SOE significantly assisted the Allied war effort and in so doing gained a reputation with the enemy as a tough-minded, effective fighting organization—even though the SOE was not as invincible as its members liked to think.

The Office of Strategic Services (OSS) was the American equivalent to both the British Secret Intelligence Service and the SOE. It was formed on 13 June 1942 by a Presidential Military Order and led by Major General William J. "Wild Bill" Donovan throughout the war. The main function of the OSS was to drop operatives behind the lines to organize and assist local resistance efforts. Secretive, professional, and jauntily daring, the personnel of the OSS, like those of the SOE, soon gained a reputation for competence and greatly contributed to the war's successful outcome.

The duties of the United States Army Air Force (USAAF) pilots who air-dropped the OSS agents behind enemy lines are carefully discussed in Ben Parnell's *Carpetbaggers: America's Secret War in Europe*. Parnell writes:

OSS intelligence gathering and covert action extended throughout the world, even into the enemy's homelands. Among its members were professors, journalists, lawyers, and common laborers. Assisting resistance forces in Europe, the OSS sent thousands of tons of arms, food, and other supplies to those underground forces. More than 5,000 officers and enlisted men of the United States Army Air Force were helped by agents of the OSS to escape from behind enemy lines.

In October 1943, when the American Joint Chiefs of Staff approved the allocation of aircraft (initially for support of the Polish underground), the USAAF agreed to supply airlift. Combat crews, flying specially converted B-24s and later C-47s, A-26s, and Royal Air Force (RAF) Mosquitoes, began to carry out agent and supply drops in concert with RAF units. These airmen took their black-painted aircraft on highly secretive nighttime missions.[2]

The German military intelligence and counterintelligence organization, the Abwehr (meaning "defense"), was formed after World War I despite a Versailles treaty moratorium on any such German agency, and in January 1935 Admiral Canaris was named its head. Considered politically unreliable by the Nazi SS and amateurish by the Allies, the Abwehr nevertheless had some notable successes in sabotage, subversion, and especially counterespionage. In the latter arena this organization succeeded in combating the large Soviet spy contingent known as the Rote Kapelle (Red Orchestra).[3] As it turns out, the SS officers who were suspicious of the Abwehr's loyalty to Hitler were correct, since Canaris played an active role in the German resistance against Hitler. The Abwehr was the conduit through which the resistance received the British explosives used in the attempts against Hitler's life, as well as other activities for the German resistance.[4]

The Gestapo, or the Reichssicherheitshauptamt or the Reisch Security Main Office (RSHA), essentially the creation of Reinhard Heydrich, was an umbrella organization with multi-faceted roles. Essentially the Gestapo was the secret police of the Nazi Party, and their activities ranged from "intelligence gathering at home and abroad; policing, including the suppression of the Nazis' political opponents, both within the Reich and in occupied territories; and the extermination of the Nazis' racial victims."[5] This police organization relied heavily on informants and collaborators to perform its duties, and these policemen never seemed to lack cooperation from people willing to turn in their fellow citizens. Employing its special unit, the Einsatzgruppen, the Gestapo was especially murderous behind the lines in occupied territory and most terrifying in Poland and the USSR, where it pursued the Nazi policy of genocide with vengeance.

The USSR also possessed an aggressive intelligence, the Rote Kapelle. The Rote Kapelle was primarily a wireless radio network stretching throughout occupied Europe and Germany. "Kapelle" was Abwehr argot for secret wireless transmissions and the countermeasures used against these transmissions. Headed by Leopold Treeper, a Polish Jew and communist, this network was organized with the help of the Soviets' primary foreign spy agency, the Glavnoye Razvedyvatelnoe Upravleniye (GRU), during the 1930s in Belgium. This network became of primary importance to the Soviets after the Germans invaded the USSR in 1941.[6]

Whereas the Rote Kapelle was primarily a communications network in Europe, the GRU, an official military intelligence organization, had a broader mission to collect strategic, technical, and military intelligence throughout the world. Along with two other Soviet (political) intelligence and counterintelligence agencies, the Narodnyi Kommissariat Vnutrennikh Del (NKVD) and SMERSH (an acronym for Smert Shpionam [Death to Spies]), the Soviets maintained extensive espionage and counterespionage activities. The NKVD eventually spun off the infamous NKGB, or KGB, agency, which had the primary responsibility for state security. The duties of SMERSH seemed to have been to ensure the loyalty of the Soviet armed forces more than anything else. Experts estimate that between 3 and 4 percent of the Soviet military were involved in either intelligence or counterintelligence and another 12 percent were either agents or informers.[7]

Indeed, Europe during World War II (and after) was thick with spies and informants.

Another component of the deception game being played by all the sides during the war had to do with codes and code breaking. During World War II the vast, mobile armies required the wireless radio to communicate with their forces all across the globe, and signal encryption became an essential element in keeping those communications secure. Similarly, code breaking, whereby the opposing force could figure out what the enemy was saying, increased in importance as well.

John H. Waller, in *The Unseen War in Europe*, asserts that "British Ultra intelligence gained from intercepting German ciphers and the Double-Cross system used to gain control of German spies were the greatest secrets of the war."[8] The most important of the secret coups was the deciphering of the German Enigma code machine. The Enigma was a cipher machine that theoretically encoded German message traffic with an unlimited number of possible solutions. Breaking the Enigma system meant the Allies were able to read secret German message traffic clearly.

Waller explains that a key figure in the British systematic penetration of the Nazi-ciphering program was German bureaucrat Hans-Thilo Schmidt,

> who sold German military secrets, including cipher secrets, to the French. As Schmidt's purloined documents were subjected to the genius of Polish cryptanalysts between the world wars, then improved upon and systematically exploited by British intelligence in World War II, there would be very few moves made by the German war machine that were not known in advance by Western Allies. And because of a remarkable effort for the purpose of doubling German agents and through playing back misinformation, the German High Command unknowingly depended on intelligence fabricated in Britain.[9]

Why would this member of the German government, who proved so valuable to the Allied cause, sell out to the enemies of his country? The answer is greed.

Schmidt "lusted for good wine and lovely women," living a high lifestyle that he could not ordinarily afford.[10] His first exchange with the French intelligence was on 8 November 1931 in Verviers, Belgium. Schmidt had risen through the ranks with the aid of his brother Rudolph, who had become head of the German Army Signal Corps unit in charge of cryptology. Schmidt gave the French "startling" examples of cryptological materials.[11] Poland, the most proficient of the pre–World War II Allies at breaking the German codes until the introduction of the Enigma machine, found the new information provided by Schmidt invaluable in deciphering German communications.

For seven years French intelligence carefully managed Schmidt, their extremely valuable asset who was given the code name "Asche." Schmidt's chief French contact, M. Lemoine, himself an expatriated German who had become a French citizen in between the two world wars, controlled "Asche" with intense security.[12] During this period "Asche" provided both the French and British cryptologists with information that eventually allowed them to exploit the Enigma machine.

In 1937 the Germans started using the Enigma machine in all military services, "and within eight months Enigma messages were spotted in police and Nazi security intelligence (Sicherheitdienst, or SD) traffic as well."[13] Although, unlike the Poles, the French and British had not yet broken the Enigma machine, they clearly understood from other intelligence information given to them by Schmidt that the intention of the German leader was to create a Germanic Europe.

In a secret meeting in the fall of 1937 with his top military leaders, Hitler described his vision for German expansion over the next decade, including the annexation of Austria and Czechoslovakia.[14] Schmidt summoned French intelligence and passed on the information, but the Germans, themselves adept at counterintelligence, intercepted the enciphered message. After quickly deciphering the message, German intelligence learned that there was a highly placed leak in their midst; but when Schmidt reported back to the French, they were also able to learn, in addition to Hitler's vision for Europe, that German intelligence was breaking their own intelligence. Deception was everywhere, but no one truly seemed to be deceiving anyone.

When Polish intelligence (to their horror) finally discovered Hitler's impending plans to invade their own country, they gave to the French and British reconstituted working models of their Enigma machine. Because of the Polish efforts, the British deciphering capabilities intensified. Organized in Bletchley Park, a converted manor house outside of London and code-named Station X, England's cryptological center developed into a key component of the war effort. This intelligence organization is credited with helping to save Britain against the massive German air assault in the Battle of Britain; protecting critical sea lanes from German U-boats during the Battle of the Atlantic; prevailing in Germany's aborted invasion of Britain, Operation Sealion; defeating Rommel's Africa Corps; and defeating General Gunther Hans Kluge's army in the Battle of Falaise in France, August 1944. Furthermore, this British cryptological organization aided in the so-called Double-Cross counterespionage operations.[15] This operation induced Abwehr spies abroad unwittingly to deceive their masters about the real locations of the Allied landings for both the Allied North African invasion (Operation Torch) and the invasion of Europe (Operation Overlord).

Schmidt's leaking of German secrets to the Allies was indeed a critical factor in eventually defeating the Nazi war effort. However, because it was limited to the European Theater, the breaking of the Enigma code machine was not the entire solution to the defeat of all the Axis Powers because the Japanese had a different code system. The breaking of Japanese codes was divided into two distinct sources: Ultra for the military codes and Magic for the diplomatic.

Although throughout the war America remained the main source of opposition against the Japanese in the Pacific, the British provided great assistance in code breaking. After the BRUSA (Britain and the United States of America) agreement of 14 May 1943, the British and the Americans worked together to break the code system of all the Axis Powers.[16] The U.S. Army, with its cryptological center in Arlington Hall, Washington, D.C., was given primary responsibility for the Pacific Theater; the British cryptological center at Bletchley Park was assigned Germany and Italy. Even among the different branches of the military from the same country, the sharing of intelligence (especially signal intelligence) was difficult because of rivalries and compartmentalization. For example, the U.S. Navy, historically suspicious of its rival service, made accommodation with the British rather than with the U.S. Army for its Pacific operations. However successful they eventually were in breaking Axis codes, the integration of the Allied code-breaking effort was done reluctantly.

After Pearl Harbor and the loss of the Philippines, the U.S. Navy intensified efforts to break the JN-25 codes of the Japanese Navy. The JN-25 were enciphered codes that made use of a numerical substitution system from two different books of codes, and the Allies were never able to break it completely and systematically. However, using an IBM computer with up to three million punch cards a month, by 1942 the Allies were able to decipher usable parts of JN-25 enciphered messages. Early American carrier operations such as the infamous James Doolittle raid, when the U.S. first bombed the Japanese mainland, were especially helpful in deciphering the JN-25 because they generated a lot of signal traffic among the Japanese forces, giving U.S. intelligence that much more information to analyze.

The Battle of Midway demonstrated the value of the Ultra intelligence by providing the Pacific Fleet's commander in chief the critical information that Yamamoto's main objective was Midway Island; therefore, the Americans were able to concentrate limited resources around the island. The Americans were also able by radio deception to fool the Japanese into believing that the only two remaining U.S. aircraft carriers in the Pacific Fleet were not in the area of Midway.[17] Thus, the Ultra code-breaking effort, and other signals intelligence tactics as well, proved an essential element in the key naval victory early in the American war effort.

OCCUPATION AND UNDERGROUND RESISTANCE

The degree of inhumanity perpetuated by both the Nazis and the Japanese against citizens of occupied territories was horrifying and warrants examination.

The Japanese invasion and sacking of Nanking is an especially important story. In *The Comfort Women: Japan's Brutal Regime of Enforced Prostitution in the Second World War*, George Hicks writes:

In December [1937], the [Japanese] Army converged on Nanking, the capitol of China then under the Nationalists, or Kuomintang, led by General Chiang Kai Shek. The Japanese took the city in an orgy of death and destruction.

Following the Rape of Nanking, the Japanese authorities were compelled to take stock. They were concerned because this bloodbath had failed to break Chinese resistance. Rather, it had stiffened it. . . . As one of the measures introduced to improve discipline, and set up a long campaign, the comfort station plan first mooted in Shanghai in 1932 was revived. . . .

The station consisted of ten barrack block-like huts, together with a supervisor's hut, all enclosed by a fence. The huts were divided into ten small rooms, each numbered and with a separate door. This was to be a prototype for the design of many subsequent comfort stations.[18]

The women whom the Japanese forced into these comfort stations (or brothels) were taken not only from Nanking but from other

countries the Japanese occupied as well. The plight of these comfort women remained obscured until very recently. Hicks notes
that in 1991 "Kim Hak Sun was the first former comfort woman
to announce she was willing to publicly tell her story, as part of
legal action against the Japanese government. . . . As the women
continue to speak out, this deliberate historical blindness will become part of the larger story of World War II."[19]

All the countries under Axis domination experienced significant
resistance activity. However, as experts point out, contrary to the
post-war myth, a large, united resistance movement never existed.
Each nationalistic entity responded according to its unique heritage. Some countries experienced more widespread resistance participation than others, but as the liberation forces moved near any
of the occupied territories, the level of resistance rose.

Experts categorize resistance activity as either active or passive.
Active resistance was similar to a militia organization in which the
citizens were involved in spying, aiding the escape of fugitives, or
sabotage.[20] Allied organizations, such as the OSS and SOE, were
integral in the success of local citizens involved in active resistance.
Because the occupiers were highly interested in eliminating active
resistance, the participants in active resistance had to be constantly
on guard. Collaborators and informants, the silent enemy, were
more a threat for the security of local resistance organizations than
any overt surveillance activity.

Passive resistance—through the use of such activities as strikes,
go-slows, demonstrations, non-cooperation, symbolic acts of alle-
giance to the original government, hiding of escapees, and dissem-
ination of important underground information—followed a more
nonviolent path.[21] Railway workers on strike in France, massive
strikes in Holland, and orchestrated non-cooperation in Norway
were acts of passive resistance that helped make the Allied war
effort successful.

THE ATTEMPTED ASSASSINATIONS OF ADOLF HITLER

The German resistance movement made several attempts against
the life of Hitler, including one whereby bombs made of British
plastic explosives were hidden in Cointreau liqueur bottles stowed
away on Hitler's private airplane. Mysteriously, like all the other

attempts against Hitler's life, this one failed. The main conspirators of this particular plot, Major General Hans Henning von Treskow, chief of staff of the German Central Army Group at Smolensk, Ukraine, and his personal staff officer, Fabian von Schlabrendorff, a German resistance activist, had to retrieve the Cointreau bottles from the plane before they were discovered by Hitler's attendants.[22] If the unexploded bomb had been discovered, all of the conspirators would have been killed since only a very limited number of people had access to Hitler's private airplane.

Treskow, a leading figure in organizing the "official" resistance against Hitler, was once again disappointed in attempts to eliminate the German dictator. Waller observes:

> It was not surprising that there had been so many attempts on the Führer's life; what is strange is that none of them succeeded. In 1935 a Jewish medical student from Switzerland named Felix Frankfurter, intent on killing Hitler, failed to get close enough so he shot Wilhelm Gustloff, a Nazi leader in Switzerland, instead. A Swiss Catholic theological student, Maurice Bavand, planned to shoot Hitler in 1938 on the occasion of a parade celebrating the abortive Nazi putsch in 1923 but could not find the opportunity. Exactly one year later, . . . Georg Elser, leftist laborer, planted a bomb in the Munich beer hall where Hitler and his followers were to hold another commemorative reunion in celebration of the same event. The bomb went off with a resounding explosion, killing several Nazi functionaries, but missing Hitler, who had just left the hall.[23]

Another failed assassination attempt involved a group of officers in the Karkhov who were astonished at the severe German casualties in the Russian theater. These officers planned to kill Hitler when he arrived on a visit to their military unit. However, after a sudden change of plans Hitler failed to arrive, foiling their planned assassination. In yet another incident a German officer, Baron Rudolph Cristoph von Gersdorff of Army Group Central, was scheduled to escort Hitler through the new Heroes' Memorial Observation. The plan was for Baron von Gersdorff to detonate a bomb strapped to his body that would kill Hitler as well as himself. Treskow himself assisted von Gersdorff in strapping on the bomb. However, because Hitler hurriedly left the exhibit before the baron could arm the weapon, which had a ten-minute fuse, Hitler once again escaped a death that could have saved millions of lives.

The most serious attempt on Hitler's life, however, came a little over a month after the Allied invasion of German-occupied Europe when the eventual defeat of the Wehrmacht was within sight. One of the prominent leaders of this attempted assassination was German aristocrat Count Claus von Stauffenberg. John Keegan writes:

> Stauffenberg was a brilliant young officer who had served with great bravery in the Polish campaign, France and North Africa. In April 1943 he was severely wounded by bullets from a low-flying aircraft in the Western Desert. He lost an eye, his right hand and forearm and some fingers on his left hand, but as he lay in hospital he told his wife, "I feel I must do something now to save Germany. We General Staff officers must all accept our share of the responsibility."[24]

As this brief description demonstrates, the fictional depiction of Stauffenberg in West's novel closely resembles the "real" one. His wounding was the final motivation to act against Hitler for the sake of his family and country.

Stauffenberg was a member of the Schwarze Kapelle, the group of German aristocrats, senior officers, and diplomats who wanted to rid their country of Hitler. The primary figurehead of this group was the Wehrmacht's former chief of general staff, General Ludwig Beck. Keegan describes Beck as "a man with genuine moral courage. . . . [H]e gladly joined with Stauffenberg in the active conspiracy that culminated in the Bomb Plot of 20 July 1944."[25] Another central figure "in addition to Colonel General Beck, was Dr. Carl Goerdeler, former mayor of Leipzig and now the Reich government Prices Commissioner."[26]

This loosely organized group had primarily been responsible for all the "official" assassination attempts against Hitler. Experts note that by mid-1944 most German generals were deeply concerned about the outcome of the war and the future of their homeland, and they blamed Hitler for their troubles. Field Marshall Rommel, Germany's greatest war hero, was no exception, and he had not been quiet, even to Hitler, about his concerns.[27] Beck, Rommel, Treskow, and the other concerned generals found in Stauffenberg an officer determined to rid his people of the man who was bringing absolute disaster to his country and the world. It was Stauffenberg who developed the plans for Operation Valkyrie, which they hoped would be the final solution to Hitler's disturbing "superman" complex.

After recovering from his wounds, Stauffenberg was reassigned on 1 November 1943 to duty as chief of staff in the General Army Office, a position that put him in proximity not only to Hitler but to the organizational center of the Wehrmacht as well. Peter Hoffman, in *Stauffenberg: A Family History, 1905–1944*, writes:

> The orders for "Operation Valkyrie," along with similar ones codenamed "Rhinegold," were first conceived during the winter 1941 catastrophe on the Russian front as a way of mobilizing reserves. "Valkyrie I" was designed to raise reserves for the front; Stauffenberg had worked on it in the General Staff Organization Branch in the summer of 1942. "Valkyrie II" organized combat-ready divisions, brigades, reinforced regiments, and combat commands in three stages for "deployment locally, at home or in frontier regions," to protect the coasts or to combat airborne forces. The orders carried a high level of secrecy: "Under no circumstances may agencies and individuals outside the Wehrmacht be informed of the intentions or of preparatory work." This denied the police and the Secret State Police any knowledge of these measures (although they would inevitably be concerned in any internal emergency); nor is there any hint Waffe-SS was to be regarded as within the Wehrmacht. The "Valkyrie" orders lay ready in sealed envelopes in the safes of the deputy corps commands and military district commands, and also in the safes of the military governors in the occupied territories.[28]

As soon as five of these divisions were sent into combat at the Eastern Front, October 1942, these particular "Valkyrie" orders became obsolete. However, new orders were eventually drawn up, and the Valkyrie operation was back on track again.

In his biography of Stauffenberg, Joachim Kramarz observes that

> Stauffenberg was able to base his planning upon the "Valkyrie" plan, which had been worked out in 1942 with Hitler's full agreement. [General Friedrich] Olbricht [who was head of the Supply Section of the Reserve Army] had told the dictator that there was a danger of internal disturbances from the large numbers of foreign workers in Germany or as a result of enemy commando raids. Plans must be prepared for such eventualities, Olbricht said, providing for the mobilization of the replacement army even should communi-

cations between him, Hitler, and the home army be cut. In such circumstance the commander-in-chief of the replacement army should be authorized to set "Valkyrie" in motion on his own initiative. Hitler accepted the proposal and authorized the plan to be worked out.[29]

Unbeknownst to Hitler, Valkyrie was really the plan to carry out an organized and effective coup d'état against Hitler.

Besides the Valkyrie plans, "Stauffenberg and his friends had to ensure there were a sufficient number of officers determined to carry out the orders for the coup during the decisive phase."[30] Stauffenberg eventually located thirteen reliable officers for the seventeen military districts. Although Stauffenberg had established a relationship with the military commander-in-chief of France, the conspirators never worked out a similar relationship with any of the other theaters, a serious flaw that contributed to their ultimate failure on 20 July. With these plans worked out in detail, the only aspect of the elimination of Hitler by the regular army was the actual assassination attempt itself.

After working through his conscience the act of murdering Hitler—which could be a mortal sin—the devout Catholic Stauffenberg finally made up his mind to take matters into his own hands— even at the risk of his soul. Instead of asking someone else to risk perdition, he would assassinate Hitler himself. He reasoned that whereas it would not be a sin to rid the world of this monster, it would be a sin to ask someone else to do the killing.

Finally at peace with his decision, Stauffenberg carried two bombs with him in the airplane and landed on 20 July 1944 at the East Prussian Rastenberg airfield near Wolfsschanze, Hitler's headquarters when he was not in Berlin.[31] Arming one of the bombs to go off in ten to fifteen minutes, Stauffenberg carried the briefcase holding the bomb to the hut where Hitler and his entourage were in the middle of the daily briefing. Stauffenberg's presence was announced, and Hitler greeted him. To ensure that the bomb would have the intended lethal effect, Stauffenberg forced his way to the table next to where the Führer was seated. After placing the bomb under the table, Stauffenberg immediately left the conference room, thinking that the bomb was well placed. The bomb exploded with a very noticeable blast not long after he left the hut.

Stauffenberg, ditching the spare bomb along the way, headed

for the airfield to make his escape. After getting past several check-points, he arrived at his airplane and got airborne. Unaware that the bomb had not killed Hitler, Stauffenberg did not realize that his plans for the coup were already in shambles. Hitler was alive, but no one outside of his immediate entourage was aware of it. Communication from the Wolfsschanze to the Wehrmacht signal office was garbled at best; the conspirators in Berlin did not know whether Hitler was dead or alive.

The fact that Hitler did live through the powerful explosion was nothing less than miraculous. Although the bomb exploded with tremendous force, Hitler was saved from certain death by the massive conference table he was leaning on at the time of detonation. Experts say the explosion tore an eighteen-inch hole in the floor underneath, yet Hitler suffered only a bruised leg and arm and two ruptured eardrums.[32] Although he did not know the true fate of Hitler, General Olbricht realized that the detonation of the bomb meant there was no turning back. It would easily be deduced that Stauffenberg had planted the bomb. So Olbricht had no choice but to activate the Valkyrie plan.

While in the process of activating the Valkyrie plan, Olbricht heard that Hitler was dead; emboldened by this information (although it proved to be false), Olbricht went to General Friedrich Fromm. The ever-equivocating Fromm, however, refused to sign the Valkyrie orders upon hearing that the Führer was not only alive but just slightly wounded.[33] Learning that Fromm was now balking at carrying out the coup, Stauffenberg (back in Berlin from his adventure at the Wolfsschanze) placed Fromm under house arrest.

Fromm's equivocation was an ominous sign: as soon as word spread that Hitler was indeed alive, the whole conspiracy collapsed. The double-dealing Fromm, easily escaping from his quarters, managed to lead the execution of the most prominent figures of the coup. He wanted to eliminate anyone who could implicate him in the conspiracy.

Despite his bravery and piety, Stauffenberg's efforts to rid his country of Hitler failed miserably. Countless people continued to suffer because Hitler lived almost another year. Kramarz accurately describes the historical legacy of Stauffenberg's sacrifice:

> His persecutors thought that his name could be effaced from all memory, but they were wrong. The name of Stauffenberg has its

place in German history as that of a man who perceived that his duty as a soldier and General Staff officer lay not within the strict confines of military matters, but who was conscious of his "supreme responsibility" to the German people as a whole.[34]

Stauffenberg will always be a model for those who choose to follow their conscience rather than political expediency.

NOTES

1. I. C. B. Dear and M. R. D. Foot, *The Oxford Companion to World War II* (New York: Oxford University Press, 1995), 1018–1019.

2. Ben Parnell, *Carpetbaggers: America's Secret War in Europe* (Austin: Eakin Press, 1993), ix–x.

3. Dear and Foot, *Oxford Companion*, 3.

4. Ibid.

5. Ibid., 969.

6. Ibid., 967.

7. Ibid., 1017.

8. John H. Waller, *The Unseen War in Europe* (New York: Random House, 1996), 27.

9. Ibid., 22.

10. Ibid., 23.

11. Ibid.

12. Ibid., 24.

13. Ibid.

14. Ibid., 26.

15. Ibid., 27.

16. Dear and Foot, *Oxford Companion*, 1171.

17. Ibid., 749.

18. George Hicks, *The Comfort Women* (New York: W. W. Norton, 1994), 45–46.

19. Ibid., 11.

20. Dear and Foot, *Oxford Companion*, 945.

21. Ibid.

22. Waller, *Unseen War*, 333–335.

23. Ibid., 335.

24. John Keegan, *Who's Who in World War II* (New York: Oxford University Press, 1995), 148.

25. Ibid., 11.

26. Joachim Kramarz, *Stauffenberg* (New York: Macmillan, 1967), 132.

27. Waller, *Unseen War*, 338.

28. Peter Hoffman, *Stauffenberg: A Family History, 1905–1944* (Cambridge: Cambridge University Press, 1995), 198–199.

29. Kramarz, *Stauffenberg*, 134.

30. Ibid., 140.

31. Ibid., 186.

32. Waller, *Unseen War*, 344.

33. Kramarz, *Stauffenberg*, 190.

34. Ibid., 200.

WAR AND PURPLE PROSE: AN INTERVIEW
WITH PAUL WEST

Born in an English mining town on 23 February 1930, Paul West writes with grace, wit, and intelligence. Besides displaying an attentive, high style, West writes with a fine and sympathetic sense of humanity; his characters, often taken from the fringes of society, all display a robust and compelling sensibility.

A prolific writer, West has written over thirty works of fiction, poetry, and criticism and has received numerous awards for his work, including the Guggenheim and National Endowment for the Arts fellowships, the Aga Khan Fiction Prize, an Award in Literature from the American Academy and Institute of Arts and Letters, and the Hazlet Award for Excellence in the Arts. He was also a fiction judge for the 1990 National Book Award. Educated at Oxford and Columbia universities, he became a Literary Lion of the New York Public Library in 1987.

Thomas McGuire is the primary interviewer here (with contributions from James Meredith). This interview was conducted through correspondence as well as a face-to-face meeting during the fall of 1997, in Ithaca, New York.

FROM THOMAS McGUIRE, "AN INTERVIEW WITH PAUL WEST"
(War, Literature & the Arts: An International Journal of the
Humanities 10, no. 1 [Spring/Summer 1998])

INTERVIEWER: Mr. West, thank you for taking the time to answer questions about your work and career. You've mentioned that you hadn't realized how prevalent war is in your writing. Is your frequent focus on war largely unintentional? Why do you suppose you return to the subject of war so often?

WEST: I don't set out, always, to write a novel about something; I'm more like the Frenchman Julien Gracq, who works away and sees where the metaphors take him. In this way, stuff hitherto hidden from your formal, Apollonian gaze comes into view or rather into use. As I've said before, I'm not always in control of what comes through; I write in a highly controlled trance. No wonder, then, that war and other traumas keep on coming out. We're not exactly sequestered from war in our daily lives anyway. Humans are a warlike bunch. I was a mere child in the period of World War II (1939–1945), but I could read at age four, and I devoured all the war magazines, pictorial things in black and white. Over my shoulder, my father, the semi-blinded veteran, peered at the same stuff and reminisced about his war days. We stuck pins and flags into maps, and he recited to me again and again his autobiography, which was almost entirely that of a soldier, a machine gunner who after three years was blown up by a shell. My father was one of those reported missing or dead, and then he reappeared. Having a war hero as a father brainwashes you a good deal, and it also liberates part of your martial imagination. Let me just add that from being a tot, I grew up in the presence of myth; my father, the soldier, was mythic, and so was my pianist mother, who appeared on stages for money.

INTERVIEWER: How did your RAF experiences shape your opinion of officers and the military?

WEST: Excellent question! When I'd been at the RAF OCTU [Officer Candidate Training Unit] about a year, Vince Gough, the Adjutant, showed me the wide group portrait that hung in his office: maybe a hundred fresh-faced lads, many with the DFC [Distinguished Flying Cross] ribbons on their chests. It was like a vision of the future, and I hero-worshipped these guys, who among other things had won the Battle of Britain, an epic that rouses me still, "Well, they're all dead but me," he said. "All of them. I've checked." Stunning stuff. I was only a young guy myself, but these guys, much younger than I, had already bought the farm before even reaching twenty. You can guess how I felt about the few of them who'd survived, belatedly becoming officers or actually on the staff already. I was a boy Socrates among giants. I (whose eye muscles are lazy) flew with them as often as I could, once with Freddy Knapper over the North Sea catching a wave with the Anson's wing-tip; we reeled about but didn't plow in, which was just as well. Some of these guys were reckless flyers. I just felt honored to be with them, whether they killed us or not. It was extraordinary atmosphere in that OCTU, with heroes training the sergeant heroes and the scholarship boys (some of whom, like me, had already been to an American university) making life difficult for them by insisting on good English, good speech. What a farce.

INTERVIEWER: Many of your works contain extremely unsavory portraits of military figures, especially officers. (Stauffenberg is, of course, a notable exception.) How did your experiences with the RAF officers shape your attitude toward officers and the military in general?

WEST: One senior officer, a Wing Commander, a light colonel [lieutenant colonel], tried to get me court-martialed for insubordination, but it didn't work. Actually, the proposed court-martial would charge me, as the base "Stationary Officer," responsible for all paper, with losing a bargeload of toilet paper in the North Sea. It never left Liverpool, as a matter of fact, as the inquiry found out!

Another got me into a court-martial to defend a couple of sodomites caught in the act; I was told they had no chance, and it was true, though I must thank the [Royal] Air Force for acquainting me with the law, and military law too, especially that concerning prisoners of war, which knowledge I use in *Terrestrials* [West's novel published in 1997].

INTERVIEWER: Can you describe some other experiences during the Blitz—what you saw, heard, felt?

WEST: My father would escort me outside as soon as we heard the un-synchronized engines of Nazi bombers, six out of seven nights. Each of us would have a brisket sandwich to munch on while looking up into the brilliant patchwork of the searchlights, our mouths no doubt open for shrapnel. Perhaps I was being blooded. My father was always con-temptuous of the bombers, and his constant brave self; myself, I found the brisket slices slithering about the breads as I tried to chew while craning my neck. How reckless we were, as my mother said. One night, when we were all together at the kitchen table, a bomb screeched down and we all without a word ducked underneath. "Well," my mother said, "if we have to go, we go together." Those who have taken on the Brits always underestimated the folly of the Churchills (brilliant stylist as one may have been), but also the sheer obtuseness of the breed, unhabituated to losing.

INTERVIEWER: Much of your writing deals with war's aftermath—espe-cially the psychological and physical scars left over from war. From a creative standpoint, do you find it more interesting to portray *mutiles de guerre* [war wounded] than individuals engaged in combat?

WEST: Probably: I never fought in a war, but I saw war's aftermath in many human lives. If war is a natural human state, then I am staggered by how much we have achieved in spite of it. I heard at first hand a large amount about air combat and had some experience in ground maneuvers (as taught by the RAF Regiment, whose main job was to defend airfields). I knew how to do all that, but I never did it for real. *Love's Mansion* and *The Place in Flowers Where Pollen Rests*, I seem to recall, show quite a bit of actual combat, though. From a creative standpoint, everything ap-peals to me, but as I say, I'm not that calculating. I go with what sways me.

INTERVIEWER: Your emphasis on the primacy of language and purple prose notwithstanding, there is certainly a moral dimension to your writ-ing. Do you feel a moral obligation or need to write about war and vio-lence?

WEST: Call it moral, if you want. I prefer epistemological. So many people, organs, institutions busily try to protect readers from what life is like. One women's magazine devoted to the notion of white won't print certain words (boxer, beer, for example). One glossy magazine, whose name seems to imply a menstrual ocean, sent out my Ripper novel [*The Women of Whitechapel and Jack the Ripper*] to someone they hoped would savage it. He turned in a rave, so they refused to print it as my novel, they claimed, was anti-woman—alas, for that opinion, [another woman's magazine] recommended the novel as wholly feminist. The literary world is full of these wimps, who want to shield their unsuspecting readers from the horrors that abide. Myself, I like to remind readers of what in the round the world is like. Myself, I am a relatively peaceable ex-jock who grew into an esthete and intellectual, but I did train RAF officers for three years. I like to think that a novelist can reveal a cross-section of life, can center a novel not just on family and suburban matters but on history, biology, astronomy, even politics. I can see the force of some exquisite extrusion from the mess, but only if it's a figure against the mess's ground. The synecdoche novel, in which a hiccup does duty for atrocity, is hardly worth typing out. So there is a moral emphasis in that I think the novelist is obliged to know things and to reflect that knowledge in prose. That's why I say epistemological. Most novelists don't know anything of the world they inhabit, but only the equally restrictive novels of their friends. Without a wide and highly developed sense of the world, what kind of a novelist can you be? It's not essential to know gunplay or the music of Schnittle at first hand, or chocolate-making or the techniques of whereof you speak. The post-modern generation of American novelists, if it exists at all, spends its time delightedly licking its own froth, and maybe it's cruder stuff than froth. You can do your world view almost entirely in symbols, as Faulkner did (he schooled in the French Symbolists), but you need to draw the symbols from the known. And the quality of your known rapidly establishes you as an ignoramus or a diligent observer.

INTERVIEWER: As someone who experienced the wrath of Hitler during the Blitz, how do you feel about the German people now?

WEST: Not friendly; I still hold it against them, to have bombed my boyhood nightly for two years and more.

INTERVIEWER: Why did you choose Count von Stauffenberg not only as the subject of your novel, *The Very Rich Hours of Count von Stauffenberg*, but as the dominant perspective as well?

WEST: Because I associated him with my one-eyed father. I knew about blinded war heroes, or so I thought. Stauf also struck me as an almost good Nazi, although, to be sure, he rather reveled in the Polish invasion, until a certain point. He was a man of parts turned man of fragments. Spoiled but zealous, I mean spoiled in both senses: pampered and ruined. A quasi-Hamlet. He also knew English. It was odd to have a German thinking in German, writing in English, narrating his own death twice. I got some hate mail from Germany, saying, "Why glorify a Nazi?" I have no friends, either, among German publishers, most of whom I'd gladly concentrate behind barbed wire to be fed a diet of Swift and Proust.

INTERVIEWER: Although the Count is a sympathetic German officer, he still is a member of an army that perpetuated and enforced Nazi atrocities. Is there something in the character of the Count that makes him an everyman—a representative man who is perpetually duped or put on the spot by the politician? You go to great lengths to demonstrate the aristocratic nobility of the man—and the aristocratic naiveté as well. Is there something for the modern military man to learn here?

WEST: His idealism, his sneaking regard for socialism. If he hadn't linked up with two socialists, Leber and Reichwein, whom the Gestapo were watching, his plot might have succeeded. He loved the arts, philosophy, knew Stefan George, was a fine horseman: enough to work with. Oh, that the so-called heroes of contemporary American fiction had such ballast. I think Stauffenberg was one of those gifted men who, swaddled in hubris and hauteur, had a tremendous capacity for both self-delusion and belated humility. An odd, but not unknown, mix. His concern was always for his people, his men—something drummed into us at the OCTU and worth cherishing. You always put them first.

INTERVIEWER: The Stauffenberg novel seems to exonerate the common people as a whole. Were they any different from us? (Recent scholarship about the Holocaust implicates a vast majority of the German people.) Was Hitler expressing an insane obsession of a whole nation? Was he an aberration or a tragic paradigm? Are we capable of such horror? Is our culture vulnerable to a potential fascist takeover?

WEST: Recent scholarship substantiates my view that the Germans knew and eagerly took part, as did Poles. I think it's fair to say Hitler, after Dryden, was "in the van of circumstance, seiz[ed] the arrow's barb before the tense strong quiver[ed]" (John Dryden, *Absalom and Achitophel*, 1681). He emerges as the consummate epitome of a national malaise. Everyone knew the Jews were running the newspapers and nobody liked the fact. He was an aberration only to us, who presumably are sane. Are we capable? Only in rages, I think, like Aussie soldiers crucifying Japanese on the northern beaches of Australia with a bayonet through each hand and foot. I think the "Allied" *Weltanschauung* is woolier, more sentimental, less endowed with Heideggerian streamlining filched from an imaginary fifth-century Greece. Best answer I have is what I'm writing now, a huge panorama novel in which Admiral Canaris figures as a part-imaginary figure, both twerpy dog-lover and master spy, together with (maybe) Pfitzner the composer.

Is our culture vulnerable? Only if there are enough crazies. No clique, but it's already got what it wants: a country of billionaires run by millionaires, the rest of the population besotted with a so-called American dream. Look how the airwaves belong to the merchandisers of everything.

INTERVIEWER: Where do art and history intersect, or do they? When does the novel (as an art form) become a better medium to represent history than a history itself?

WEST: When a novelist has the style to make his imagined world supplant the real one. Art and history intersect all the time; the trick, I suppose, is to separate them, but how, if you have an eye, an ear, open? We are surrounded by hoax and swindle. It's all history, and cumulatively so. Carlyle has the answer, and it has to do with history done through expressionism—how you feel about it being just as important to you as what happened.

VOICES OF SUBVERSION AND ESPIONAGE

THE SOE AND OSS

The globalness and complexity of World War II demanded a much more sophisticated intelligence-gathering operation than had ever been done before. Intelligence operatives from all sides responded with imagination and courage, but none more than the SOE and OSS. The following excerpts are a sample of some of the fascinating exploits of these two intelligence groups.

FROM IAN DEAR, *SABOTAGE & SUBVERSION: STORIES FROM THE FILES OF THE SOE AND OSS*
(London: Arms and Armour, 1996)

The SOE's objective was, in Churchill's well-known phrase, to "set Europe ablaze"—the prime minister's order to [(Edward) Hugh] Dalton, Minister of Economic Warfare, who was SOE's first political head. Its inspiration were the Fifth columnists who were supposed to have been so active throughout Europe, including Britain, and were much feared at the time (although except for the examples of *Volksdeutche* activity . . . , they proved to be largely a myth). It was, of necessity, a secret organization. By that is meant that it was not one that the government would officially acknowledge as existing. (9)

• • •

The OSS became operational much later than SOE, but its record is also an impressive one. The first SO [Special Operations] London agent to enter the field was E. F. Floege, code-named "Alfred," who, with his wireless operator, an SO officer called André Bouchardon, was first parachuted into France on 13 June 1943 to organize a sabotage circuit in the area of Le Mans-Nantes-laval. . . .

When SO was formed it was [Bill] Donovan's intention that it should handle black propaganda and similar methods of subversion. But SOE and PWE, which handled British political warfare, had different political heads which made it difficult for PWE to liaise with SO satisfactorily. Therefore, in January 1943, Donovan created the Morale Operations (MO) Branch to mount black propaganda operations of all varieties into enemy territory. "Persuasion, penetration, and intimidation," he said of this type of warfare, "are the modern counterpart of sapping and mining in the siege warfare of former days." (17)

One of the most prominent soldiers to serve in the OSS was Jack Hemingway, the oldest son of Ernest and Hadley Hemingway. Hemingway was selected for these special forces because, having grown up with his expatriate parents, he was fluent in French. Brave and adventurous, Jack Hemingway was a perfect choice for covert work behind the lines. In his memoirs, *Misadventures of a Fly Fisherman: My Life with and without Papa*, Jack writes about his perilous drop into occupied France and the duties he performed there.

FROM JACK HEMINGWAY, *MISADVENTURES OF A FLY FISHERMAN: MY LIFE WITH AND WITHOUT PAPA*
(Dallas: Taylor Publishing, 1986)

We'd been dropped from way too high, about fourteen hundred feet above the DZ, because the rough terrain had made the pilots nervous about going as low as they should have. For the moment it seemed wonderful to me but we would have to pay a price. Jim realized immediately that the wind was taking us away from the signal fires of the drop zone and he slipped away below me to try to land as close to them as possible. I followed as best I could but suddenly, I was below the horizon and, an instant later, trying to fight the impulse to reach for the invisible ground with straight legs, the rod line went slack and I was tumbling through a thicket of bushes to the bottom of what proved to be a deep gulch. I had landed in France, whether safely or not remained to be seen.

I was unhurt, save for some bumping around on the rocks. Moreover, the rod [the fly rod for fishing Jack took into combat with him] was unbroken. After hiding the chute and striptease in some bushes and covering them with stones, I started climbing up the steep of the deep ravine. It was a hell of a climb, about three hundred feet through brush and thorn thickets to the crest of the ridge between me and the reception area. The night was moonless with a clear starlit sky, as planned. That was just as well because it was practically the only thing that did go according to plan. (140)

Hemingway later states that his experiences with the OSS in France were some of the most difficult and memorable events of his life. For example, he was eventually wounded and captured by the Germans. Sent to a POW compound, Hemingway was liberated from his incarceration at Hammalburg, only to be re-captured while attempting to reach the Allied front lines. He finally experienced true liberation just days before the Germans' surrender. Jack Hemingway today lives in Sun Valley, Idaho.

WOMEN SPIES

From counterespionage behind enemy lines to compiling extensive analysis at home, women played a vital role in the Allied intelligence mission. Elizabeth McIntosh joined the OSS in 1943 and served in places such as Burma and China. In *Sisterhood of Spies: The Women of the OSS*, McIntosh develops, through extensive interviews and research, some of the fascinating experiences she and other women encountered while serving their country as members of the intelligence community. In the following excerpt she describes the work of Amy Thorpe (code-named "Cynthia"), who worked as a "Mata Hari" for both American and British intelligence. In the operation McIntosh recounts here, Cynthia penetrated the Vichy French embassy in Washington, D.C., to obtain vital naval codebooks in the embassy safe. Obtaining these codes was essential to the pending invasion of North Africa, Operation Torch. Assisting Cynthia on this mission was Ellery Huntington, Jr., a prominent New York attorney before the war; the Georgia Cracker, a former convict who was highly competent in opening safes; and Charles Brousse, a Frenchman who was an attaché in the Vichy embassy. Although Brousse was married to another woman, he and Cynthia were romantically involved and later were married after the war. Their relationship provided them a cover for access to the embassy after normal duty hours. In the following excerpt Cynthia and her team have just gotten the codebooks out of the safe, and she and Brousse are in the embassy waiting for Cracker to return from the Wardman Park Hotel, where the stolen material was to be photographed before being returned.

FROM ELIZABETH P. McINTOSH, *SISTERHOOD OF SPIES: THE WOMEN OF THE OSS*
(Annapolis: Naval Institute Press, 1998)

It was a long, tense wait for Brousse and Cynthia. As he wrote later, "I do not wish to underline what could have been the consequences, outside the physical danger from the armed guard, if we had been caught."

They waited in darkness, Cynthia sometimes slinking over to the code-room window to watch for the Cracker. Their nerves on edge, they smoked one cigarette after another, anxiously watching the doors, not daring to dress until they had heard from their teammate. Their deadline had been 4 A.M., and it was now almost 4:30. Had something gone wrong? Had the FBI picked up the Cracker? With his past record, they could easily incarcerate him. Would the guard return?

Finally, at about 4:40, Cynthia heard a movement under the window: the Cracker was back with the books. Swiftly he climbed through the window with an agility he had not lost since his early days as a second-story man. The books were replaced, the safe locks back in the position they had found them. Fingerprints were wiped clean, and the Cracker was out the window and gone. They arrived at Apartment 215B at the Wardman Park Hotel and entered a busy room filled with photo equipment, two cameramen, Huntington, and, most important, photographs of the code pages spread out to dry on several tables. (24–25)

TOPICS FOR WRITTEN AND ORAL DISCUSSION

1. Research some recent examples of espionage during the Cold War. Write an essay discussing the motivations of the individuals who sold secrets to the enemy. Is there a common factor in all their cases? Could deception be a habit for those individuals who deceive professionally?

2. Write an essay discussing the moral implications of assassinating the leader of a country who has taken the nation, and the world, to the brink of disaster. The news today is full of examples of leaders who have put their countries in danger.

3. In today's terms, is there ever a reasonable justification to occupy another nation? It is easy to criticize Nazi Germany's occupation of Europe, but historically the United States has also been seen by others as an occupation force. U.S. military forces are present all over the world. Imagine that you are working for the president and you have been asked to prepare a speech explaining to the American people why the United States must occupy another country. Give at least ten different reasons, and explain them. Now give ten reasons why the United States should never be an occupying force.

4. Do you think you have what it takes to be a secret agent? Imagine that you have always wanted to be a spy, and now you have a chance. Prepare for a job interview with the CIA by writing down at least ten personal characteristics that qualify you for the job. Compare your characteristics with those of others in your class. Are there many differences?

5. Is Count von Stauffenberg a hero for attempting to assassinate Hitler? Think about your answer before you respond. What took so long for the resistance against Hitler to develop? Why didn't they respond before the war began? Is one ever justified in assassinating anyone? Is there a difference between assassinating a leader such as Hitler and killing someone on the battlefield? Explain your answers. Remember that it is much easier to see an issue in hindsight.

SUGGESTIONS FOR FURTHER READING

Céline, Louis-Ferdinand. *Castle to Castle*. Trans. Ralph Manheim. Normal, IL: Dalkey Archive Press, (1957) 1997.

———. *Rigadoon*. Trans. Ralph Manheim. Kurt Vonnegut Jr., introd. Normal, IL: Dalkey Archive Press, (1969) 1997.

Dear, Ian. *Sabotage and Subversion: Stories from the Files of the SOE and OSS*. London: Arms and Armour Press, 1996.

Hemingway, Jack. *Misadventures of a Fly Fisherman: My Life with and without Papa*. Dallas: Taylor Publishing, 1986.

Hicks, George. *The Comfort Women: Japan's Brutal Regime of Enforced Prostitution in the Second World War*. New York: W. W. Norton, 1994.

Higgins, Jack. *The Eagle Has Flown*. New York: Pocket Books, 1990.

Hoffman, Peter. *Stauffenberg: A Family History, 1905–1944*. Cambridge: Cambridge University Press, 1995.

Ludlum, Robert. *The Rhinemann Exchange*. New York: Bantam, 1989.

Maclean, Alistair. *The Guns of Navarone*. New York: Fawcett Crest, (1956) 1984.

Montagu, Ewen. *The Man Who Never Was*. Alan Stripp, introd. New York: Oxford University Press, (1953) 1996.

Parnell, Ben. *Carpetbaggers: America's Secret War in Europe*. Austin, TX: Eakin Press, 1993.

Southworth, Samuel A., ed. *Great Raids in History: From Drake to Desert One*. New York: Sarpedon, 1997.

Waller, John H. *The Unseen War in Europe: Espionage and Conspiracy in the Second World War*. New York: Random House, 1996.

West, Paul. *Tent of Orange Mist*. Woodstock, NY: Overlook Press, 1995.

———. *Terrestrials*. New York: Scribners, 1997.

Whiting, Charles. *Death on a Distant Frontier: A Lost Victory 1944*. New York: Sarpedon, 1996.

4

The Holocaust

An Analysis of William Styron's *Sophie's Choice* and Elie Wiesel's *Night*

LITERARY ANALYSIS

SOPHIE'S CHOICE

In broad terms, *Sophie's Choice* is a novel about discovering just how dark, how evil, the human heart is capable of being—themes very similar to those of Joseph Conrad's *Heart of Darkness*. In more specific terms, *Sophie's Choice* is about the evil of the Holocaust and how it destroyed many lives, even those of survivors. The Holocaust and its aftermath affected an enormous amount of people, and the more we understand about the horrors of that dark time, the better prepared we are not ever to let it happen again. Like the novel's narrator, Stingo, readers discover that the Holocaust was not a sudden inexplicable phenomenon that attacked an isolated group of people, coming on quickly and leaving just as fast. Rather, like a powerful disease, its buildup was deliberate and gradual, leaving massive destruction in its path. Layer by layer, like peeling an onion, Stingo steadily discovers humanity's baffling cruelty against its own kind, as he realizes that a lot more people than he ever imagined are implicated in these and other crimes.

A young man from North Carolina, Stingo has moved to predominantly Jewish Brooklyn, New York, and retrospectively narrates the story in the first person. He is living in Yetta Zimmerman's rooming house, "a large rambling wood and stucco house of the nondescript variety erected. . . . [I]t would have faded into the homely homogeneity of other large nondescript dwellings that bordered on Prospect Park had it not been for its striking—its overwhelming—pinkness."[1] Stingo, who is a Protestant white southerner, is a stranger in this land. He lives in the rooming house because he cannot afford an apartment in Manhattan, where he works as a fledgling editor in a publishing company; his true ambition is to be a writer.

Soon after moving into Yetta's rooming house, Stingo overhears the sounds of loud, passionate lovemaking and the music of Beethoven's Fourth Symphony coming from the room directly upstairs. He soon befriends this amorous couple, Nathan Landau and Sophie Zawistowska. Nathan is a diagnosed manic-depressive who can be charming one minute and ruthless the next. Sophie, a developing alcoholic, is the most charming woman Stingo has ever met. Stingo, smitten by the beguiling Sophie, begins an intense friendship with this couple that does not end until Nathan and Sophie commit suicide.

Yetta's boarding house, where these three individuals—each with a dark history to relate—meet and learn about each other's experience, is a microcosm of the world. Although Stingo is the narrator of the story, it is Sophie's life that is paramount, as the title indicates. Thus, Nathan serves more as a function of the plot than anything else. His manic ravings and brutal behavior remind readers that tyranny is everywhere: that although the Nazis, through modern technology and efficient bureaucracy, raised inhumanity to a higher level than at any time in history, insanity and brutality have not disappeared from the world. Ironically, Nathan, a Jew who is fully aware of the Holocaust, should be sensitive to the darkness in the human heart. His own insanity, however, has blinded him to his actions; he cannot fully control the evil that consumes him. Besides being a foil for both Stingo and Sophie, Nathan (who at times is a sympathetic character) has another purpose. He forces Stingo to confront the evil in his own heritage—particularly the issue of field slavery in the South.

Stingo, a sensitive, caring friend of Sophie, spends a lot of time

listening to the story of her life in Nazi Europe and the concentration camps. Through the retelling of her story to him, readers learn
not only of Sophie's tragic life but also that she is not always truth-
ful about her experiences. Ironically, however, there is more truth
in her lies than readers at first can imagine. Her lies tell the story
of how she would have liked her life to be, had she been able to
relive it. The reconstruction of her life is something to which she
has given a lot of thought. Stingo narrates this point:

> As will be seen in due course (and the fact is important to this
> narrative), Sophie told me a number of lies that summer. Perhaps
> I should say she indulged in certain evasions, which at the time are
> necessary in order for her to retain her composure. Or maybe her
> sanity. I certainly don't accuse her, for from the point of view of
> hindsight her untruths seem fathomable beyond need of apology.
> (104)

Narrating this story retrospectively, Stingo himself may have indulged in a few misdirections—although the novel does not spare
many details about his relationship with Sophie, it would have
been impossible to tell it all. The very nature of telling a story
demands selection—*choices*. Although the actual reason behind
the title is entirely different from this point, Sophie's choice (or
lack of choices) in telling her story is one of the ironic meanings
of the title.

Sophie is not the only liar in this novel. John Kenny Crane observes that the lies

> perpetuated by various characters in this novel are so inventive that
> they ultimately defy classification, but they appear to fall into three
> broad categories. First, there are those which are simply fundamen-
> tal conscious attempts to make facts seem other than they are.
> Among these would be simple untruths, such as Sophie's claim that
> Nathan is the only man other than her husband she ever made love
> to; her omission that she had two children, not one, at Ausch-
> witz. . . .
>
> The second category of lies are those which dull the mind so that
> truth cannot be felt or comprehended. Sophie is virtually an alco-
> holic by the time of her death. Nathan is a drug addict. . . .
>
> The third category of lying incorporates all those activities that
> attempt to rewrite reality in a different form, as opposed to denying

it (the first category) or blinding oneself to it (the second). Prevalent in this group are dreams which various of the characters have.[2]

Because the truth seems so hard to live with, lying becomes a major element in the novel.

All three main characters in this novel have a history, even if it is based on lies; they have a past that crowds in on their present lives. Each has a burden to bear. Because Sophie is forced to make the biggest choices in the book, she has the biggest lies to perpetuate. Despite her guardedness, the most horrible truth imaginable eventually comes out about *the choice* she once had to make. During her almost accidental incarceration in the concentration camps, Sophie was forced to make a choice between the life of her son and that of her daughter. Styron describes this horrific adjudication:

> Sophie, with an inanity poised on her tongue and choked with fear, is about to attempt a reply when the doctor said, "You may keep one of your children."
>
> "*Bitte?*" said Sophie.
>
> "You may keep one of your children," he repeated. "The other one will have to go. Which one will you keep?"
>
> "You mean, I have to choose?"
>
> "You're a Polack, not a Yid. That gives you a privilege—a choice."
>
> Her thought processes dwindled, ceased. Then she felt her legs crumble. "I can't choose!" She began to scream. Oh how she recalled her own screams! Tormented angels never screeched so loudly above hell's pandemonium. "*Ich kann nicht wablen!*" she screamed. . . .
>
> "Send them both over there, then," the doctor said to the aide, "*nach links.*"
>
> "Mama!" She heard Eva's thin but soaring cry at the instant that she thrust the child away from her and rose from the concrete with a clumsy stumbling motion. "Take the baby!" she called out. "Take my little girl!" (529)

Who would ever want to make this choice? It is no wonder Sophie attempts to reconstruct a different past than the one she was given, and it is no wonder she now looks for escape in alcohol and sex.

Although the novel is more about Stingo's discovery of the extent of the horror of the Holocaust than the actual Holocaust itself, the book is unsparing in its condemnation of inhumanity. With its haunting themes about evil, horror, and lies, the novel is a reminder that one cannot forget the truth—about the Holocaust and about humans' potential for cruelty.

William Styron, winner of the American Book Award, Howells Medal, Edward MacDowell Medal, and Pulitzer Prize, is not a Jewish survivor of the Holocaust. He is not even Jewish. Moreover, although *Sophie's Choice* is largely about the Nazi pogrom against the European Jewish community during World War II, Sophie, a survivor of Auschwitz, is not Jewish either. In fact, before the war Sophie's father was a Polish intellectual who had published a harshly anti-Semitic pamphlet. These "facts" should not detract from the truth that the Holocaust was overwhelmingly targeted at the Jewish community and that Jews were most savagely persecuted; these "facts" broaden readers' understanding of the scope of the Nazis' activities.

NIGHT

Whereas Styron's novel is a complex unraveling of a Holocaust story, Elie Wiesel's first-person retrospective is a distilled story about one man's nightmarish experience. Yet despite the differences between the two novels, both describe with amazing power the Nazis' atrocities against the Jews.

Night seems to cross genre lines. In *Elie Wiesel*, Ted Estess writes:

> *Night* is autobiographical; indeed, Wiesel has said that the story should be read in view of this statement: "I swear that every word is true." But there is a difference between Eliezer of the book and Elie Wiesel the storyteller. The reader's clue to this is the difference in names: the character in the story is "Eliezer," while the storyteller uses the name "Elie." The difference in names relates to Wiesel's recognition that he cannot adequately convey what happened to him and to millions of others. There would inevitably be discrepancies between the story he would tell and the events he suffered. It is more truthful for him to acknowledge this by creating a slight distance between himself and his "character."[3]

The novel begins with an anecdote about Moshe the Beadle, a man of whom the whole town is fond. A poor man, Moshe is a "past master in the art of making himself insignificant, of seeming invisible."[4] Moshe teaches the narrator, Eliezer, about religious matters, the mysteries of Hebrew mysticism, and the cabbalistic texts:

> "And why do you pray, Moshe?" I asked him.
> "I pray to the God within me that He will give me the strength to ask Him the right questions." (3)

When the local authorities ban all foreign Jews from this Hungarian town, Moshe is put on a train and taken away. Several months later Moshe returns to the city, and he tries to explain what happened to him and the other deportees. He tells the villagers that the deportees were taken to Poland and made to dig their own mass graves. He explains that the Gestapo then shot them all. Moshe escaped because he had only been shot in the leg and mistaken for dead. But people in the town refuse to listen to him. Such is the narrator's first discovery that things are terribly wrong. More is yet to come.

In the spring of 1944, when the tide of war is turning against Hitler, the Germans arrive. On the seventh day of Passover, the Jewish leaders of the community are arrested. Jews are then forced to wear yellow stars, and all their properties are divested. The narrator goes on to lament, "Then came the ghetto" (9). In the ghetto, life returns to a semblance of normalcy and the community hopes to remain there until the Red Army can rescue them. But eventually time runs out for these Jews, like it has for Jews all over occupied Europe. The ghetto is emptied, and the Jews are deported by train to Birkenau, an annex of Auschwitz. Before the train leaves the station, a Hungarian lieutenant collects their very last possessions.

At their arrival at Auschwitz, the SS immediately take charge, ordering them into lines. Here, the narrator remembers seeing the infamous Dr. Joseph Mengele (who is further described later in this chapter). He describes the encounter:

> (a typical SS officer: cruel face, but not devoid of intelligence, and wearing a monocle); a conductor's baton in his hand, he is standing among the other officers. The baton moved unremittingly, sometimes to the right, sometimes to the left.
> I am already in front of him:

"How old are you?" he asked, in an attempt at a paternal tone of voice.

"Eighteen." My voice is shaking.

"Are you in good health?"

"Yes."

"What's your occupation?"

Should I say that I am a student?

"Farmer," I heard myself say.

This conversation cannot have lasted more than a few seconds. It had seemed like an eternity to me.

The baton moved to the left. I took half a step forward. I wanted to see first where they are sending my father. If he went to the right, I would go after him.

The baton once again pointed to the left for him too. A weight is lifted from my heart.(29)

Although the narrator did not know it at the time, he and his father have escaped death in the crematory by having been chosen for the left side. On his way to prison, he sees flames coming out of a ditch as a truck filled with dead children arrives and dumps its cargo into the fire. It is a scene from the worst of nightmares.

Witnessing such an unbelievable atrocity, the narrator has to pinch his face, but the worst is yet to come. Eventually they are transferred to the main camp at Auschwitz, where they are given prison garb and tattooed; the narrator becomes A-7713. They stay at Auschwitz for three weeks until the iron gates at their new camp, Buna, close behind them.

In Buna, which is described as being "empty and dead" (45), the narrator and his father, despite their attempt to look out for each other, begin experiencing a familial dissolution on account of the horrors of Nazi cruelties. When their guard beats the father, the son gets angry with his father for not being able to avoid the guard's cruelty: such is the absurdity of concentration camp life.

The life of the father and son, like that of the other Jews, consists mainly of hard work and very short rations. Under these harsh conditions their bodies begin to diminish, especially the father's. One day a guard takes the father's "number," and he is told to stay behind in camp instead of going to the work yard. Afraid that this action means he has been selected for death, the father gives the son his inheritance—a knife and spoon. But when the son returns from work, a day he spends in great anxiety, the father is found alive; he has avoided selection for death by somehow proving he can still be useful. Others are not so lucky, however.

The winter of 1945 comes, and with the Soviet Army nearing the camp, Buna is evacuated. The father and son, along with the other Jews in the camp, are marched out of the gates into the icy wind. The SS march them relentlessly. On this march, the narrator discovers the limits of human endurance. When a heavy snow falls, many Jews succumb to exhaustion and lie down to freeze to death. There is no one to say prayers for them—even "sons abandoned their fathers' remains without a tear" (87).

Living without food—only snow brings them nourishment—these poor creatures are eventually forced into cattle cars, an evacuation train to Buchenwald. The narrator states that although 100 Jews are forced into the railroad car, only a dozen eventually get off. Even Eliezer's father barely manages to escape certain death when two gravediggers mistake him for a corpse. At Buchenwald his father's health further deteriorates to the point that fellow inmates beat him because he is too weak to go outside to relieve himself. Eliezer gets advice from the head of his block concerning his father: "Don't forget that you're in a concentration camp. Here, every man has to fight for himself and not think of anyone else. Even of his father. Here there are no fathers, no brothers, no friends" (105). On 28 January 1945, Eliezer goes to sleep, only to awaken the next day to discover that his father has been carried away to the crematory. The son does not weep.

Eliezer stays in Buchenwald until the camp is liberated on 11 April 1945. The last anecdote in the book recounts the first time that the narrator sees himself in the mirror after leaving the ghetto: "From the depths of the mirror, a corpse gazed back at me. The look in his eyes, as they stared into mine, has never left me" (109). Notice the narrator's confusion in the personal pronouns *his* and *me*. They are the same set of eyes being reflected, but the image of the narrator is someone he cannot recognize as himself. The inhumanity of his treatment by the Nazis has disfigured him beyond human recognition. Whereas Styron's complex novel relies on art to convey its story, Wiesel's novel relies on the story to convey the art.

Winner of the Nobel Peace Prize in 1986 and the 1985 Congressional Gold Medal, Wiesel is today a powerful voice in the fight for human rights. Just as one must never forget about the horror of the Holocaust, one must never fail to listen to survivors, such as Wiesel, when they warn about contemporary atrocities.

NOTES

1. William Styron, *Sophie's Choice* (New York: Vintage, 1979), 35. All subsequent quotations of this text come from this book.

2. John Kenny Crane, *The Root of All Evil: The Thematic Unity of William Styron's Fiction* (Columbia: University of South Carolina Press, 1984), 31–32.

3. Ted L. Estess, *Elie Wiesel* (New York: Frederick Ungar Publishing, 1980), 17–18.

4. Elie Wiesel, *Night* (New York: Bantam, (1960) 1982), 1. All subsequent quotations of this text come from this book.

HISTORICAL CONTEXT

KRISTALLNACHT (9 NOVEMBER 1938)

Recriminations against the Jews in Germany began as soon as Hitler and the Nazi Party took power in January 1933. Emboldened by his successes in annexing territory at Munich, in September 1938 Hitler intensified his anti-Semitic policies by expelling 18,000 German Jews who had been born in the Polish provinces of the former Russian empire, even though they had been living in Germany since the end of World War I.[1] These people were deported to the eastern border of Germany and told to leave the country. Holocaust historian Yehuda Bauer notes that even though they were denied passage into Poland by the Poles, "many were nevertheless forced across the border illegally by the Nazis; others, some 5,000, to camp in a tiny Polish frontier village, Zbazsyn."[2] Left to manage for themselves in rustic Polish frontier towns, the Jews suffered greatly. One of these victims, Zindel Grynszpan, sent a postcard to his son, Hirsh, who was studying in Paris. Enraged by the deplorable conditions his family had been forced to endure, on 6 November 1938 Hirsh went to the German embassy in Paris and shot the first German official that he could find, Ernst vom Rath.[3]

Bauer argues that vom Rath's death turned out to be a convenient excuse for the Nazis to punish the Jewish people in Germany. Bauer observes that some sort of recrimination had already been planned before vom Rath's shooting.[4] On the night of 9 November, Hitler and Josef Goebbels met to discuss the "proper" response to this murder. Goebbels, eager to lead on the Jewish Question, "activated the SA and tens of thousands of loyal party members to burn all the synagogues in Germany, destroy and loot Jewish shops, and physically abuse large numbers of Jews."[5] The SA were Sturmabteilung (or the Stormtroopers), who were also known as the Brownshirts for the uniforms they wore. Hitler had formed this group of fanatical fascists on 3 August 1921 to control members of his own Nazi Party and to harass opponents.[6] These men were the official bullies of the party and the Nazis' primary source of physical abuse against the Jewish people.

Martin Gilbert describes the destruction that occurred during the Kristallnacht recriminations:

In twenty-four hours of street violence, ninety-one Jews were killed. More than thirty thousand—one in ten of those who remained—were arrested and sent to concentration camps. Before most of them were released two to three months later, as many as a thousand had been murdered, 244 of them in Buchenwald. A further eight thousand Jews were evicted from Berlin: children from orphanages, patients from hospitals, old people from old people homes. There were many suicides, ten at least in Nuremberg; but it was forbidden to publish death notices in the press.

It was not by the killing, however, nor by the arrests or the suicides, that the night of November 9 was to be remembered. During the night, as well as breaking into tens of thousands of shops and homes, the Stormtroopers set fire to one hundred and ninety-one synagogues; or, if it was thought that fire might endanger nearby buildings, smashed the synagogues as thoroughly as possible with hammers and axes.[7]

As one would imagine from such demolition, the streets of Germany were full of broken glass that the Nazis used derisively as a symbol of their punishing of the Jews. This night, 9 November 1938, thus became known as Kristallnacht, or the "night of broken glass."

A majority of German citizens were shocked by this violence against the Jews—although there was little assistance given to the victims.[8] Gilbert conveys a poignant story about one German gentile, Pastor J. Von Jan, who spoke out against the tyranny. This pastor's vicarage was destroyed by the SA, and he was sent to prison as well.[9]

Bauer notes three significant changes in social policy against the German Jewish population after Kristallnacht. First, the Germans worked out a completely new Jewish policy after this incident that had not been in place before. Second, the Jews were forced to pay the Nazis one billion Reichsmarks for the death of vom Rath. They also had to pay insurance benefits for the destroyed property because the German insurance companies were upset over the amount of damages incurred (250 million Reichsmarks). Third, the Jews were disenfranchised completely from Germany's economy.[10] Gilbert observes that German Jewish children were also now completely barred from public schools.[11] Bauer writes that by 1 January 1939, only Jewish-run organizations could hire Jews, and that if a business was taken over by Germans, then no Jewish person could work for that company again. The ultimate goal of this process was to force all Jews out of the country. The results were panic and a massive migration of Jews, people who had once been good citizens of either Germany or Austria.[12]

THE NAZI CONCENTRATION CAMPS

When the Allies were liberating the concentration camps at the end of the war, the most notorious image of the remains of Nazi Germany were photographs of the hollow-faced survivors of the Holocaust.

From as early as 1921, Hitler warned the world that concentration camps would be a major part of his new society.[13] Almost immediately after coming to power, the SA established small detention centers throughout Germany. Gilbert notes that on 9 March 1933, a scant two months after Hitler took national power, "the SS sent thousands of critics of the regime, including many Jews, to a so-called 'concentration camp,' at Dachau, near Munich."[14] Dachau was the first major concentration center, expanding to accommodate 5,000 prisoners by the end of March.[15] Other state-sponsored camps quickly sprang up throughout Germany. By the early fall of 1934, fully 80,000 people had been incarcerated.[16]

The biggest impetus for the Nazi concentration camp system occurred in May 1934 when the SS took over operation from the SA, and they consolidated most of the camps into larger concentrations. Theodor Eicke, the former head of the Dachau camp, was appointed by Himmler to the position of Inspector of Concentration Camps.[17] His job was to reorganize the system. A highly competent administrator, Eicke closed all the SA camps, standardized the operations of the camp system, and created the SS Death's Head guards. The administration of the camps remained under the control of Eicke, and the Gestapo was in charge of the incarceration and release of prisoners. By the early summer of 1935 five major camps existed in Germany: Esterwegen, Lichtenburg, Morgingen, Dachau, and Sachsenburg.[18]

Buchenwald was created in the summer of 1937 near Weimar in

Thurgia when Sachsenberg and Lichtenburg were closed. Buchenwald

had the distinction of being the first major concentration camp to fall into the hands of the Western Allies while it still had a full population of prisoners. The U.S. Army had earlier discovered an abandoned Nazi camp at Natzweiler, France, near the end of 1944; the Soviets had come upon Auschwitz, Poland, in January 1945. On April 5, the U.S. Army, however, found fresh evidence of atrocities on a large scale when they overran recently abandoned camps at Ohrduf and Nordhausen-Dora. But these discoveries had not fully prepared Allied troops and their commanders for the sight of the sprawling camp at Buchenwald near Weimar in central Germany, which they reached on April 11, 1945. It held 21,000 starving and ragged prisoners and was complete with crematoriums, execution rooms, and a hospital used for medical experiments on prisoners.[19]

As Hitler propelled Germany toward war, the concentration camps grew even more full, as they became sources of forced labor as well as prisons for Jews and other political unwanteds for the Nazis. Camps closer to SS factories and industrial centers, such as Sachsenhausen north of Berlin, began to spring up when prisoners also became sources of forced labor. More pressure was put on the camp system as Germany expanded its territory.

After the invasion of Poland and the USSR (with three million and one million Jews, respectively), the population of the camps exploded. Additional camps, including Auschwitz, were quickly and efficiently constructed in the newly occupied territory. Poland, which had a legacy of anti-Semitism even before the war, became a nightmare of historical proportions as extermination and concentration camps littered the landscape. Auschwitz, located near Cracow, was established in June 1940 with Rudolf Hoess as the founding commandant. He and five other SS men arrived in Auschwitz on 29 April. Thirty more Germans, all convicted criminals from Sachsenhausen, arrived on 30 May to serve as Kapos, the title given to prisoners in charge of other prisoners. Jews from the town of Auschwitz eventually were forced to fix up the site, which had been an Austro-Hungarian artillery base during World War I.[20] Auschwitz became a large complex of three different camps and thirty-six subcamps. One of the camps held political prisoners; another one, Birkenau, which could house up to 100,000 prisoners, held the Final Solution gas chambers and used Zyklon-B gas as the method of mass extermination; and the last one maintained crematoria capable of simultaneously cremating 2,000 bodies.[21] There was no limit to the inhuman treatment at Auschwitz—even the medical staff, people trained and sworn to alleviate human suffering, administered their own version of cruelty against the Jews and other prisoners.

The infamous Dr. Joseph Mengele, also known as the "Angel of Death," was the chief medical officer at Auschwitz. Mengele, ambitious for notoriety in medicine, performed medical experiments on living Jews, "injecting them with phenol, petrol, chloroform or air, or [ordered] SS medical officers to do so."[22] Mengele was also interested in genetic experiments with twins, reportedly hoping to increase the German race. Gilbert reports that among some of Mengele's experiments were two twins who died as a result of an experimental operation, a Jewish women who was killed on his command so he could perform a comparative autopsy with her dead twin sister, and a triplet sibling on whom he performed a "postmortem" while the child was still alive.[23]

Gilbert notes that following his arrival at Auschwitz, Mengele took responsibility for the selection of which new arrivals or patients in the infirmary were sent to their immediate death in the gas chamber. Mengele managed to avoid capture after the war, fleeing first to Argentina and then to Paraguay in 1960, when Israeli agents were closing in. Mengele's remains, removed from a grave in Brazil, were positively identified in 1985.[24]

Auschwitz did eventually develop a rather extensive resistance movement. Reports of the genocide practiced in Birkenau did not reach the rest of the world until 1944, when three Jewish prisoners managed to reach Slovakia. A major escape was attempted, but all 250 escapees were eventually shot and another 200 were killed as accomplices.[25] As the Soviet Army was closing in on the camp, SS soldiers started dismantling the camp, and on 18 January orders were given to evacuate the remaining prisoners into Germany. As described in *Night*, this evacuation was mostly done on foot, and many prisoners were too weak to survive. The death march from Auschwitz proved to be a nightmarish trip, as the SS shot tens of thousands of Jews along the way. Although a few Jews managed to escape and find hiding places until they were rescued by the advancing Soviet Army, for most people the march became an agonizing dance with death.

Despite the harsh treatment by the SS, there were some Germans who did help some Jews escape death. Oskar Schindler is reported to have saved over 1,500 Jews by having them work in his factory. Steven Spielberg made a movie, *Schindler's List*, about his efforts to save Jews, and it won the Academy Award for Best Picture in 1994.

THE FINAL SOLUTION

Like a rage that ran through Nazi Germany and occupied Europe, the Final Solution attempted to annihilate the Jewish people. This Nazi process followed several stages. In their concerted effort to make whole areas of Germany "Jew-free," the Nazis at first tried to expel the Jews from their homes and villages. Emigration was the next step in the process. Forced to sell their property for whatever they could get, more than half of the 1933 German Jewish population, 500,000 people, had emigrated by 1938. Emigration was further complicated by the fact that other countries wanted proof that those wishing to emigrate could support themselves. And more often than not, there were strict limitations on the foreign exchange of money. What was exchanged was done so at exorbitant rates.[26] By the time even the wealthiest Jew had emigrated, not much of their estate was left.

Despite the unfair hardships being placed on them, the rest of the world's acceptance of German Jews was less than enthusiastic. During the 1930s the whole world was in an economic slump, and no one seemed very willing to increase the number of people in their labor markets. Those that were accepted usually were farmers and miners; the German Jewish professional class was not particularly welcomed at all. Anti-Semitism played a large part in the limits of Jewish immigration as well; this attitude has never been an exclusively German phenomenon. The Jewish people really had no place to go.

In 1938 the condition of the German Jews reached a crisis point. As the Nazis moved toward war with their European neighbors, their policies toward the Jews grew more radical. Concerned about the problem, President Roosevelt organized an international conference, but the conference ended up "largely stating what they could *not* do.''[27] After the Kristallnacht brutality, which made it abundantly clear that the Nazis' actions against the Jews would continue to become increasingly extreme and violent, emigration exploded and the Jews went to any place they could find: Palestine, Britain, the Americas, even Shanghai.

Interestingly, in the 1930s the idea to mass murder the Jews was an option that seemingly had not been widely discussed. Yet experts note that when the killings did take place in the 1930s, they were mostly isolated within the concentration system; no fewer than 100 Jews were killed then among the several thousands of other political prisoners murdered at places such as Sachsenhausen, Buchenwald, and Dachau.[28] When Germany annexed Austria in March 1938, and Bohemia and Moravia in March 1939, murder as a policy for resolving the Jewish Question still did not exist— even though the number of Jews under Nazi control increased by another 250,000.[29] In pre-war Germany emigration remained the primary policy, but only if other nations would continue to take in the migrating Jews. Another problem for the Jewish people leaving the Nazi menace was that Germany was seemingly gaining territory as rapidly as people could flee.

As Germany's conquest of Europe developed, the murder of Jews in the expanding concentration camp system multiplied. Experts observe that when the Germans were planning for the invasion of the Soviet Union, they realized they would have to do something with the 5 million Jews in that territory. The brutal treatment of the Jews by Nazis also had not been protested by the United States or the Vatican, so there was no reason to suspect any reaction if the brutality were to intensify.[30] Some experts argue that until early 1941 the Nazis, with the possible exception of Hitler, had not given the murdering of all Jews a prominent place on their agenda. The rapid conquest of eastern Europe and Russia not only made it possible to destroy a huge portion of European Jewry, but the successful invasion made it a necessity, according to the deranged mentality of Hitler and his henchmen.[31]

Because SS documentation was destroyed, there is no written order in the archives to be found specifically directing the annihilation of the Jewish people. Bauer notes that Hitler probably gave the order to destroy European Jewry to Himmler sometime between October 1940 and May 1941. The order to destroy the Jewish people, as well as all Soviet officials and all communists, was then passed down to the Einsatzgruppen (Action Groups) commander, Otto Ohlendorf.[32] Thus began mass murder of historical proportions. Kiev, where 33,000 victims died, is the best-known site of Jewish massacre in the former USSR. By the end of 1942, fully 1.4 million Jews had been murdered in the USSR.[33]

In *Ordinary Men: Reserve Police Battalion 101 and the Final Solution in Poland*, Christopher Browning writes:

> In mid-March 1942 some 75 to 80 percent of all victims of the Holocaust were still alive, while 20 to 25 percent had perished. A mere eleven months later, in mid-February 1943, the percentages were exactly the reverse. At the core of the Holocaust was a short, intense wave of mass murder. The center of gravity of this mass murder was Poland, where in March 1942, despite two and half years of terrible hardship, deprivation, and persecution, every major Jewish community was still intact, and where eleven months later only the remnants of Polish Jewry survived in a few rump [remnant] ghettoes and labor camps. In short, the German attack on the Jews of Poland was not a gradual or incremental program stretched over a long period of time, but a veritable blitzkrieg, a massive offensive requiring the mobilization of large numbers of shock troops.[34]

The Einsatzgruppen was given the primary responsibility to round up and murder the Jews in occupied territory:

> In preparation for the invasion of Russia and the "war of destruction" Hitler intended to wage there, four special mobile units of the SS known as Einsatzgruppen were formed and trained in the late spring of 1941. The core of these units came from Heydrich's Security Police (Gestapo and Kripo) as well as his intelligence apparatus (Security Service, or SD). They were supplemented by small units of Waffen-SS (the military branch of Himmler's SS). In addition, however, the three companies of Order Police Battalion 9 were distributed to three of the four Einsatzgruppen.[35]

The Order Police was a military formation used to maintain order behind the front lines; they were primarily an occupying force. Bauer observes that of the first four Einsatzgruppen commanders, three had Ph.D.s, including Ohlendorf. In addition, quite a few of the subordinate officers were university educated and one was a pastor. Only 12.5 percent of the total men were Nazis; 87.5 percent remaining were just "ordinary men."[36]

On 20 January 1942 the Nazi leadership held the Wannsee Conference near Berlin. At this conference the Nazis discussed strategies for the complete annihilation of the 11 million Jews in Europe. Although specific methods were not debated, it was determined that the same procedures they had already used to kill the 1.4 million Jews would be inadequate to kill the remainder. The primary importance of this conference is that it marked the time when the German bureaucracy focused on the extermination of the Jews. On 8 December 1941, the same day that the first death camp was established at Lodz in Poland, poisonous gas was first used to kill Jews in Chelmo, Poland, five weeks before the conference.[37] Death camps would soon dot the countryside throughout occupied Europe, killing as many Jews as quickly as the death machinery could manage it. The Germans maintained these death camps right up to the very last days of the war.

AFTERMATH

The Jews, who had suffered so greatly during the war, did not find the world particularly sympathetic immediately after Germany's surrender either. Of the 200,000 Jews who had managed to survive in the Nazi concentration camps, most tried to go back to their home country; but 65,000 Jews from Poland and Lithuania could not do so because they were not welcome anymore.[38] The newly formed Jewish Brigade, a group of Palestinian Jews who had served in the British Army, began searching Germany and Austria for surviving Jews to be smuggled across the Italian border for eventual emigration to Palestine. It took groups like the Jewish Brigade to help their own people because the Jewish displaced (DPs) were not getting adequate assistance from the Allies until President Truman stepped in. The basic issue of contention was that the Allies wanted the Jewish DPs to return to their home of origin, but the Jews who were still residing in refugee camps did not. They wanted to go to Palestine to form their own nation. Thus, the most important consequence of the Holocaust was the establishment of the Jewish State of Israel on 14 May 1948. However, Bauer argues that Israel did not necessarily originate as a direct consequence of the Holocaust; it might have been established earlier had the Holocaust never occurred. He does allow that the pressing number of Jewish DPs residing in camps accelerated the State of Israel's establishment.

Freed from Nazi terror, the Jews who survived the war were not freed from the psychic and emotional scars of the Holocaust. Out of this experience the Jewish people have developed a universal mentality of never letting it happen again. Bauer observes that remembering the Holocaust has become a dominant feature of Jewish identity everywhere.[39] The issue of the Holocaust, the recognition that humanity is not only capable of enormous inhumanity but that modern technologies and bureaucracies have made it even more convenient to do unimaginable harm to innocent people, is a touchstone for Jews and non-Jews alike. Knowing that atrocity in the modern age can explode at a moment's notice, we have to be on guard at all times.

NOTES

1. Martin Gilbert, *The Holocaust: A History of the Jews of Europe during the Second World War* (New York: Henry Holt, 1985), 66.

2. Yehuda Bauer, *A History of the Holocaust* (New York: Franklin Watts, 1982), 108.

3. Gilbert, *Holocaust*, 68.

4. Bauer, *History*, 108.

5. Ibid.

6. Gilbert, *Holocaust*, 24.

7. Ibid., 69–70.

8. Bauer, *History*, 108.

9. Gilbert, *Holocaust*, 73.

10. Bauer, *History*, 108–109.

11. Gilbert, *Holocaust*, 73.

12. Bauer, *History*, 109.

13. I. C. B. Dear and M. R. D. Foot, *The Oxford Companion to World War II* (New York: Oxford University Press, 1995), 260.

14. Gilbert, *Holocaust*, 32–33.

15. Ibid.

16. Dear and Foot, *Oxford Companion*, 260.

17. Ibid.

18. Ibid.

19. David A. Hackett, trans., *Buchenwald Report* (Boulder, CO: Westview Press, 1995), 1.

20. Gilbert, *Holocaust*, 121.

21. Dear and Foot, *Oxford Companion*, 78.

22. Gilbert, *Holocaust*, 582.

23. Ibid., 688.

24. Dear and Foot, *Oxford Companion*, 738.

25. Ibid., 78.

26. Bauer, *History*, 124.

27. Ibid., 129.

28. Dear and Foot, *Oxford Companion*, 364.

29. Ibid.

30. Bauer, *History*, 193.

31. Ibid., 194.

32. Ibid.

33. Ibid., 199.

34. Christopher R. Browning, *Ordinary Men: Reserve Police Battalion 101 and the Final Solution in Poland* (New York: HarperPerennial, 1992), xv.

35. Ibid., 9.

36. Bauer, *History*, 195.

37. Ibid., 209.

38. Ibid., 338.

39. Ibid., 348.

A HISTORICAL CASE STUDY:
THE DESTRUCTION OF THE LITHUANIAN
JEWS AT KOVNO AND VILNA

The invading Wehrmacht captured Kovno, the pre-war capital of Lithuania, on 22 June 1941. On the day before taking the city, the Soviets evacuated it, leaving it in chaos in the hands of Lithuanian nationalists. For the next several days the Jews in that community suffered greatly. And when the Germans entered the city, they intensified the atrocities; the murdering reached a peak on the night of 25 June when whole Jewish families were slaughtered in house-to-house searches.

During the first week of occupation, 6,000–7,000 Jews were murdered and buried in mass graves. Although the Nazi security police were manipulating the situation, it was the Lithuanian extremists, not the Germans themselves, who were actually committing the murders.[1]

The Germans formed a ghetto for the surviving Jews on 15 August, and Dr. Elhanan Elkes, a Zionist (a Jewish nationalist) and prominent physician, became the reluctant Judenrat (the Jewish Council responsible for executing Nazi orders) leader of the Jewish people. On 27 October an assembly of Jews was formed in the ghetto, and the next morning most were marched to huge pits, shot, and covered with lime and dirt. In November of that same year, thousands of Jews who had been deported from Germany to Kovno were ordered to undress and then were shot, buried in more mass graves. After this incident, mass murder recessed in Kovno for two and a half years.[2]

In a 1 December 1941 report about the status of occupied territories, SS colonel Karl Jaeger, chief of Einsatzkommando 3, noted that only 15,000 Jews remained in Kovno and Vilna. Jaeger went on to state that he was proud that his troops were solving the Jewish problem; his only difficulty in carrying out more deaths was the harsh winter climate: the ground was too frozen to dig sufficient graves.[3] The destruction and deportation of the Jews in Kovno continued throughout the remainder of the war. By 12 July 1944, right before the Soviets liberated the town, most of the remaining 8,000 Jews were deported to gas chambers; those who were left behind were killed in Kovno. The ghetto was then burned to the ground, and the Jewish community in Kovno ceased to exist.

The Germans captured Vilna, the pre-war "Jerusalem of Lithuania," on 22 June and quickly established two ghettos—a small one for "unproductive" Jews and another one for workers and their families.[4] A member of the right-wing Zionist Revisionist Party, Jacob Gens, was selected as chief of police. Although he was Jewish, Gens' wife was Lithuanian and lived in the non-Jewish section of town. Throughout his tenure Gens was forced to sacrifice countless Jews in order to save other Jews. In the fall of 1942, for example, Gens agreed that all the old people in the ghetto should be given up to save the younger ones. Gilbert reports that Gens later justified his actions to fellow members of the Judenrat council, saying it was a disturbing secret that everyone must learn to keep.[5] With such a man being able to make sacrifices of his own people, it is no wonder Vilna was such a difficult place for Jews during this nightmarish regime.

In the end, nothing could stop the Nazis from not only destroying the entire community but killing Gens as well. The Germans began deportations from Vilna to Estonian labor camps on 1 September 1943, and on 6 September Gens tried to maintain control of the ghetto by requesting that the remaining 10,000 Jews register with the Judenrat council.[6] While many fled for the forest to resist, those who remained in the ghetto grew even more desperate as the end drew near. On 14 September 1943, Gens was summoned to the local Gestapo headquarters and shot to death.[7] The Nazis subsequently annihilated what remained of the ghetto nine days later: 1,600 men were deported to Estonian camps, and 5,000 women and children were sent to the gas chambers at Ponar. By the end of September, only 2,000 Jews remained in Vilna, the dwindling survivors of the original 57,000 Jews who had once lived in this flourishing Jewish community.[8] The advancing Soviet Army liberated the very last remaining Jews of Vilna, only 200 of them, on 13 July 1944. The battle for Vilna lasted for five days, and 8,000 German soldiers were killed.[9]

Despite their eventual elimination, the Jews in Vilna did mount a resistance movement. Led by Yitzhak Wittenberg, this resistance cell managed to smuggle a large landmine out of town on 8 July 1943, blowing up a military train the next day. A member of the group was captured within a week, and after being severely tortured he identified Wittenberg as the leader of Vilna's resistance. At a "secret" meeting with Gens, the Lithuanian police captured Wittenberg; but when fellow Jews attacked, Wittenberg managed to escape. Gens then warned the entire ghetto that Wittenberg must be turned in or the Germans would destroy the whole community. Panic and chaos ensued until Wittenberg turned himself in to the Gestapo. It was reported that Wittenberg managed to commit suicide before the Germans could inflict punishment on him.[10]

Although there had been brief moments of good times for the Jews in Lithuanian history, they had seemingly always been at the mercy of forces beyond their control. During World War I the Russian Tsarist government had expelled 120,000 Jews from Lithuania. After the war a democratic Lithuania allowed Jewish culture to flourish for a while; there were five Jewish daily newspapers in the early 1930s. However, a more repressive, pro-Nazi nationalist government came into power soon after Hitler took control of Germany, and anti-Semitism quickly intensified. When the German Army rolled through on its way to its own desperate destiny at Moscow and Stalingrad, the Jewish community in this part of the world disappeared. Only a mere handful of Jews live in Lithuania today.

Dr. Paul Frank was a visiting professor from 1997 to 1999 at the United States Air Force Academy, teaching in the English Department. His home is in Albuquerque, New Mexico, where he is on the faculty of Southwestern Indian Polytechnical Institute. He is writing a book about his father's family in Lithuania.

AN INTERVIEW WITH PAUL FRANK: A SECOND-GENERATION
LITHUANIAN
(James Meredith conducted this interview with Dr. Frank on 27 and
29 January 1998 in Colorado Springs, Colorado.)

INTERVIEWER: How did you get interested in circumstances of the Jewish people in Lithuania?

FRANK: Although I'm originally from Los Angeles, my father migrated to this country from Lithuania when he was 18 years old. And before he died, I got him to record his life's story on tapes that I now have. I'm using these tapes to write my book. You wouldn't believe some of the experiences my father and his family had to go through. He left before World War II, but life in his community during World War I was bad enough. The Germans blew up my father's hometown of Druskininkai, right before his eyes. Druskininkai, which is near Vilna and Kovno, it was shelled in September 1915 and put under siege for such a long time. My father's family had to relocate to Vilna. Vilna, now the capital of Lithuania, at that time had a tremendously large Jewish population. It was known as the "Jerusalem of Europe." They had some of the most learned Hebrew scholars, a large center for rabbinical training. It was a real center for Judaism. I think that at the outbreak of World War II, half the population of Vilna was Jewish. My father told me that he knew the meaning of hunger from those years. He had practically nothing to eat for so long, he almost starved; in fact, he went blind temporarily from malnutrition. But I think that the depravations he experienced then toughened him for the rest of his life. He was 93 years old when he died. My aunt, who migrated to this country on the same boat as my father, lived almost to be 100 years old as well. She was about seven years older than my father was. Although my father had eight other siblings, including another sister who lived in the United States, he was extremely close to his sister Sarah. They did everything together from the day he was born until the day he died. I think it was the shared suffering during World War I that made them so close. They died within a few months of each other. They knew hardship. These are some of the experiences I'm writing about in the book. When it is finished, you can read more about it all then.

INTERVIEWER: What do you know about your extended family who remained in Lithuania after your father migrated to the United States?

FRANK: To be honest, not much because so many of them and their history completely disappeared during the Holocaust. My father had left Lithuania in 1922, long before World War II broke out, and my mother was born and raised in New York City. They did not personally experience the Holocaust, except what little they knew about my father's family in Lithuania, mostly from letters until they stopped coming. It is unbelievable that so many people, so many families, could disappear completely without a trace in such a short amount of time.

As I said, my family was from Druskininkai on the Nemanus River. All that I have left is this picture of my extended family from Lithuania. It was taken in June 1936. There are 16 people in that picture—only one, Pnina (Romanoff) Igra, of them survived the slaughter that was to come; she had escaped the Holocaust because she had migrated to Palestine with a pioneer group. She's still living. She resides in Quebec, Canada. In this photo, there are three different families represented. My father's sister Frieda—she was the eldest sister of the nine children—married a Romanoff and she is there with all her children and her grandchild. Notice how many Romanoffs were listed here. My father's sister Bashah Leah married a Kagan, and she is there with her family. My grandmother, who died not long after this photo was taken, was named Debrushka. This would be the family that would greet me when I visit Lithuania now, but they are all gone. You can imagine what it was like growing up seeing this picture, knowing what had happened to them. I traveled to Lithuania last summer to see what I could discover about my family, and what I did find was that there's not much left. Before World War II, there were 105 Jewish synagogues in Vilna; today there is one that is left standing, and the only reason it remained, I heard, was that it was used as a stable by the Nazis. The rest were obliterated. One out of 105!

INTERVIEWER: How much work have you done on reconstructing what happened to your family in Lithuania?

FRANK: I don't think that I've done very much, but there's not enough left to do very much with. To give you an example, when I was in Lithuania, I took a bus from Vilna down to Druskininkai, which is really a nice resort town. It was completely destroyed both during World War I and World War II, but now it is a rather new, clean town. It is well known for its mineral baths. There doesn't seem to be a trace of what life was like in that town during the early twentieth century. I went to Druskininkai specifically to see a Jewish museum that I saw listed in the tourist guide that I had. Well, when I went to this museum, it was closed, so I kept coming back to it, and it was still closed. Later, after returning to Vilna, I had some local people that I knew call them to set up an appointment when I could get there and visit the place. I finally got in only to find there was nothing there. Not even one picture. I think most of the records were completely destroyed. It is amazing!

Let me give you another example. Before his family moved to Druskininkai, my father was actually born in a very little village about two miles southeast of town, right on the Lithuanian/Belarusan border. Fortunately, it was just inside the Lithuanian border because if it were in Belarus I couldn't go there without a visa, and they are hard to get for an American tourist. So I visited this little village when I was over there, and I mean it really looked like an old, turn-of-the-century farming village. I walked around it a little bit, but there was no way for me to communicate with the people there. Except that someone mentioned that there was an old Jewish cemetery there in town. They said that it was the only Jewish cemetery for many miles around. I went there, and it was really strange, overgrown. The tombstones were scattered; they weren't really tombstones. They were irregular, pointed, jagged rocks. Not like we see in this country at all. The graves weren't in rows or anything. They had some

Hebrew writing on them, but I couldn't read it. I'm a totally assimilated American boy. I can't read or understand much Hebrew. A lot of the writing was faded anyway.

INTERVIEWER: You don't have any idea how old this cemetery was, do you?

FRANK: It was an old cemetery. I'm pretty sure that my grandparents were buried there. They both died before the Holocaust. So they never left the hometown there, and since that was the only Jewish cemetery for miles, they had to be buried there. I felt that I was close to their grave. Exactly which one of those irregular stones marked their grave, I had no idea. There were a couple hundred graves there. This cemetery had no building connected to it; it was just an opening in the woods. Stones marked the border of the cemetery.

INTERVIEWER: Was there a Jewish community around there?

FRANK: No, not there, but in Vilna—a small Jewish community was starting back there. On my first day in Vilna, I was standing on the street, looking confused with my guidebook in my hand. I see coming toward me two young Orthodox Jewish men. I saw them coming, and I thought about starting a conversation with them, but I didn't think we could understand each other. All of a sudden, one of them spoke to me, "What are you doing here, looking confused?" He spoke in perfect English. I answered, "Are you talking to me?" And he said, "Yes, you." He told me that I was obviously an American Jewish tourist, trying to trace his family's roots. It turns out that he was the local rabbi who was born and raised in Boston. He was trying to re-establish a Jewish community in Vilna. There were now only 6,000 Jews in Vilna.

On the outskirts of town, there are a few sights marking the mass graves of the Jews who were murdered in Vilna. They have a few monuments commemorating the slaughtered. Shrines. I didn't spend a lot of time there because I really didn't feel the need to visit these mass graves. It is too much for me.

INTERVIEWER: Thank you for sharing your family's history with me. I truly appreciate the time we've spent talking about you and your family. Good luck with your book. I look forward to reading it soon.

FRANK: You're welcome.

NOTES

1. Yehuda Bauer, *A History of the Holocaust* (New York: Franklin Watts, 1982), 183–184.
2. Ibid., 185.

3. Martin Gilbert, *The Holocaust* (New York: Henry Holt, 1985), 235.
4. Bauer, *History*, 160.
5. Gilbert, *Holocaust*, 483.
6. Ibid., 606–607.
7. Ibid., 608.
8. Ibid.
9. Ibid., 699.
10. Ibid., 593.

VOICES OF THE HOLOCAUST

Viktor E. Frankl, in *Man's Search for Meaning*, writes about his own experiences in the Nazi concentration camps. The following selection underscores the feeling of utter helplessness that he experienced.

FROM VIKTOR E. FRANKL, *MAN'S SEARCH FOR MEANING*
(New York: Touchstone, 1959)

The thought of suicide was entertained by nearly everyone, if only for a brief time. It was born of the hopelessness of the situation, the constant danger of death looming over us daily and hourly, and the closeness of the deaths suffered by many of the others. From personal convictions . . . I made myself a firm promise, on my first evening in camp, that I would not "run into the wire." This was a phrase used in camp to describe the most popular method of suicide—touching the electrically charged barbed-wire fence. It was not entirely difficult for me to make this decision. There was little point in committing suicide, since, for the average inmate, life expectation, calculating objectively and counting all likely chances, was very poor. He could not with any assurance expect to be among the small percentage of men who survived all the selections. The prisoner of Auschwitz, in the first phase of shock, did not fear death. Even the gas chambers lost their horrors for him after the first few days—after all, they spared him the act of committing suicide. (31)

The French writer Charlotte Delbo, a non-Jewish survivor of Auschwitz, wrote about her experiences in *Auschwitz and After*. In one chapter of her book, she describes the almost unimaginable pain of her thirst.

FROM CHARLOTTE DELBO, *AUSCHWITZ AND AFTER*
(New Haven: Yale University Press, 1995)

I'd been thirsty for days and days, thirsty to the point of losing my mind, to the point of being unable to eat since there was no saliva in my mouth, so thirsty I couldn't speak, because you're unable to speak when there's no saliva in your month. My parched lips were splitting, my gums swollen, my tongue a piece of wood. My swollen gums and tongue kept me from closing my mouth, which stayed open like that of a madwoman with dilated pupils in her haggard eyes. At least, this is what others told me, later. They thought I'd lost my mind. I couldn't hear anything, see anything. They even thought that I had gone blind. It took me a long time to explain that, without being blind, I saw nothing. All my senses had been abolished by thirst. (142)

Living in a culture that takes plentiful drinking water for granted, it is hard to image such a deplorable human condition: being so thirsty that you become absolutely senseless.

Born in France about ten years before the war, André Schwarz-Bart lost his entire family in the concentration camps. While serving in the French resistance during the war, he was imprisoned but eventually escaped. Schwarz-Bart's novel, *The Last of the Just*, won the Prix Goncourt. In the following excerpt the protagonist, Ernie Levy, and Golda, the woman he loves, are about to be gassed to death in an SS concentration camp.

FROM ANDRÉ SCHWARZ-BART, *THE LAST OF THE JUST*
(New York: MJF Books, 1960)

The building resembled a huge bathhouse. To left and right large concrete pots cupped the stems of faded flowers. At the foot of the small wooden stairway an SS man, mustached and benevolent, told the condemned, "Nothing painful will happen! It's a way to prevent contagious diseases. It disinfects." Most of them went in silently, pressed forward by those behind. Inside, numbered coathooks garnished the walls of a sort of gigantic cloakroom where the flock undressed one way or another, encouraged by their SS cicerones, who advised them to remember the numbers carefully. . . . There, under the showerheads embedded in the ceiling, in the blue light of screened bulbs glowing in recesses of the concrete walls, Jewish men and women, children and patriarchs were huddled together. . . . When the first waves of [Z]yclon B gas billowed among the sweating bodies, drifting down toward the squirming carpet of children's heads, Ernie freed himself from the girl's mute embrace and leaned out into the darkness toward the children invisible even at his knees, and he shouted with all the gentleness and all the strength of his soul, "Breathe deeply, my lambs, and quickly!"

When the layers of gas had covered everything, there was silence in the dark sky of the room for perhaps a minute, broken only by shrill, racking coughs and the gasps of those too far gone in their agonies to offer a devotion.

• • •

The voices died one by one in the course of the unfinished poem. The dying children had already dug their nails into Ernie's thighs, and Golda's embrace was already weaker, her kisses were blurred when, clinging fiercely to her beloved's neck, she exhaled a harsh sigh: "Then I'll never see you again? Never again?" (372–373)

TOPICS FOR WRITTEN AND ORAL DISCUSSION

1. The Holocaust, like any atrocity in history, is a very difficult topic to write about. Attempts at describing such utter horror can sound trite or hollow. Contact a survivor of the Holocaust or a member of the family of a survivor, interview this person, and write an essay about his or her experience. After you have written the essay, analyze it, paying close attention to the words you use to convey the survivor's experience. Are these words that you would use in ordinary conversation or not?

2. Research the Allies' treatment of the Jewish refugees after the war. Was it humane, or did the Allies themselves also treat the Jewish people inhumanely? Debate the issue in class.

3. Research the founding of the Jewish State of Israel and the situation in the Middle East today. Pay close attention to how the Holocaust has impacted that region of the world.

4. Contact a local chapter of any Jewish organization concerned with preventing anti-Semitism. Find out how prevalent anti-Semitism is in the community where you live, as well as in the state, the nation, and the world. Develop a detailed plan for how you and your school can help prevent anti-Semitism.

5. Ignorance is often the essential ingredient in misunderstandings between people. Visit the services of religious groups and denominations other than the one you practice. Describe some of the differences and similarities among the various faiths. Interview a religious leader in one or more of these communities. Ask questions about the history and practices of their religion, especially about things you do not understand. Write an essay about some of the differences and similarities between the religion that you have either practiced or are familiar with, and the one that you researched.

SUGGESTIONS FOR FURTHER READING

Bauer, Yehuda. *A History of the Holocaust*. New York: Franklin Watts, 1982.

Brown, Robert McAfee. *Elie Wiesel: Messenger to All Humanity*. Notre Dame, IN: University of Notre Dame, 1989.

Estess, Ted L. *Elie Wiesel*. New York: Frederick Ungar, 1980.

Frankl, Viktor E. *Man's Search for Meaning: An Introduction to Logotherapy*. New York: Touchstone, (1959) 1984.

Friedman, Ada June. *Philip Freedman, Roads to Extinction: Essays on the Holocaust*. New York: Jewish Publication Society of America, 1980.

Fuch, Elinor, ed. *Plays of the Holocaust*. New York: Theatre Communications Group, 1987.

Gilbert, Martin. *The Holocaust: A History of the Jews of Europe during the Second World War*. New York: Henry Holt, 1985.

Morgan, Ted. *An Uncertain Hour: The French, the Germans, the Jews, the Barbie Trial and the City of Lyon, 1940–1945*. New York: William Morrow, 1990.

Niewyk, Donald L., ed. *The Holocaust: Problems and Perspectives of Interpretation*. Boston: Houghton Mifflin, 1997.

Ross, Daniel W., ed. *The Critical Response of William Styron*. Westport, CT: Greenwood Press, 1995.

Roth, John K. *A Consuming Fire: Encounters with Elie Wiesel and the Holocaust*. Atlanta: John Knox Press, 1979.

Ruderman, Judith. *William Styron*. New York: Ungar, 1987.

5

The Atomic Bomb

An Analysis of John Hersey's *Hiroshima*

LITERARY ANALYSIS

John Hersey's book is about Hiroshima, the city that suffered utter devastation from the first atomic bomb to be exploded in anger. Although the book originally provided the world with the first important details of the bomb's destruction, it exists today more as a work of epic literature than straight journalism. Because of its elegantly spare, dispassionate prose, it has transcended the ordinary confines of mere journalism; having lost its immediacy, the book is now a work of art for all time.

First published in the 31 August 1946 edition of the *New Yorker* magazine, it has sold over 6 million copies in book form and now includes an afterword, appropriately entitled "The Aftermath," which doubles the original size of the work. Roger Angell, in a fiftieth anniversary commemorative edition of the *New Yorker*, writes:

> "Hiroshima" is a short piece, given its concerns, and was read everywhere, one may assume, at a single sitting. Its thirty thousand words suffice because they abstain from the smallest judgment or moral positioning, and leave the reader to deal with the consequences and the questions. Nothing in the work has been dramatized, but many

individual scenes begin with a simple few words—"Early that day," "It began to rain," "Some time later"—that sound like stage directions. Indeed, the meticulous, restrained flow of the words, the slow conversations of his handful of characters, and flattened, burned out scenery of the destroyed city contrive to shift the piece from contemporary war reporting to what feels like ancient tragedy.[1]

John Hersey first saw the destruction of Hiroshima in April 1946, about seven months after the bomb exploded.[2] Although he had already witnessed a great deal of the war as a correspondent for *Time*, nothing prepared him for what he encountered. Like an epic visit to the underworld, it overwhelmed him.

Hersey's account, his "story," concentrates on the plight of six survivors—people who are going about their everyday wartime lives until they experience one of the worst catastrophes in history. Although they never fully understand why they did not meet the same fate that so many others did, these individuals miraculously survive the immediate explosion. This story is not so much about why they survive as it is about how the human spirit can survive in a world of unimaginable horrors.

The theme of this book is survival—but not survival of the fittest, a theme the fascists used in their attempt to conquer the world. The survivors in this book are not the elite members of a master race; they are the meek, humble people of ordinary life. It is not surprising that two of them are religious people, two are women, and two are doctors. (Only one of them, Dr. Fujii, demonstrates more concern for himself than he does for others.) The fact that Hersey carefully chooses people who have not been essential parts of the Japanese war machine (in fact, most of them are caregivers of some sort) disassociates them from the evils of the Japanese military establishment—the inscrutable kamikaze pilots or the brutal samurais. Their ordinariness makes them more like us, the readers. Hersey consciously uses this strategy in his narrative, since V-J Day had occurred only a year and sixteen days prior to its initial publication. Even today, more than fifty years after the conflict, residual rancor seems to exist over the Japanese conduct in World War II.

The story begins seconds after the initial explosion, in a chapter Hersey entitles "A Noiseless Flash." Immediately after the bomb goes off, the reader is introduced to the cast of characters: Miss Sasaki, who works in personnel at the East Asia Tin Works; Dr.

Fujii, a physician who operates a private hospital; Mrs. Nakamura, a poor tailor's widow; Dr. Sasaki, another physician, who practices surgery at the Red Cross Hospital; Reverend Mr. Tanimoto, a Protestant minister; and Father Kleinsorge, a Jesuit priest. Hersey writes that these people still wonder

> why they lived when so many others died. Each of them counts many small items of chance or volition—a step taken in time, a decision to go indoors, catching one streetcar instead of the next— that spared him. And now each knows that in the act of survival he lived a dozen lives and saw more death than he ever thought he would see.[3]

Although the details fail to reveal the secrets of their survival, their experience not only makes compelling reading but offers insight into a suffering that no person should ever have to endure. When Mr. Tanimoto sees the blinding flash of light, he is about two miles from the hypocenter; having a little time to react, he dives between two rocks. Like almost every other survivor of the Hiroshima bomb, he does not recall hearing an explosion. Interestingly, people miles from the city did hear the explosion, reporting that the noise sounded much louder than the sound of conventional weapons even when they exploded much nearer by (6). Mrs. Nakamura, who has already lost a husband in the war, is looking out of her kitchen window when the bomb explodes. Her house is about three-quarters of a mile from the hypocenter. Her first reaction is to run toward her children when she is tossed about in the rubble of what was once her house. Dr. Fujii, who is the wealthiest of this group, is lazily lounging in his nearly empty hospital when he sees the flash. The next thing he knows he is in a nearby river along with the ruins of his practice, injured but amazed that he has survived. Father Kleinsorge, weakened from "a rather painful and urgent diarrhea" (11), having already finished saying early-morning Mass, is reading *Stimmen der Zeit* in his underwear when the bomb explodes; not knowing how he got out of the house, he ends up in the garden. He is only about 1,400 yards from the hypocenter when the bomb explodes. Dr. Sasaki has just stepped past an open window at the hospital where he works when he sees the flash; he falls to one knee and miraculously is left untouched by the blast, the only doctor left unhurt in the whole hospital. Hersey later reports that of the 150 doctors in Hiroshima, 65 are already dead; of the 1,780 nurses, 1,654 are either dead or too injured to assist the wounded (24). Finally, Miss Sasaki (who is not related to the doctor with the same name) is working at her job (which was 1,600 yards from the center) when the blast occurs; she is completely buried by piles of books and rubble, "her left leg horribly twisted and breaking underneath her" (16).

The next chapter, "The Fire," forms an interesting irony. Having survived the explosion of the atomic bomb, the product of the most sophisticated scientific process in history, the characters must struggle against one of the oldest and most basic human discoveries—fire. Hersey notes that "except at the very center, where the bomb itself ignited some fires, most of Hiroshima's citywide conflagration was caused by inflammable wreckage falling on cook stoves and live wires" (20). Like many other survivors, after rescuing her three children from the wreckage of her house Mrs. Nakamura heads toward Asano Park, an estate owned by the wealthy Asano family, proprietors of the successful Kisen Kaisha steamship line, near the Kyo River. Asano Park had previously been designated as a refuge in case of an air attack. On her way to the park, fleeing the growing fire, Mrs. Nakamura sees Father Kleinsorge, who is still wandering around the garden in his underwear, dazed. The bath house next to Father Kleinsorge's mission home is aflame, so after regaining his senses somewhat, although his clothes are nowhere to be found, he manages to salvage a papier-mâché suitcase containing the mission's money. Meanwhile, fires encircle his neighborhood.

Also in his underclothing, Dr. Fujii wiggles himself free from the submerged debris of his hospital and discovers two fires: one across the river from his hospital, and another one far to the south. He then notices that a large number of people are hurrying about "in an endless parade of misery," and although they are coming from an area that is not on fire, they "exhibited terrible burns on their faces and arms" (21). As new fires begin to spread, Dr. Fujii witnesses more scenes of horror; he eventually returns to the river for refuge from the heat of the flames.

Hersey shapes his narrative to depict these survivors experiencing a real hell on earth. Dante's *Inferno*, the great early Italian Renaissance masterpiece, tells the story of a poet's journey through the fiery underworld; although the parallels between these two texts are understated, there is no question that they are linked in their description of a living hell. A significant difference between them, however, is that instead of just one epic hero as in Dante's work, there are at least six real ones in Hersey's. Through no fault of their own, these individuals have skipped purgatory and gone straight to the inferno.

A large crowd of survivors gathers in Asano Park, including Father Kleinsorge, Mr. Tanimoto, and Mrs. Nakamura. In the early afternoon a fire breaks out in the forested area of the park and is ultimately brought under control after two hours of intense struggle by the weary survivors. The heat from the fire intensifies the radiation burn wounds of the victims, adding to their already excruciating pain.

Compounding their pain and fear is an overflight of a weather or reconnaissance plane; even the severely burned crawl to the "safety" of the bushes. Then it begins to rain. Instead of seeing the rain as their salvation, these frightened people, afraid the planes are returning to destroy them again, think that the great explosion had come from Americans dropping and igniting gasoline. They prepare to meet their end. But instead of another blinding flash, the heavy rain brings a whirlwind that subsequently rips through the park, uprooting trees and blowing the survivors about. By now, one wonders what other horrors of epic proportions could beset these people.

During these events Mr. Tanimoto is ferrying the injured to the park from across the river and organizing relief for the wounded. He stays at the park, "ministering to the wounded" (60), until 11 August—five days after the bomb—when he returns to his parsonage to begin the process of not only restoring his own life but rebuilding the life of his community as well. As the survivors soon realize, because of the indifference of the Japanese government, the restoration of their immediate lives will largely be a personal challenge. The title of the third chapter, "Details Are Being Investigated," is taken from the official Japanese response to the bombing, which is broadcast over the radio. The use of the passive voice in this title underscores the impersonality of the government's response. Seemingly focused entirely on continuing the war, the government lacks the immediate resolve (or compassion) to help its own people. The survivors are left to fend for themselves.

By nighttime on the day of the explosion, 10,000 victims have found their way to the Red Cross Hospital where Dr. Sasaki "aimlessly" works on the wounded (46). The scene inside the hospital is horrific: debris and rubble are piled haphazardly; blood and vomit are everywhere. After having worked non-stop all day Dr. Sasaki lies down to rest, but the suffering victims find him and he has to get up again after only an hour respite to bind the wounds of his fellow citizens. While Dr. Sasaki is able to help the wounded, Dr. Fujii, "laying on the floor of his roofless house on the edge of town" (46), surveys the extent of his injuries: a fractured left clavicle, many abrasions and lacerations on his face and torso, other deeper cuts, serious contusions on his chest and trunk, and fractured ribs.

Despite what he may think about his injuries, Dr. Fujii is not the worst of the wounded among the group; for two days and nights Miss Sasaki is stuck in the ruins of her office, pinned under the rubble. Her broken leg is "discolored, swollen, and putrid," and she has been completely without food and water since the explosion (54). Some of her friends, thinking she has been killed, come to her office to recover her body. They discover her alive and take her to the military hospital on Ninoshima, where she finds out that although she does have a severely fractured leg, she does not have gangrene. Despite the severity of her injury, the doctors attempt to send her back to Hiroshima until they discover how high her temperature has climbed. In a situation of such destruction and misery, there seems to be very little room for sympathy.

Adding insult to injury, only five days after the great flash the civilian patients at the Ninoshima Hospital are evacuated to make space for military casualties. Eventually Miss Sasaki finds some help in a makeshift hospital organized in the appropriately named Goddess of Mercy Primary School. The next day Mrs. Nakamura discovers that her mother, brother, and older sister are all dead. As distressing as this news is for Mrs. Nakamura, it represents a turning point in her life and a turning point in the book as well. Her discovery marks the beginning of the immediate aftermath and the partial restoration of order in the survivors' lives. As in any catastrophe, when the worst news has been heard, the victims at least know what they have to deal with. Throughout the book to this point, the worst news has had very little to do with material possessions (except in Dr. Fujii's case), but what has mattered most for these people is the fate of their loved ones. Now Mrs. Naka-mura can give up hoping for the best and learn to live with the worst; her bad news reminds readers that these people are alone in the world.

Although the Red Cross Hospital's resources are completely taxed—patients are resting on the floor, in stairwells, or on any other space left open, while the cremated remains of the dead, stuffed in makeshift envelopes ordinarily used to store x-rays, pile up around the hospital's shrine—the absolute worst also appears there as well. On 15 August, order is given the ultimate chance to succeed when Emperor Hirohito himself broadcasts, in a "dull, dispirited voice," the announcement that Japan, defeated both on the battlefield and now at home, has surrendered (64).

Until this point, the main theme of the book has been survival. The fourth chapter, which was originally the final one, concerns recovery, healing, and starting life anew—although the road to full recovery is a winding one. Underscoring the metaphor of the wind-ing road to recovery, the chapter begins with Father Kleinsorge, who has found temporary refuge in a novitiate outside of Hiro-shima, walking back to the destroyed city with the papier-mâché suitcase he had salvaged. It is 18 August, a mere twelve days since the explosion, and the Yokohama Specie Bank has already re-opened—a symbol that life is beginning again.

On the way to the bank he grows unusually tired and weak, displaying symptoms of the onset of what is now called radiation sickness. But he is not alone in this, as Mrs. Nakamura soon loses her hair and feels continually nauseated, and Mr. Tanimoto expe-riences a general malaise, weariness, and feverishness. Miss Sasaki, who is now under the care of Dr. Sasaki at the Red Cross Hospital, not only has a traumatic leg wound and associated problems but also experiences spot hemorrhages, symptomatic of many Hiro-shima survivors. Eventually Dr. Sasaki and his colleagues form a theory about this widespread disease, which comes from the body being bombarded by neutrons, beta particles, and gamma rays. This bombardment was so lethal that it immediately killed 95 per-cent of the people within a half-mile of the hypocenter (76). The others who initially survived the bombardment not only developed the discomforting symptoms already mentioned but acquired other serious blood disorders about thirty days later as well. In almost all cases the patient's white blood cell count dropped below 4,000, and if it dropped below 1,000 death was certain to occur (77). The lowered white blood cell count resulted in increased and more protracted infections. Paradoxically, those who suffered the worst initial burns, as well as those who were injured and remained inactive immediately after the explosion, were more immune from disease than those who were more active initially. As the specifics of this man-made disaster convey, in a world turned upside down by the nuclear physics, one can never be certain about the reason for survival.

A year after the explosion these six survivors remain deeply affected by their experience. Miss Sasaki is still a cripple; the poorest of the group originally, Mrs. Nakamura remains utterly "destitute"; the priest is in the hospital; Dr. Sasaki remains exhausted; Dr. Fujii has started another private practice, but not as large as the former one; and Mr. Tanimoto has lost not only his church but his extraordinary drive as well. It is almost too much of an understatement to say that the "lives of these six people, who were among the luckiest in Hiroshima, would never be the same" (87).

Parallel to the personal experiences of these six representative Hiroshima citizens, the city itself also comes back to life, as uneven as that recovery might be. A new municipal government organized by the Allied Military Government sets into motion many projects to rebuild the city. Despite what Hersey seems to imply about the Japanese government, the efforts of Shinao Hamai (chief of the Municipal Distribution Section at the time of the explosion, and later the mayor of Hiroshima) in finding food for the survivors of his city has been miraculous.[4] Whereas the local government provides immediate help, it takes the Japanese national government years to begin to assist these people.

In *Day One: Before Hiroshima and After*, Peter Wyden conveys a special vignette concerning Mr. Hamai, illustrating Hiroshima's recovery:

The turning point along the road to rebirth arrived when Hamai looked out his office window one morning in April 1946. Just about all surviving trees had been burned as firewood in the course of the winter, but city administration had sentimentally preserved a cluster of scrawny, smoke-blackened cherry trees on the south side of the municipal building. Now Hamai thought he saw something he had not dared to hope for. He ran down the steps, up to the trees—

and yes, the first white traces of cherry blossoms were in evidence. The trees created a great stir throughout the city; hundreds came to view the wonder that confirmed the reality of survival.[5]

"The Aftermath," the last chapter in the revised edition, was written by Hersey forty years after the original. In this chapter he carefully updates the lives of these Hiroshima survivors, the *hibaskusha*, during the interim. Whereas the original details failed to reveal the exact reason why they were able to survive the immediate blast, one thing is certain about their long-term survival: they possess an indomitable spirit. Because her survival, and the lives of her three children, would have been the most tenuous, this chapter aptly begins with the personal history of the poorest of the poor, Mrs. Nakamura. Moments after the initial explosion, Mrs. Nakamura "unthinkingly" (20) had thrown her sewing machine into the cement tank of water in front of her house for "safekeeping." After repairing the rusted machine, Mrs. Nakamura uses it to make ends meet by taking in sewing from her more affluent neighbors. However, she is ultimately forced to sell her only valuable possession after falling seriously ill from roundworm. Eventually, despite the initial inactivity on the part of the Japanese government and the outside world, help begins to arrive for people like Mrs. Nakamura. She ends up working for the Suyama Chemical Company, and by 1966 she is able to retire on a 30,000-yen-a-month pension (about $240 at the 1999 rate of exchange). By the time of the fortieth anniversary celebration of surviving the bomb in 1985, she is enjoying an additional $256 in pensions provided by the government. Money has always been tight, but she and her children have survived.

Dr. Sasaki has taken ten years to finish his doctoral degree, twice as long as it normally takes. He never fully recovers his former energy level, and by 1951 he has left the hospital and started his own private practice in his hometown of Mukaihara. Unlike Mrs. Nakamura, Dr. Sasaki never had to worry about money; his practice has grown into a thriving concern. Forty years after the bomb the doctor, a widower, is a prominent practitioner who has lived by a simple creed: "Do not work primarily for money; do your duty to patients first and let the money follow; our life is short, we don't live twice; the whirlwind will pick up the leaves and spin them, but it will drop them and they will form a pile" (108). His only regret about the disaster is that he failed to keep track of the identities of the bodies cremated en masse at the Red Cross Hospital; their souls are unhappy with their fates.

To no one's surprise, Father Kleinsorge's health never regains its vigor, but the priest has actively maintained his ministry. Like Dr. Sasaki, he ends up in the village of Mukaihara, living as inconspicuously, "as Japanese," as possible (114), and changes his name to Father Makoto Takakura. In 1976, Father Takakura slips on ice and is bedridden, and by November 1977 he dies. The priest is buried at the top of a hill above the novitiate in Mukaihara, and Hersey carefully notes that there are "almost always fresh flowers at that grave"(118).

Miss Sasaki never fully recovers physically from the bomb either. In addition to physical changes, she experiences spiritual ones. Father Kleinsorge aids her in her conversion to the Catholic faith, and she enters the convent and takes her vows in 1957. She also changes her identity to become Sister Dominique Sasaki, a member of the Society of Helpers. She has not only found her place in the world but has made peace with the violence she once experienced.

Although Dr. Fujii rebuilds a practice over the remains of his old one, it is a more modest one. Nevertheless, over the years his practice flourishes with help from his new American friends. His favorite diversion is drinking alcohol, which he prescribes to all his *hibaskusha* patients. Dr. Fujii also enjoys other diversions of modern Japan: baseball, golf, and money. Much to his pleasure as well, his five children have all grown up to be connected to the medical profession. On New Year's Eve 1963, Dr. Fujii's health fails catastrophically when the pilot light on a gas heater goes out and he is found unconscious. Was it a suicide attempt? Although he recovers consciousness and seems to be regaining his health, by 25 January he loses consciousness again; a condition he will maintain for 11 years. The doctor dies on 11 January 1973, and his family feuds over his property.

The last *hibaskusha*, Mr. Tanimoto, has spent the four decades since the bomb attempting to rebuild his shattered church. Like the ancient Greek warrior Odysseus, Mr. Tanimoto's odyssey propels him into the company of many strange people and into many strange lands. In 1948, while aboard the USS *Gordon* on his way to the United States to raise money, he resolves to devote his life to peace. In a world more used to war and violence, no one seems to be more dangerous than someone who is devoted to peace. His resolution leads him to meet such notables as Pearl Buck (a Nobel Prize winner) and Norman Cousins (the editor of the *Saturday Review of Literature*) and gets him on the "This Is Your Life" television program. It also puts him at odds with General Douglas MacArthur, the supreme commander of occupying forces; Mayor Hamai, the prefectural general; the U.S. State Department; and the Pentagon. During the television show, which relives the major events of his life, it is his good "fortune" to meet a member of the airplane crew that dropped the bomb on Hiroshima, Robert Lewis, who has gotten drunk and is upset over not being paid for his appearance on the show.

Thanks to the courageous efforts of people like Mr. Tanimoto, the threat of nuclear annihilation seems extremely remote.

NOTES

1. Roger Angell, "Hersey and History," *New Yorker*, 31 July 1995, 66.
2. Peter Wyden, *Day One: Before Hiroshima and After* (New York: Simon & Schuster, 1984), 332.
3. John Hersey, *Hiroshima* (New York: Vintage, 1989), 2. All subsequent citations from this text come from this book.
4. Wyden, *Day One*, 262–264.
5. Ibid., 331–332.

HISTORICAL CONTEXT

THE MANHATTAN PROJECT

Although the actual dropping of the atomic bomb on Japan was an American operation carried out by an American plane with an American crew, the origin of this weapon was not strictly American. French scientist Henri Becquerel discovered radioactivity in 1896. In 1903 British scientists Ernest Rutherford and Frederick Soddy correctly hypothesized that the atom contained enormous amounts of energy, concluding in 1904 that this energy might lead to a very devastating weapon. Scientists later speculated that fusing a hydrogen nucleus with a helium nucleus would release tremendous amounts of energy, the main source of the stars.[1]

Another British scientist, James Chadwick, advanced the study of nuclear energy with the discovery of the neutron in 1932; unlike either protons or electrons, the neutron can more easily penetrate the nucleus of an atom because of its neutral charge. Later in the 1930s scientists from Germany, Denmark, and Sweden further advanced atomic discoveries to the point that physicists entertained the notion that with the right chain of events fission could produce atomic weapons.

Jewish scientists Otto Frisch and Rudolph Peierls made the next great leap toward the bomb. Escaping from Hitler's Europe, they were given asylum by the British. These two men hypothesized that if Uranium-235 could be separated from Uranium-238, a bomb could be manufactured by using only a few kilograms of uranium (a fraction of the amount scientists previously had considered effective). Also during this time other scientists discovered a process to produce plutonium, a new element that became the primary explosive material of future atomic bombs.[2]

Meanwhile, in the United States scientists (who, like Frisch and Peierls, were also refugees from the Nazis) made some progress toward an atomic bomb. American developments, however, still lagged far behind those in England. Finally, on 11 October 1939, President Roosevelt formed a committee funding uranium research in American universities, after receiving a letter from Albert Einstein describing the possibility that the Germans were working on an atomic weapon that would lead to world domination.[3]

Not much happened in America toward the creation of an atomic weapon until May 1942, when the S-1 group of the Atomic Committee, headed by Vannevar Bush, met to determine the final direction of the U.S. atomic bomb program. Five different methods of bomb production were considered at that meeting. Three methods involved the separation of Uranium-235; the other two methods entailed the production of plutonium.[4] As a result of this meeting, all five methods were allowed to progress until an operational weapon was produced. The U.S. government then created the secret Manhattan Project, a massive government program to build a working bomb as quickly as possible. Brigadier General Leslie Groves, a West Point graduate who graduated fourth in the Class of 1918, led this $2 billion project.[5] Stephane Groueff, in *The Manhattan Project: The Untold Story of the Making of the Atomic Bomb*, writes that "in the opinion of most engineers, scientists and industrialists interviewed by me, [the development of the atomic bomb was] the greatest single achievement of organized human effort in history."[6]

By early 1945 this massive project successfully produced two different types of atomic weapons: "Little Boy" and "Fat Man." The "Little Boy" bomb, which was dropped on Hiroshima, used uranium as it explosive source. This bomb, detonated by firing one component of critical mass at the other, kept the two halves of the critical mass separated from the other until the moment of explosion. The other type of bomb, which was dropped on Nagasaki and nicknamed "Fat Man" after Churchill, used plutonium as its explosive source. It was a much more powerful bomb. Plutonium, with a much higher radioactivity speed than uranium, could not be detonated by using the gun method because its two critical mass components would melt before they could explode. Instead of using the "Little Boy" method, "Fat Man" compressed plutonium by using conventional explosives. Compressed plutonium creates a much denser target for the neutrons to hit. The initial explosion compresses the plutonium beyond its critical volume, and a nuclear explosion occurs.[7]

On 16 July 1945, the United States exploded the world's first atomic weapon at the Trinity test site in Alamogordo, New Mexico; the bomb was plutonium with a yield of between 15 and 20 kilotons. The explosion was observable up to 180 miles away.[8] With the successful explosion of the weapon, the next stage in the nuclear process was to select target locations. Because the Americans felt it was primarily important for the Japanese government to realize the full damage this weapon would inflict, Hiroshima was chosen as the first target since it had been largely spared by the U.S. Army Air Force.[9] The other location, Nagasaki, not even the first choice on the day that the bomb exploded, was bombed as a secondary target because the primary target, Korkura (which has since been merged with five adjacent cities to form Kitakyushu), was under heavy clouds and visibility was too low.

On 6 August 1945 at 8:15:17 A.M. (local time), the American B-29 Superfortress bomber *Enola Gay* released its single weapon, an atomic bomb, which exploded 43 seconds later at an altitude of 580 meters (plus or minus 20 meters), precisely over the Shima Hospital, 160 meters southeast from what is now the Atomic Bomb Dome in downtown Hiroshima.[10] This explosion generated heat at a maximum air temperature of several million degrees centigrade and an atmospheric pressure of several hundred thousand bars.[11] Three days later, on 9 August, the second atomic bomb exploded over Nagasaki at 11:02 A.M. (local time). The altitude of this explosion has been estimated at 503 meters (plus or minus 10 meters), and the epicenter at approximately 90 meters east-southeast of a large Matsuyama township intersection, where today sits the Hypocenter Monument at the Peace Park.[12]

A reckoning of the destruction varies. A 1956 study from the Atomic Bomb Casualty Commission estimates that at Hiroshima 60,000 people were killed immediately, with an additional 70,000 people receiving "overt" injury from the explosion. This estimated number of deaths at Hiroshima is conservative. Many more people might have been killed. Hiroshima was a military staging area, and the strict military secrecy at the time has made it difficult to get an accurate accounting. In contrast, Nagasaki "merely" suffered 33,000 immediate deaths, and 25,000 were severely injured.[13] I. C. B. Dear and M. R. D. Foot, using data taken from *Hiroshima Genbaku Sensaich* (Hiroshima, 1971), estimates that 118,661 people were killed immediately at Hiroshima, with 30,524 severely injured. Another 20,000 probable deaths of military personnel occurred, but because of a concern for secrecy at the time, no one knows for certain.[14] Dear and Foot estimate that at Nagasaki 73,884 people were killed immediately, and another 74,909 were injured.[15] Although the plutonium explosion was significantly greater that the first uranium one, the destruction of Hiroshima was much more pronounced because of geographical factors. Whereas Nagasaki has a long bay and a mountain range running down the middle of it, splitting the city in half, Hiroshima is a triangular, flat delta. At Nagasaki the bomb exploded on one side of the mountain, which blocked the destruction on the other side. At Hiroshima nothing shielded the entire city from the enormous blast.[16]

THE GERMAN HEAVY WATER PROGRAM

Although the Germans never developed an operational weapon from their nuclear program, the fear that they would makes it a topic worth reviewing. According to Ronald W. Clark in *The Birth of the Bomb*, until 1942

> when the time was past—it was never seriously considered either by Hitler or by the German High Command that German forces would need the aid of a nuclear weapon to win whatever war they wished to wage; and, since the Fuhrer thought thus, it would have been unwise for anyone to suggest that the reverse might be the case.[17]

After the German conquest of the European continent, including the Norwegian Norsk Hydro Works, word leaked back to the Allied scientific community that the Germans had increased heavy water production from 3,000 pounds a year to 10,000.[18] Heavy water, which is a "mixture of oxygen and the heavy isotope of hydrogen," reduces "the speed of neutrons but rarely absorbs them."[19] It is a critical element in creating plutonium, and it has no other industrial use except the production of nuclear weapons. Although it appears that the Germans may have had plenty of heavy water, for a variety of reasons their weapons program never got off the ground. Some historians have speculated that German scientists, themselves fearful of what the Nazis would do with such a weapon, sabotaged their own program. During the war the Allies had no way of knowing the status of the German program, so they launched a preemptive raid against the Norsk Works at Rjukan. The raid, using glider forces for the first time, was a dismal failure.[20]

Eventually, another attempted raid and an air attack prompted the Germans to move the heavy water back home to the fatherland, but the ferry carrying this cargo sank while crossing Lake Tinnsjoe. The Germans subsequently abandoned their development of the atomic bomb.

THE ATOMIC BOMB CONTROVERSY

President Harry S Truman's decision to drop the atomic bomb not once but twice on the citizens of Japan has not been without controversy. A Smithsonian event commemorating the fiftieth anniversary of the first bomb caused a furor, and a U.S. Postal Service stamp showing the mushroom cloud over Hiroshima was canceled before being issued.

The defenders of Truman's decision, many of them combatants who were grateful that the war ended when it did, argue that it saved American lives. Because the Americans were essentially the only troops committed to the Pacific front at that time, it is a compelling argument, especially since some estimates are that it would have cost at least one million casualties to finish the job. Iwo Jima, a small island 650 miles southeast of Tokyo, took about 23,000 casualties in only 36 days of fighting.[21] The conquest of mainland Japan would have taken considerably more. For Truman and the Allies, nothing less than unconditional surrender was demanded, and nothing more than an invasion or the bomb was going to force the Japanese to those terms. Although it was not announced until the Potsdam Declaration on 26 July 1945, unconditional surrender had been the goal of the Allied policy since 1943. In a routine press release just hours after the blast, Truman told the American people what had happened:

Sixteen hours ago an American airplane dropped one bomb on Hiroshima, an important Japanese Army Base. That bomb had more power than 20,000 tons of TNT. It had more than two thousand times the blast power of the British "Grand Slam," which is the largest bomb ever yet used in the history of warfare.

The Japanese began the war from the air at Pearl Harbor. They have been repaid many fold. And the end is not yet. With this bomb we have now added a new and revolutionary increase in destruction to supplement the growing power of our armed forces. In their present forms these bombs are now in production and even more powerful forms are in development.

It is an atomic bomb. It is harnessing the basic power of the universe. The force from which the sun draws its powers has been loosed against those who brought war to the Far East.[22]

Opponents of Truman's decision argue that besides forcing the Japanese to surrender, the real reason for dropping the bomb was to counter the Soviets and to assert American post-war dominance. Robert Jay Lifton and Greg Mitchell, in *Hiroshima in America: A Half Century of Denial*, systematically debunk the elaborate thought processes the White House and the U.S. government went through that brought about the chain of events leading to Hiroshima and Nagasaki. They write that this

subject is charged with emotion. When the atomic bomb was dropped over Hiroshima, Americans felt both deep satisfaction and deep anxiety, and these responses have coexisted ever since. Half a century later, Americans continue to experience pride, pain, and confusion over the use of the atomic bomb against Japan. Part of each of us wishes to believe that the decision to use the bomb was reasonable and justified, but another part remains uncomfortable with what we did.[23]

Despite the continuing support for Truman's decision, recent declassification of U.S. government documentation about the bomb shows that Truman did indeed have more in mind than the numbers of American casualties when he allowed the bomb to drop.[24] He was also concerned about a military rivalry with the Soviet Union in the post-war political world.

NOTES

1. I. C. B. Dear and M. R. D. Foot, *The Oxford Companion to World War II* (New York: Oxford University Press, 1995), 69–70.

2. Ibid., 71.

3. Stephane Groueff, *The Manhattan Project: The Untold Story of the Making of the Atomic Bomb* (Boston: Little, Brown and Co., 1967), xi.

4. Ibid.

5. Ibid., 5.

6. Ibid., xi.

7. Ibid., 73.

8. Brigadier Peter Young, ed., *The World Almanac of World War II* (New York: World Almanac, 1986), 351.

9. Dear and Foot, *Oxford Companion*, 530.

10. Ibid., 23.

11. Ibid.

12. Ibid., 29.

13. J. V. Neel and W. J. Schull, *The Effect of Exposure to the Atomic Bomb on Pregnancy Termination in Hiroshima and Nagasaki*, Publication no. 46 (Washington, D.C.: Atomic Bomb Commission, 1956), 28.

14. Dear and Foot, *Oxford Companion*, 531.

15. Ibid., 773.

16. Neel and Schull, *The Effect*, 29.

17. Ronald W. Clark, *The Birth of the Bomb* (New York: Horizon Press, 1961), 145.

18. Ibid., 142.

19. Ibid., 68.

20. Dear and Foot, *Oxford Companion*, 1244–1245.

21. Ibid., 604.

22. Robert Jay Lifton and Greg Mitchell, *Hiroshima in America: A Half Century of Denial* (New York: Avon, 1995), 4.

23. Ibid., xi.

24. Dear and Foot, *Oxford Companion*, 75.

EYEWITNESS TO GROUND ZERO: AN INTERVIEW WITH BRIGADIER GENERAL JESSE GATLIN, UNITED STATES AIR FORCE, RETIRED

Jesse Gatlin was born in Creswell, a small town in eastern North Carolina, the only citizen from that town ever to attend the United States Military Academy. He graduated from there in 1945. He served in the United States Air Force for thirty-two years, retiring in 1977 as permanent professor and head of the English Department, United States Air Force Academy, with the rank of brigadier general.

This interview was conducted in Colorado Springs, Colorado in 1997.

FROM JAMES HUGHES MEREDITH "AN INTERVIEW WITH BRIGADIER GENERAL JESSE GATLIN"

INTERVIEWER: General Gatlin, when did your Air Force career start?

GATLIN: Actually, my career started in the Army. I graduated from the United States Military Academy in 1945, but because I got my pilot's wings before I graduated, I went into the U.S. Army Air Force or the Army Air Corps (which is what it was originally termed until 1938, when it was redesignated). We all still referred to it as the Air Corps until it became a separate branch of service after the war in 1947 [when President Truman, aboard the C-54 Sacred Cow airplane, signed the National Security Act of 1947, officially establishing the U.S. Air Force as a separate service]. Well, as I said, in those days we all got our wings before we graduated from West Point. About 280 cadets (out of the 470 who began the training), a fourth of my whole class of 852 (which was the largest ever to graduate up to that time), were pilot qualified. We were all on a separate academic program because we had to spend so much extra time in flight school. My primary flight training was in Texas. I was in class 44-J, which meant that I was the tenth class in the 1944 training year. (We took it during the summer leading to my senior year.) I had to go to night school during the academic year to catch up because of flight training. I went to advanced training at Stewart Field near West Point. We all flew the T-6, a single-engine training plane, and we were awarded our pilot's wings about a week before graduation from West Point, so we could wear them on our gray cadet uniforms during June Week of 1945. I was so proud of those wings; we all were. We thought we were big men on campus. Flyboys have always thought that they're special. After graduation I trained on the B-25 and the B-17.

INTERVIEWER: I'm sure the ground forces graduates were envious.

GATLIN: They'd have never said it to us. The ground officers who had graduated a year ahead of me, the Class of 1944, had experienced rough going. A lot of them were killed during the Battle of the Bulge. The Army had put these young, "green" troops in the safest spot they thought they could find, which was the Ardennes Forest during the early winter of 1944. However, no one told the Germans that it was a safe spot, as that is exactly where the Panzers came rolling out of Germany. Of course, the strength of this German offensive caught everyone by surprise—no one thought that they had that much punch left, but they certainly had enough to kill so many of these inexperienced second lieutenants. Being a replacement lieutenant was bad enough, the new "leader" of war-hardened troops, but to have to face what was left of the whole Wehrmacht on the Western Front must have been terrifying.

INTERVIEWER: Did you ever see combat during World War II?

GATLIN: By the time I was fully qualified enough to see combat, Truman had dropped the bombs over Hiroshima and Nagasaki, and the Japanese surrendered—much to the relief of not only me and my wife (I had gotten married right after graduation) but to every other American soldier as well. The estimate for troop casualties to invade Japan was enormous. No one that I knew questioned Truman's decision to drop the bomb.

INTERVIEWER: What was your first assignment in the Army Air Force?

GATLIN: In February 1946 I was assigned overseas to Europe as a part of the Army of Occupation. Until that time I'd been finishing some flight training down in Albany, Georgia, and then Sebring, Florida. After a short delay in Germany I was stationed in Austria, near Linz, and then later stationed in Bad Kissinger, Germany. Because of the devastated state of society over there then, I was unaccompanied at first. My wife would join me about seven months later. The lack of confidence in the local currency, the lack of confidence in the new, provisional governments, meant that everything ran on a cigarette economy. I remember that I bought a Willys jeep, a U.S. government surplus item, and a local Austrian craftsman installed a sheet aluminum body on it (the aluminum salvaged from downed aircraft in the local area) for two cartons of cigarettes, a box of Hershey bars, and five gallons of gasoline.

INTERVIEWER: What were the German people like then? Were they resentful of Americans or were they resigned to their plight?

GATLIN: The German people that I had dealings with were very kind people indeed; they seemed humbled by what they had caused the rest of the world. A lot of them were temporarily dispossessed of their homes to accommodate the American soldiers who were over there (the U.S. government was compensating them for their inconvenience, however), but they did not seem resentful. I'm sure that they were tired of not only the war but the aftermath as well. I can't image what they had been through—just like I can't imagine what the rest of Europe experienced as well. However, it wasn't the German people in the area that I served who had the most problems; it was the displaced people, mainly from eastern Europe, fleeing the Soviet occupation forces, who had the most difficulty. No one wanted to be caught in a country held under Russian occupation. My wife and I were friends with two Romanians whom we paid to help us around the house, and they were such nice people. They were so grateful for being on the Western side of the Allied occupation, instead of the Eastern, the Communist side.

INTERVIEWER: With the war over, what was your job?

GATLIN: In Europe at that time, there were a lot of airplanes and gasoline in surplus, and we couldn't bring it all back in a hurry. Getting the infantry back was the first priority. Besides, I think we needed to keep some troops, weapons, and supplies over in Europe because the situation was still so unsettled. I don't mean that the Germans were still an organized threat—they weren't. But the Russians consciously maintained a huge standing army, right across the dividing line, and no one was certain what they were going to do. I don't think we had any intentions to be aggressive, but the situation was still very complicated since the Russians had just been our allies. Well, to answer your question, I got to fly a lot. I flew every multi-wing aircraft we had on base and the P-47 Thunderbolt as well. Flying during those days was very different than it is today in the Air Force—easier, less restricted, especially in Europe.

INTERVIEWER: I wanted to ask you about your experiences in nuclear bomb testing. I'll have to come back and ask you more about the immediate post-war Air Force.

GATLIN: I'm so glad, amazed even, that you're interested in my career experiences since I really didn't do that much; not like so many others. Everything then was a lot more relaxed in Europe. I never flew a combat mission until I went to Vietnam. I was lucky not to have to fly a combat mission until then. A lot of good men died flying or fighting for their country during World War II. They were the heroes.

INTERVIEWER: I agree. I'm glad that I've never had to be tested in combat. When did you start your work with nuclear bomb testing?

GATLIN: In the early 1950s, after we came back from Europe, I trained to be a radiological monitor at San Dia, which is now a part of Kirkland Air Force Base, New Mexico, which was in charge of nuclear training; nuclear surety I think is what they call it today. It was a part of what we then called Radiological Defense. I eventually was assigned to the 97th Bomb Wing's Aviation Squadron at Biggs Air Force Base, Texas, near El Paso. My wing commander there was Colonel John Ryan, who later became the Chief of Staff of the Air Force and his son is also now the Chief. We were flying the B-50 bomber then.

INTERVIEWER: Did you ever get the chance to witness any nuclear blasts?

GATLIN: Yes, as a wing radiological officer, I volunteered to go to Nevada where we were holding above-ground test blasts. These were the days before we had treaties to stop this kind of testing. It was at Camp Mercury. I witnessed three series of tests (seven or eight blasts in total). I flew over in an airplane in one. I was directing the airplane pilot around the mushroom cloud. Our job was to follow and report the direction of potential radioactive fallout on the ground below, which was very difficult to do with any degree of accuracy.

During another blast I had to retrieve an instrument, which was very near ground zero. It was after a tower burst. I was in a jeep with a fellow officer when we bogged down in powdery sand near the crater. Our radiac instruments, measuring radiation intensity, were off the scale on the high side, but I managed to push the jeep while my companion drove, and we got the vehicle moving out of the high-intensity area—though only after a fairly high radiation exposure. I still feel as if I have been living on borrowed time—neither of my parents lived as long as I have. Covered with radioactive dust, we drove quickly back to the decontamination center, where several showers were needed to wash away the radioactive particles, especially out of our hair, ears, and nostrils. It sounds crazy now, doesn't it? But those were different times then. Despite what has been widely portrayed, the fifties were not the contented, peaceful, conformist times. We were genuinely concerned—even afraid—that the United States was vulnerable to an atomic attack. The Soviets had the bomb by then, which would have been a devastating catastrophe. We knew what had happened to Britain, only a few years ago, under the attack of Hitler's Luftwaffe bombers. Moreover, we knew the devastation the British and we had rained upon the Germans in retaliation as well.

INTERVIEWER: You said that you were involved in three series of tests. In the third one, how close were you to the blast?

GATLIN: I didn't plan it this way, but I guess that I've saved the best for the last. I was crouched in an open trench. This is easily the most memorable of the testings I witnessed, within two miles of ground zero, which is at the exact spot where the bomb explodes. I was only wearing GI coveralls, cotton gloves taped at the wrist where the sleeves joined, and a standard-issue gas mask. The device, a polite word for a bomb, that was exploded was several times more powerful than the bomb dropped on Hiroshima. My job was to lead the troops from the trench toward ground zero after the explosion, ostensibly to familiarize them with the after-effects and to dispel their fear of tactical nuclear weapons, which might be used on the battlefield.

I remember how, even though we all were crouched at the very bottom of the trench with our hands pressed tightly over our eyes for protection, the intense flash of light clearly exposed the bones of my hands and fingers at the instant of the blast. Simultaneously came a sudden, intense flash of heat all over my body. Seconds later, the pressure of the blast wave hit with a great boom and maelstrom of desert rocks and sand showering into the trench, and I clearly remember seeing the trench wavering like a crawling snake, as the earth rocked under the force of the blast. It was simply amazing.

Once the blast wave passed, I gave the signal for the soldiers to leave the trench, and we began our advance toward ground zero. I also remember a Joshua tree off the end of the trench that had burst into flames from the intensity of the heat wave. As we moved forward toward our pre-determined radiation intensity level, I noticed a large jackrabbit hopping. It was completely charred—as though roasted—on the one side, which had been exposed to the heat wave when the bomb exploded.

That experience was merely a hint of the potential devastation a nuclear war may bring. Unwittingly x-rayed hands, a hot flash, a sinuous trench, a burning tree (not unlike the one Moses experienced), and a still-alive roasted rabbit—strange images all, but images that have persisted all these years as cautionary omens. I'm glad the Cold War is over, and we may be able to live in peace.

INTERVIEWER: Have you noticed any physiological after-effects at all?

GATLIN: None that I know of. Even after all those exposures, our youngest son, born some years later, is a normal and healthy adult. And I still don't glow in the dark.

A COMBATANT'S PERSPECTIVE ON THE DROPPING OF THE ATOMIC BOMB

Alfred Kern, born in 1924, is a World War II veteran, English professor, novelist, and poet and writes on a wide variety of subjects. Kern served in the U.S. Army Air Forces from 1942 to 1946. During World War II, he spent most of two years in the Pacific Theater. About his experience in the combat zone, he writes that "I was close enough to understand what being closer could mean."

ALFRED KERN, "HANG THE *ENOLA GAY*"
(War, Literature, & the Arts: An International Journal of the Humanities, 7, no. 1 [Spring/Summer 1995])

General Tibbetts, the man who flew the airplane, surely is right. Exhibit the *Enola Gay* and say nothing. But then I'm a writer (mere crewman to Tibbetts' authentic Moment) and argue that saying something constitutes duty. As one version of the recent story got played, the people arranging the Smithsonian's exhibit of the *Enola Gay* had made some perfectly reasonable comments about the war in the Pacific. These historians and archivists wanted to bring us the truth that a fifty-year perspective could now allow us to accept: the American war in the Pacific was one of vengeance and cruelty against the Japanese, who fought only to protect their culture and way of life. Furthermore, the United States did not drop the bomb out of any strategic necessity, but to impress the Soviet Union with both the might and willingness of American power. The dropping of the second bomb (about which some question might be asked) is proof of American perfidy, a perfidy made all the more emphatic if only because the American Legion rose up in its predictable chauvinism to deny it. And so the *Enola Gay*'s last mission—its own hanging—would reveal the truth of America's evil intentions.

To argue against this premise risks endowing it with a respect it doesn't deserve. Still, a sentence or two might be helpful. The decision to drop the bomb was not made easily; neither was it a callous message to impress the Soviet Union. From Port Moresby—only a long spit from Australia itself—we had come all the way to Okinawa and Ie Shima. While the Japanese still put airplanes into the air, including the suicide missions that attacked American naval vessels off the harbor at Naha, we prevailed in the air war. Our B-29 raids were producing the kind of damage that

should by then have persuaded the Japanese, and so—yes—by early
1945, the question remaining was just how and when we would win the
war. Still, the Japanese had not surrendered, and if you had come the
whole way or a fair hunk of it (I began at Nadzab, New Guinea, a few
miles inland from Lae), you were not all that certain if or when the Japanese would ever surrender. The argument that we justified the dropping
of the bomb by deliberately overestimating the number of American casualties to be suffered by an invasion of the Japanese home islands is
worse than specious. As measured by the number of American casualties
in the island wars, Japanese resistance against an invasion of the home
islands certainly could not be expected to diminish. Does anybody need
to be reminded that the Japanese were fierce fighters? Ask the Marine
veterans who recently marked the fiftieth anniversary of Iwo Jima.

Then, too, how many American casualties were to be suffered in order
to justify the use of the bomb? At a cocktail party a year ago, I heard an
acquaintance condemn our dropping the bomb as having been cynically
unnecessary. Speaking about an American invasion of Japan, he said
something like the following: "The estimate of one million American casualties was never even close to the truth. At worst, there might have
been fifty thousand casualties. Less than fifty thousand. Maybe thirty to
thirty-five thousand." My unit was scheduled to go in D + 2; with respect
to what would have been suffered by the first waves, those two days
would have been like a century later. But I'm still impressed enough with
D + 2 not to have said anything at all to the man at the cocktail party.
Anyhow, what are you supposed to say to somebody arguing that at worst
we would have lost only fifty thousand American lives?

In agreeing with the calm and measured tones of the American Legion—far softer than I would have spoken—I say first that I am not a
member of the Legion or the VFW. Back in civvies after WWII, I joined
the American Veterans Committee, the veterans association founded by
people like Bill Mauldin, Gilbert Harrison (then publishing the *New Republic*) and Chet Bolte. Just as the far left despised anticommunist socialism more than it feared the right wing, so, too, did it live easier with
the American Legion than with us AVC liberals. In fact, the left did its
best to destroy the AVC, whose motto was "Citizens first; Veterans second." Nearly fifty years later, I haven't much changed my political stripes
and am among those who have not grown more conservative with age.
Whether you think my brand of politics to be wisdom or senility depends
on your own politics, but let's get one notion straight from the start. The
revisionism that makes the United States the bad guys in the Pacific war
is in no way a premise of American liberalism. Neither is the view of the
Smithsonian historians an argument between liberal Democrats and conservative Republicans. I remind you that it was Harry Truman who gave

the order for the mission of the *Enola Gay*. If you need your memory refreshed, David McCullough's work on Truman will provide the historical perspective.

For my generation, this foolishness about the *Enola Gay* flying an evil mission has refreshed memories. I remember the day. I'd been working on the strip we ran on the Motobu Peninsula on Okinawa. Somebody came into the engineering shack and said that this enormous bomb had been dropped. *So how enormous is enormous? They got it into an airplane, didn't they?* No, not enormous in size. Small in size—enormous in the power to destroy. One bomb knocked out most of a city. Tokyo? No, not Tokyo. Some other city with a funny name. *And one bomb did all that?* One bomb. The guy said this bomb implodes. Ask the armorers what that means. *Our armorers? Our armorers don't know shit from shinola about anything.* What the guy really said was that troops stationed on Okinawa had better keep a tight asshole cause there's no telling how the Japanese will react to whatever-that-thing-was. *You say it implodes itself. And that's why it blew up a whole city? Cause it implodes? Was this implosion supposed to happen or just some kind of lucky screw-up?*

That flight of the *Enola Gay* has got to be the most impressive single mission ever flown. Nothing can compete with its awesomeness. Unlike a routine mission, the *Enola Gay* was History from the start, and those involved knew it. But for those of us who served in the Pacific, the A-bomb mission was an ending that in some ways seemed to have little to do with the Pacific war as we had fought it. For example, during the New Guinea campaign, I worked at the strip where still only Captain Richard Bong's P-38 squadron returned from missions. By the time Bong had knocked down eleven or twelve enemy planes, GIs from all over the base began to line that strip like cheerleaders at their high school football game. We waited for that P-38 to come in hot, level out flat what seemed only a dozen feet above the strip, and then climb into its victory roll. And on numbers of those days, Bong flew back around for a second victory roll. We would look at each other, nodding and smiling and holding up two fingers. "Two. He scored two."

For me, a Dick Bong victory roll remains in memory as a thing of beauty, and those moments were an enormous lift to morale in what was a difficult war. Look at a map of the Pacific. Find Port Moresby on the southern New Guinea coast and then calculate the distance in miles to the Japanese islands. And while you're at it, calculate that distance in time. I mean the amount of time it took us to get there. We had already used up *Never More in '44* and were hoping for *Back Alive in '45* though the squadron pessimists predicted *Home or Heaven by '47*, or even *Golden Gate in '48*. We were ready for the miracle we didn't begin to comprehend, a miracle involving something called atomic fission. For Fifth Air Force veterans, the years of scrounging to get airplanes in the air, the awesome distances to be traveled, the ersatz food, names never before heard like Buna and Pelelieu and Samar, the holding on to a civilization from which we had been removed: all of these represent the war in the Pacific more than the flight of the *Enola Gay*, and I have a hunch that nobody knows that better than General Tibbetts himself.

Our pilots flew the requisite number of missions (and more), but GIs didn't get rotated home. Most of us had been at it for a long time when The Bomb was dropped. Not yet twenty-one, I'd already been in territories designated as combat zones for nearly two consecutive years. If some old infantry veteran is reading this, let me say here and now that us air corps types aren't making any claims. At least in your presence we aren't making any claims. Being in a combat zone usually meant only that you were close enough to understand what being closer could mean. My squadron did get a bit closer, stupidly a time or two, but that was because I served in something called an airdrome squadron.

The idea for such a unit was borrowed from the British, and like a British aircraft engine was more to be admired in design than lived with. An airdrome squadron was to arrive the moment an air strip was taken or completed for use by our engineers. We were staffed and equipped to run the strip for a month, after which—in theory anyway—bomb and fighter groups would move in safely with their own personnel and heavier equipment. Until then, we did everything: control tower, crash crews, weather, communications, armament, and aircraft maintenance far beyond minor repairs and pre-flight once-overs. We took our squadron's assignments and the general mission of the Fifth Air Force as being perfectly sensible; fifty years later the wonder is how we did it. I understand more keenly now than I had time to understand then that our airdrome squadron was to move itself up to the next air strip and function. Instantly. Snap a finger. Just like that. And we did it, did it before a tent got pitched or a latrine got dug. We also learned what could be the real meaning of a "moment too soon." The airdrome squadron that had been on the boat with us arrived at Hollandia more than a moment too soon and got shot up. We disembarked at Lae and went inland to Nadzab. In addition to running a strip there, we were assigned to do the maintenance for the Fifth Bomber Command's flight section. A bit more about that later.

I always figured that somebody at the command level had fought against the very idea of these airdrome squadrons. Having lost the argument, he figured out another way to make his point. My impression of that unit—unchanged more than fifty years later—was that you were assigned duty there only if you had impressed someone in charge of you—fairly or unfairly—that you were or could become a square peg. Surely, we had more people who had done prison or guardhouse time than the typical Fifth Air Force unit. Other of our people had flunked out of air corps training schools or, to put it as kindly as possible, had not been among the class leaders. Anyone who had told us to our faces that we were at best a collection of shanghais would have committed a grave diplomatic error; he would not, however, have been entirely inaccurate.

I had done nothing terrible, yet I see now that from the very start of service I was destined for assignment to the 92nd. My first summons to a CO's office occurred as early as basic training; I was told that in Ohio a warrant had been issued for my arrest because I had not registered for the draft. Why had I not done so? I explained that I had volunteered after my eighteenth birthday, which fell months before my age group was supposed to register. Rightfully unimpressed, the CO grunted and said that he'd do his best to keep me out of jail. Next, having taken the battery of tests, I was sent to the Buick motor division in Flint, Michigan, where after eleven weeks of instruction I would become a specialist in Pratt-Whitney aircraft engines. The Flint assignment was wonderful. Our nightly retreat ceremonies were held on a public street and watched by girls working in GM war plants. These young women not only produced the equipment and weapons we would soon be using, but respected our future bravery with a patriotism that could inspire from toe-to-head.

About a month after I arrived, I was again summoned to the CO's office. I still remember his name—Lieutenant Balch. In appearance and mildness of manner, Lieutenant Balch looked as if he had taught General Science at some Midwestern high school. After about thirty seconds of sighing, he explained to me that I had made one of the highest scores of any soldier ever to be sent to his school. He then said that my performance also placed me among the most inept students ever assigned there, and he might well have to get rid of me. How had I done so well on the test only to do so wretchedly in his school? I tried to explain that the test had been simple. For example, you might be given an illustration of interlocking gears. You were told the direction of the first gear and asked whether the last of the gears was moving to the right or left; I explained that such a test had nothing to do with fixing an airplane engine. On the line, your hands seemed to be more important than your head. And the tools had funny names. Somebody kept asking for his ratchet or Philips' head. Who was this Philips anyway? By the end of the eleven weeks I did know the difference between a ratchet and a hatchet, but anybody who flew an airplane I had worked on would have flown more easily if he did not know that I had done the safety wiring.

My final move to the 92nd Airdrome Squadron occurred at Hunter Field, Georgia, still an army airfield. In a replacement squadron there waiting to be assigned, I was once again summoned to the CO's office. He was Major Robinson, a West Pointer, called out of retirement to what for him had to be an unfulfilling assignment. Little did either of us know that indifferent gods had destined each of us to find the other. The first sergeant advised me to be scrubbed and starched, and like most GIs I wondered what I had done wrong. In posture and bearing, Major Robinson impressed me as never once in his entire life having been at ease. I stood at attention and did my best not to breathe. The major first explained that he himself was a graduate of West Point. He then said that the army had issued a new directive. Any GI who met the requirements— age, IQ, physical condition, educational background, score on the GCT, and whatever else—could qualify for West Point. He had ordered his clerks to go through the entire roster, and I was the only man currently assigned to him who met the requirements. He was proud to have a man in his outfit who qualified for the Point and he was going to back me all the way. That's what he said, "And, soldier, I'm going to back you all the way."

The requirements weren't that steep; there were just a number of them, including a year of college. I had graduated from high school at sixteen (a bad idea) and so had been a college sophomore when I entered the service. At that moment anyway, Major Robinson was unlucky enough to find only one person assigned to his outfit who qualified. But I didn't want to spend those years in school. Stupid as it may sound to most current potential candidates in both political parties, I didn't want to miss the war. But what I said then to Major Robinson came out wrong—wrong for both of us. "But, sir," I said, "I don't want to be at West Point." Only four hours later, I threw my duffel bag into the back of a 6 × 6 and headed for the other side of the base. That's how I came to spend the war with the 92nd Airdrome Squadron, surely the only GI in the 92nd who got there not by robbing a bank, but by declining a chance to attend West Point. My friend, Brigadier General Jesse Gatlin, retired head of the English department at USAFA and himself a West Point graduate, thinks what Major Robinson did was terrible. Had I said yes, Jesse and I would have been classmates. About a year and a half later, by then in the Philippines, my orders for OCS came through. But I didn't want to go to school in Australia then because the squadron was about to leave for Okinawa. No, Major Robinson may have been right about me. And then you never know about a shift in assignments. The old major may have saved my life.

Those first few weeks in New Guinea, we experienced what surely was the typical shakedown of any initial combat duty. Some people cracked up, not one of those being somebody I would have figured to do so. The people I thought were loony bin candidates all did fine. Our squadron

physician, a Cleveland Heights obstetrician-gynecologist and thus a typical assignee to my airdrome squadron, lasted a bit longer—three or four
months. Wisely, I was taken off the line and assigned to the engineering
shack. Soon after, the NCO in charge was moved up to command headquarters, and I was given his duties. Then, over the next few weeks, what
I discovered about our squadron is hopefully typical of any organization,
military or civilian. We had the dozen necessary people who knew what
they were doing and also how to make do. In a month, we were func-
tioning adequately. A month after that, we were good.

The planes we serviced regularly were those of Fifth Bomber Command
Headquarters. The tactical aircraft flown on missions were B-25D2s, a
medium bomber and marvelous airplane. But bomber command headquarters was also a sort of WWII menagerie, and so at one time or another
we also worked on the B-26, B-24, A-20, and one stripped down fat-cat
B-17. We also had a couple of those wonderful little two-seater Taylor-
crafts. When one of the pilots discovered that I was still a kiwi, he took
me up in a Taylorcraft and once off the ground immediately initiated me
by demonstrating stalls and loops; that flight was not a gentle initiation,
but I enjoyed it. No, it's more than fifty years later, and I no longer have
to say that I enjoyed it. I did not, however, get sick.

A few of our pilots had been rotated out of their combat groups. While
waiting for transportation home, they continued to fly missions. More of
our pilots had been detached from their squadrons for a variety of other
reasons. I had a bit of air time with them, and I can attest to their having
been first-rate fliers. They were also—how to put this politely?—apt to
prefer their own war plans to those of Fifth Bomber G-2, and a time or
two saw something on their way to a target that appealed to them more
than the object of the briefing. Perhaps these days they might be court-
martialed, but remember that we are talking about a bunch of civilians
fighting the war in the Pacific. In retrospect, I think they were handled
just right, but then for us they fit perfectly with the 92nd Airdrome Squadron. Put all the nonconformists in the same outfit and don't bother to
kick butts about minor infractions, and you just might get yourself an
outfit that can be called upon for bigger stuff.

The only two regular army people in our squadron were the first sergeant and the line chief. I suspect each had been chosen with us in mind.
The first sergeant was tough and unyielding. At Hunter Field before leaving for embarking at San Francisco, he had played tackle football wearing
only fatigues, and he had broken his collar bone. (Do I dare say by now
that I never regretted having been in on that tackle?) The first sergeant
could be one unpleasant s.o.b., but when the war ended and he had
more points than anybody else in the squadron, he stood in the mess
hall, tears streaming down his face, and said good-bye by telling us that

he loved us. The first sergeant was an archetypal career soldier, and I'll tell you how much I respected him. When I saw him standing there and weeping, I believed that he meant what he said but still thought he was an s.o.b.

The line chief, Master Sergeant Morris Jones (Sarge Mo), a big and handsome Georgian, was quiet and self-possessed. Although we had an engineering officer, Mo Jones ran the strip and in doing so rarely spoke at all. Mo and I became good friends and with others shared quarters. Mo was determined that we would always put planes in the air, and we never failed to do so. Meeting such assignments wasn't easy, but we were superbly staffed for it. The 92nd Airdrome Squadron excelled in its use of the moonlight requisition. While he could not be represented on the table of organization, we came to employ a full-time scrounge-spy. At a midnight meeting in the engineering shack attended only by enlisted men, the scrounge might say, "The 101st Bomb Group just received a dozen new 1830-radials. They've been sitting there for a week, still crated and pickled." We never stole just to steal, and we never stole a whole engine—just the parts needed to get our own planes in the air. In that sense, the Pacific war belonged to us civilian enlisted types. I assume our officers knew what we were doing, but not even Mo Jones came to a requisition session. Mo could call for a meeting, however; all he had to do was raise an eyebrow.

After a few months in Nadzab, we moved north to Owi, an island just across a strait from Biak and maybe an hour off the New Guinea coast from Hollandia. Biak is another of those places long forgotten that saw intense fighting. We were told that the air strip on Biak changed hands two or three times so that before the island was secure, we and the Japanese had actually taken turns flying off it. Owi was a barren hunk of coral, desolate and sun-drenched. With nightfall, the moon merely replaced the sun for more hours of white-on-white. Such constant light can be as depressing as darkness. Owi is the only place I know where the phrase "like pissing on a flat rock" is not a figure of speech.

Mo Jones did not care for the Owi assignment either. He told me that the Fifth Bomber Command was to send a detachment of three B-25s including flight crews and ground support to Anguar in the central Pacific and that he had volunteered our services. When one of the pilots overheard my saying "I hope to God they won't fly up there in formation," that is exactly what they did. But by then I knew what to worry about. I assigned myself to the lead plane, climbed into the bombardier's forward station in the nose and enjoyed the flight. One does learn. And as it turned out, that is why we were being sent to Anguar; the Seventh Air Force fresh from Hawaii and new to combat had use for a few of us nineteen- to twenty-five-year-old veterans.

We were assigned to a B-24 group that had too often failed to reach target, and we were going to fly pathfinder missions for them. I remember how healthy they all looked in contrast to us. Despite our hours in the tropical sun, we wore those Atabrine-yellow faces. But by then we were also different in other ways. Landing at Anguar, one of our B-25s needed a bit of work done; I went to the tech supply tent for some parts only to discover that nobody was there. I found the squadron technical supply sergeant and told him what was needed only to learn that tech supply was closed on Sunday. For me, duty at places like Nadzab and Owi in wartime pretty much did away with my sense of calendar time, and so my question to the supply sergeant was in no way sarcastic. "Today is Sunday?"

I then found my way to the squadron's engineering officer, told him what we needed, and politely asked if he would request his tech supply noncom to be open for business. I must have managed to say it in the proper tone of voice because no captain ever responded quicker to the request of a three-striper. In speaking to that captain, I mixed the appropriate enlisted man's umbrage with the right seasoning of disrespectful battle weariness. But so, too, did everybody else in our Fifth Air Force detachment play that same role. After all, we had been dispatched here to bring just such experience. By then, we were no longer impressed that we had such experience to bring. We kept those three B-25s in the air, flew the pathfinder missions and got the B-24s to their targets. A month later—maybe less, maybe three weeks—they didn't need us.

From Anguar we flew to San Jose on the Philippine island of Mindoro. The mission now was to fly China coast reconnaissance missions, a far piece of flying for a B-25. I've still no idea how they managed to rig it, but our mechanics put an extra gas tank in the crawl space between the front and midsection of the airplanes. While I still was not to be trusted with either a ratchet or hatchet, I had long before begun to read the tech orders rather than just file them away. Typically American perhaps, I had kept all sorts of unreported data on these planes and knew their individual eccentricities. Along with our crew chiefs, I was possessively jealous; as far as we were concerned, these were our planes which we consented to lend to the pilots who flew them. I suspect that sense of ownership hasn't changed to this day.

The pilots to whom we lent our airplanes accepted our ownership. For months, we had been advising them about the best settings for any particular flight, and they were now especially interested in asking our help for their China coast missions. Even more than on previous assignments, we waited nervously at the strip for the return of the mission. On some days, only one plane was designated to fly, and it was one of those days that the plane did not return from its mission. I hung around the oper-

ations shack most of that night. In the morning we were told that someone had seen the plane go down, not all that far off shore but nearer to
a small island than to Mindoro. The problem was that these were still
contested waters, and if the crew did manage to get itself to the smaller
island, we could not be sure they wouldn't be captured.

Next day—sing for joy—they returned, rescued by a navy patrol boat.
The pilot stared at me not quite menacingly and said, "We ran out of
gas, Sergeant." But his radioman stopped by later. "We were maybe fifteen minutes from base," he said, "and he saw some Japanese shipping
and went down after it. We made three or four passes and then had to
climb back up." I was immensely grateful for his honesty, but that's how
closely we had figured the safe completion of those missions. You simply
could not vary the course without risk—well, maybe we allowed for some
manageable two-minute finagle. This pilot not only had the customary
individualistic daring-do of a Fifth Bomber Command Pilot, he was also—
if you don't mind my saying it, sirs—a stupid jerk. I was thankful for his
return, but now that he and the crew had returned, I wanted to tell him
that he had lost one of my B-25D2s, an airplane we had been flying since
the Nadzab, New Guinea, days.

From Mindoro, we went to Luzon where we ran the strip at Clark Field.
Some brilliant army tactician located our quarters just behind the infantry
but in front of the artillery. That was not the first occasion for our involvement in ground alerts, but we did—for us—have a fairly extensive
go of it. Luzon was the first place we'd been stationed that had a large
and fluent civilian population, and in that sense we'd returned to civilization. But we also saw some of the horrifying consequences of Japanese
occupation. A friend, the master sergeant in charge of communications,
had an aunt, a Roman Catholic nun, who had been a nurse in a Manila
hospital. He had promised his mother that he would try to find his aunt
and asked me if I'd go to Manila with him. We found the hospital where
Sister had worked but could not find her or anybody who had known
her. We had only an overnight but did see the extent to which the city
had been devastated. The Intramuros—the old walled inner city—had
been hit particularly hard and was still smoldering. Even in its ruins, we
could tell how beautiful it had been.

And so we were running this strip on Okinawa the morning the *Enola
Gay* lifted off with this enormous thing that imploded. We were still
scrounging for supplies, and we were weary with the whole business,
including each other. Our camp site sat on a high bluff from which you
could look down on Ie Shima, another tough fight and the place where
Ernie Pyle, the GI's war correspondent, got killed. My college roommate
was also on Okinawa, and we managed an afternoon's reunion. We had
entered the service and gone through basic together, but we had not

seen each other for more than two years. My old roomie was a second lieutenant in the infantry and while Okinawa had been taken, there was still fighting. Some of you may remember how MacArthur handled that sort of thing. The press release would read, "General MacArthur has stated that the island is now secure except for minor mop-up operations." We were getting weary with that nonsense as well. My roommate observed that day, "If this is the mop-up, I'm glad I wasn't here for the battle."

We were ready for that miracle. And then the *Enola Gay* made its flight. And then the second bomb. And it was over. Traffic was very heavy the next couple of weeks with flights to and from Japan. Many of the American POWs flown from Japan to Okinawa landed on our strip. I watched General Skinny Wainright being helped from the airplane. He managed to stand tall and erect even as he accepted the needed help. Shortly after, the first sergeant wept his I-love-you valedictory in the mess hall and departed. Most of the squadron went on to Japan, but those of us who had been in the detachment that served on Anguar, and later in Mindoro, were credited with time in additional battle areas and had extra points. We stayed in Okinawa and waited for a ship. On the way home, I edited the ship's paper to get an early chow pass. The ship received a news service which I used for the paper. The war being over, the United Automobile Workers Union had gone on strike, and I wrote an editorial assuring the GIs that the UAW was just getting us a raise before we got discharged. The ship's captain sent his exec to bawl the hell out of me and tell me not to write that sort of unpatriotic drivel again. I toned it down, but to honor the captain and the ship's speed, I changed the name of the paper to *The Daily Creeper*. We disembarked January 1, 1946, in Seattle where German POWs were working in the mess hall. Unlike Skinny Wainright, they looked both healthy and at ease. Ain't the United States terrible?

Now then, there's one thing I haven't talked about, and it's what motivated my writing this in the first place. Without making a big psychological deal out of it, I may well have been putting it off for years. But the nonsense about the *Enola Gay* compels me. So here goes.

After I read that in the Pacific war, the United States was compelled by vengeance and cruelty, I began again to see the faces of friends who did not return. Any war veteran knows what I'm talking about. From my freshmen dormitory alone, I count seven people. I'm going to list a few names. You won't know them and by now their parents are also gone. But indulge me. I just want to put some names in print. There was Pat Murphy, our class president, a bright and athletic kid who led us in the annual pants fight against the sophomore class. And Emmett Corrigan, who had prepped at some fancy private eastern school and had a surer sense of who he was at age eighteen than I have now; I never thought

anything could happen to Emmett Corrigan. And Don Turk, the upper-
classman who lived in our section of the dorm and who gave me some
help for a course I shouldn't have taken; I couldn't believe it when I
heard that he'd been killed in a navy training mission—*not* Don Turk.
And from my home town Billy Kline with whom I double-dated in high
school, a B-24 pilot who didn't return from a mission. When I got back
home, I went into his father's small clothing store to say how sorry I was
about Billy, but his father saw me coming and went into a back room
and couldn't talk to me.

There is one other incident, though. In Nadzab, New Guinea, our first
overseas assignment, I met a kid exactly my age who had also graduated
from high school early and gone on to college. We'd managed to put
together a kind of day room there, and this kid and I had a series of late
night ping-pong games. We were both good players, and we kept ongoing
statistics from night to night about wins and losses and scores. After a
session, we also talked. We even discussed the possibility of going back
to college together after the war. The kid was a radioman/gunner, and
he was especially eager to play for hours any night before he had a morning mission. Well, by now you know where I'm going. On one of those
missions, he didn't return. I've been referring to him as that kid because
I cannot remember his name. I kept thinking that when I got to this point
in the writing the fingers would simply type out the letters. He was killed
in early 1944, and I've been telling myself that it's perfectly sensible if I
cannot remember a name from fifty-one years ago. Maybe I'll remember
later, just sit up one night and say it.

I could tell a number of these stories about each of those stopping
points on the way from New Guinea to Okinawa. For example, on Anguar, December 31, 1944, the detachment celebrated New Year's Eve.
Somebody had managed to bring some liquor from Australia. Inspired, I
removed the astrodome from a B-25 and used it as a mixing bowl. What
the hell, why not? But the CO of the B-24 group heard about what we
were doing and came down himself to put a stop to it. He confiscated
the booze and told me to replace the astrodome immediately. We cussed
him out pretty good later and did not wish him a happy new year. And
the Colonel did not return from the next mission.

On that same island, we also had a series of ground alerts. Not far from
the hospital tent in which we were all sleeping, a half-dozen sailors—
also detached—were running a navy weather station. As our ground
troops pulled out for other places, the Japanese intensified their forays.
Sixty thousand of them were still on the island of Yap, skillfully bypassed
but hungrier by the day. One of those nights I had taken the jeep and
driven somewhere to see a movie. I even remember that it was *Rhapsody
in Blue*. (If I can remember the name of that movie, why can't I think of

the ping-pong player's name?) When the signal for a ground alert lit the sky—red puff, puff—I drove back to our camp site. Mo Jones told me that he'd had to set up a perimeter and had given my carbine to somebody serving on it. I said okay then, I'd take his Thompson sub, but he'd also lent it to somebody on the perimeter. Just then we heard gunfire and decided we'd relieve the people who had our weapons. Well, these air corps stories about ground war are surely both inane and amusing to anybody who served in the infantry. I'm telling this particular story because that night the little navy weather station got wiped out. They were stationed a bit closer to the shore, and from the looks of it, the Japanese had simply walked up to the door and tossed in grenades. Not one of the navy guys survived.

Enough of stories. Most everybody has them to tell. And I haven't mentioned that many names. Maybe a dozen is all. Now what I want you to do is take any one of these names—just one. Or choose a name of your own, a name from one of your own wars. I'm going to go with the radioman/gunner ping-pong player from Nadzab. When you're sure that you see the face and hear the voice as if he's in the very same room, multiply it by fifty thousand. Or as my acquaintance at the cocktail party said, *only* fifty thousand.

I prefer to end on another note. Almost sixteen years ago, I spent a year teaching at the Air Force Academy. For one of the formal occasions, an officer friend there got all my campaign ribbons replete with battle stars and explained that civilians might wear them for formal occasions on a tuxedo. Most of those ribbons and battle stars were awarded to types like me not for any bravery but for survival. Still, they looked prettily impressive even to me. During the evening and standing with the USAFA brass, I was presented to an older man in dress uniform who lived in Colorado Springs. He was General Crabbe, none other than the CO of the Fifth Bomber Command. We shook hands, and I said to him, "The General has no reason to remember me, but I once flew with you out of Nadzab, New Guinea." Eyes bright and as alert as I remembered him years ago, he gave me a quick inspection including the campaign ribbons. "Well then," he said even better than David Niven could have said it, "I take it the mission was successful." He was smiling.

"Well, Sir, it wasn't exactly a mission. It was in the fat-cat B-17 to Australia. I don't know what you were doing there, Sir, but we were getting booze." There was the slightest ripple of movement among my USAFA hosts. Had the civilian professor gone too far with the general? General Crabbe stared a few seconds more. Then the smile grew broader. "92nd Airdrome Squadron?" he asked.

"Yes, sir," I said. And we both burst into a laughter that neither bothered to explain to our colleagues. When we said good night, we held the handshake an extra second. If General Crabbe was astonished that anybody from the 92nd Airdrome Squadron could have become a distinguished visiting professor at his own United States Air Force Academy, he didn't seem to be displeased.

What else? In Pittsburgh we live in an apartment complex that houses mostly older types like us and young Japanese professionals and their families. Unlike us older folks, the Japanese move in and out of the building. Numbers of them are physicians who are specializing or doing a residency in one of the hospitals or taking courses at Pitt's medical school. Others are computer types studying at Carnegie Mellon University, and there's also a batch working toward MBAs at both schools. Those with small children send them to American schools. There is also a group of little Japanese toddlers who impress me as being exactly like little American toddlers, and I'm on special hugging terms with a number of them. These families are, of course, a very bright and special group of people, and I am very glad they are here with us and willing to be part of America's evil intentions.

And a last word to General Tibbetts. Sir, I agree. If they choose to do so, just hang it up there at the Smithsonian for a few weeks and say nothing. We don't owe the Japanese an apology. Neither do they owe us one. It's over. So let the *Enola Gay* fly its last mission, and people can make of it what they will. With no disrespect intended, Sir, I do not myself need to give it a gander. But I do heartily agree that it would be better if everybody kept his mouth shut. Even me. (63–79)

The Allied cemetery at Oosterbeek, the Netherlands. In memory of those who gave the ultimate sacrifice.

TOPICS FOR WRITTEN AND ORAL DISCUSSION

1. Interview people from different war generations: one from World War II, one from the Korean War, and one from the Vietnam War. Find out if they have differing views on dropping the atomic bomb.

2. Read the *New York Times* news coverage of the bombs that were dropped over Hiroshima and Nagasaki. Have our perspectives changed about the bomb from wartime America until now?

3. Research and debate whether the United States should or should not have dropped the bombs on Japan. Do not just rely on emotional appeal; there are plenty of facts to support both sides of this debate.

4. Discuss the worst natural disaster you either lived through or at least read or heard about. Are there any similarities to the disaster that befell the *hibaskusha* of Hiroshima? What are they? What are the differences?

5. Read Book II of Virgil's *Aeneid*. In this epic, are there any similarities to the sacking of Troy and the destruction of Hiroshima? What are some differences? In a 500-word essay, describe how humankind has or has not progressed in over two thousand years of western civilization. Has technology changed us, or has it just altered the way we go about doing our business? How do we maintain control over technology? The recent controversy over nuclear bomb testings in Asia is a fertile topic to research. Should we try to limit nuclear proliferation or not? How do we do it? Debate this topic fully.

6. *Writing Topic*: Is it fair or even necessary to judge actions of the past on contemporary standards and distanced perspectives? What might we be doing today in America that fifty years from now future generations will critique? Look no farther than the Internet for this information.

7. *Writing Topic*: Is there a greater obligation to one's own country or to humankind in general? Discuss the practical as well as the ethical aspects of the decision to drop the atomic bomb. What ethical role about this vital question does the military have in a democratic society?

SUGGESTIONS FOR FURTHER READING

Akizuki, Tatsuichiro. *Nagasaki, 1945*. New York: Quartet Books, 1981.

Clark, Ronald W. *The Birth of the Bomb*. New York: Horizon Press, 1961.

Committee for the Compilation of Materials on Damage Caused by the Atomic Bombs in Hiroshima and Nagasaki. *Hiroshima and Nagasaki: The Physical, Medical, and Social Effects of the Atomic*

    Bombings. Trans. Eisei Ishikawa and David L. Swain. New York: Basic Books, 1981.

Groueff, Stephane. *The Manhattan Project: The Untold Story of the Making of the Atomic Bomb*. Boston: Little, Brown and Co., 1967.

Groves, Leslie R., Lieutenant General, U.S. Army. *Now It Can Be Told: The Story of the Manhattan Project*. New York: Harper and Brothers, 1962.

Lifton, Robert Jay, and Greg Mitchell. *Hiroshima in America: A Half Century of Denial*. New York: Avon Books, 1995.

Nobile, Philip, ed. *Judgment at the Smithsonian: The Bombing of Hiroshima and Nagasaki*. New York: Marlowe, 1995.

Selden, Kyoko, and Mark Selden, eds. *The Atomic Bomb: Voices from Hiroshima and Nagasaki*. New York: East Gate Books, 1989.

Wyden, Peter. *Day One: Before Hiroshima and After*. New York: Simon & Schuster, 1984.

Index

About the Author

JAMES H. MEREDITH is Associate Professor of English at the United States Air Force Academy. He is also an Associate and Book Review Editor for *War, Literature & the Arts: An International Journal of the Humanities*, and has served as Guest Editor as well. He has published on Ernest Hemingway, Ambrose Bierce, Stephen Crane, and war literature. He is currently working on several book-length projects, including one on Joseph Heller's fiction, which will be published in 1999.